C000138388

NAVIGATING THE TRANSITION FROM HIGH SCHOOL TO COLLEGE FOR STUDENTS WITH DISABILITIES

Navigating the Transition from High School to College for Students with Disabilities provides effective strategies for navigating the transition process from high school into college for students with a wide range of disabilities. As students with disabilities attend two- and four-year colleges in increasing numbers and through expanding access opportunities, challenges remain in helping these students and their families prepare for and successfully transition into higher education. Professionals and families supporting transition activities are often unaware of today's new and rapidly developing options for postsecondary education. This practical guide offers user-friendly resources, including vignettes, research summaries, and hands-on activities that can be easily implemented in the classroom and in the community, and that facilitate strong collaboration between schools and families. Preparation issues such as financial aid, applying for college, and other long-term planning areas are addressed in detail. An accompanying student resource section offers materials for high school students with disabilities that secondary educators, counselors, and transition personnel can use to facilitate exploration and planning discussions. Framing higher education as a possible transition goal for all students with disabilities, *Navigating the Transition from High School to College for Students with Disabilities* supports the postsecondary interests of more than four million public school students with disabilities.

Meg Grigal is Senior Research Fellow and Co-Director of Think College at the Institute for Community Inclusion at University of Massachusetts, Boston, USA.

Joseph Madaus is Director of the Center on Postsecondary Education and Disability, Professor in the Department of Educational Psychology and Associate Dean at the Neag School of Education, University of Connecticut, Storrs, USA.

Lyman L. Dukes III is Professor, Program Coordinator, and Graduate Program Advisor, Special Education, College of Education, University of South Florida St. Petersburg, USA.

Debra Hart is Director of Education and Transition at the Institute for Community Inclusion at University of Massachusetts, Boston, USA.

NAVIGATING THE TRANSITION FROM HIGH SCHOOL TO COLLEGE FOR STUDENTS WITH DISABILITIES

Edited by Meg Grigal, Joseph Madaus,
Lyman L. Dukes III, and Debra Hart

Routledge
Taylor & Francis Group

NEW YORK AND LONDON

First published 2018
by Routledge
711 Third Avenue, New York, NY 10017

and by Routledge
2 Park Square, Milton Park, Abingdon, Oxon, OX14 4RN

Routledge is an imprint of the Taylor & Francis Group, an informa business

© 2018 Taylor & Francis

The right of Meg Grigal; Joseph Madaus; Lyman L. Dukes, III; and Debra Hart to be identified as the authors of the editorial material, and of the authors for their individual chapters, has been asserted in accordance with sections 77 and 78 of the Copyright, Designs and Patents Act 1988.

All rights reserved. No part of this book may be reprinted or reproduced or utilised in any form or by any electronic, mechanical, or other means, now known or hereafter invented, including photocopying and recording, or in any information storage or retrieval system, without permission in writing from the publishers.

Trademark notice: Product or corporate names may be trademarks or registered trademarks, and are used only for identification and explanation without intent to infringe.

Library of Congress Cataloging-in-Publication Data
A catalog record for this title has been requested

ISBN: 978-1-138-93472-6 (hbk)
ISBN: 978-1-138-93473-3 (pbk)
ISBN: 978-1-315-67776-7 (ebk)

Typeset in Bembo
by Apex CoVantage, LLC

Visit the eResource: www.routledge.com/9781138934733

CONTENTS

INTRODUCTION

*Joseph Madaus, Meg Grigal, Lyman L. Dukes III,
and Debra Hart*

The intent of this book was foreshadowed by Herbert Rusalem, who more than 50 years ago described a cohort of students who were attending college in increasing numbers – students with disabilities. In 1962, he wrote:

> [C]ollege students [with disabilities] requiring one or more special educational services are no longer a rarity on the American campus. Having the same goals as other students, they are enrolling in increasing numbers, encouraged by better public and private school preparation, improved rehabilitation services, the availability of scholarship funds, and a changing attitude toward disabled persons in our society. Since these sources of encouragement will probably become more influential in the future, it seems likely that the problems of educating the student [with disabilities] will be receiving increasing attention.
>
> *(1962, p. 161)*

As Rusalem predicted, postsecondary services for students with disabilities has received increased attention over the past 50 years and great progress has been made with regard to access and available services. Originally, services were largely directed at veterans with disabilities and students with physical disabilities (Jarrow, 1993; Scales, 1986), but because of changes in legislation and societal attitudes, increased expectations, and improved services at the K–12 level, students with a range of disabilities now attend college.

However, these opportunities also bring new challenges, and more needs to be done to continue the progress that has been made. The chapters in this book are designed to describe these issues, and to present practical and adaptable solutions for students and their families and teachers, to enhance the transition to postsecondary education. An overview of some key statistics, trends, legislation, and emerging research provides an important bird's-eye perspective before we survey the content of each chapter.

An Overview of the Situation

The Evolution of Access

In what was perhaps the first national look at the availability of programs for students with disabilities in postsecondary education, Condon (1957) surveyed 181 institutions nationally. She reported that only 17 percent offered an organized program for students with disabilities, while 58 percent reported not having a program but offering some services, and 25 percent not offering any programs or services. Another survey, conducted by Ayers in 1962, found that only 27 percent admitted students using wheelchairs (cited in Blosser, 1984).

Significant progress occurred in the 1980s and 1990s due to the passage of Section 504 of the Rehabilitation Act of 1973 and the Americans with Disabilities Act in 1990. Madaus (1998) reported that of 567 disability service offices in institutions nationwide, 89 percent came into existence after the passage of Section 504. Sixty-eight percent of these were started in the 1980s alone, and 21 percent began after the passage of the ADA. By the 2008–2009 academic year, 88 percent of all institutions, and 100 percent of public two- and four-year institutions, reported enrolling students with disabilities (Raue & Lewis, 2011).

Data at the student level also reflects significant progress. The National Longitudinal Transition Study (Blackorby and Wagner, 1996) indicated that only 14 percent of students with disabilities accessed postsecondary education in the early and mid-1990s. Nearly fifteen years later, the National Longitudinal Transition Study 2 reported that this figure had increased to 60 percent (Newman et al., 2011). The National Center for Education Statistics (2015) found that 11 percent of all full-time college students reported having a disability, a more than threefold increase from 3 percent in 1978 (Henderson, 1999). McGregor et al. (2016) analyzed responses from nearly 64,000 students in large, research-based universities and found that 6 percent reported having a learning disability. Proportionally, students with hearing impairments (75%) and visual impairments (71%) are most likely to attend postsecondary education, followed by students with speech and language impairment and learning disabilities (67% each). Two rising cohorts in postsecondary education that will be discussed throughout this book are students with autism (44% of whom enroll) and students with intellectual disabilities (29% of whom enroll) (Newman et al., 2011).

Key Legislation

These encouraging numbers are, to a significant degree, the result of several pieces of federal legislation related to children and adults with disabilities. At the K-12 level, the Education for All Handicapped Children Act was passed in 1975 and mandated a free and appropriate public education for *all* students with disabilities. Now known as the Individuals with Disabilities Education Improvement Act of 2004 (IDEA), the law has provided special education services for several generations of students with disabilities, and more recently, has emphasized the importance of secondary transition planning, including planning for postsecondary education. Transition planning must include "appropriate measurable goals" for each student, and must be based on student preferences, goals, and needs (34 C.F.R. § 300.320 (b)(1)).

Once a student graduates or exits the public school system, the supports and protections of the IDEA no longer apply. Qualified students with disabilities who attend college are eligible for protection under two closely related civil rights laws, Section 504 of the Rehabilitation Act of 1973 (Section 504) and the Americans with Disabilities Act Amendments Act of 2008 (originally the Americans with Disabilities Act of 1990). These laws require that colleges and universities provide both physical and instructional access to qualified students with disabilities, through the use of reasonable accommodations and auxiliary aides. It is important to note that neither law requires postsecondary institutions to provide special education services, or to modify instruction or grading for students with disabilities.

Additionally, although Section 504 covers high school students with disabilities under Subpart D, college students with disabilities are covered under Subpart E. Therefore, accommodations and services that might have been received under Section 504 at the high school level might not carry over to the college level. Students, their families, and their teachers should be aware of the differences in these laws, as they impact the services that are available, or are not available, for students. Importantly, they place increased responsibility on the student to seek out and to self-advocate for services.

Importance of Expectations

College expectations permeate the academic and social experiences of college-bound youth throughout their secondary education experiences (Grigal & Hart, 2012). Transition-aged students base their desired future plans largely upon what they have been told is and is not possible by their family and their teachers. Higher expectations for academic and career success have been found to relate to better high school completion rates and higher postsecondary school attendance rates (Boser, Wilhelm, Hanna, 2014; Grigal & Deschamp, 2012; Wagner, Newman, Cameto, Levine, & Marder, 2007). Teacher expectations may be directly or indirectly influenced by the type or severity of a student's disability (Newman, 2005), their race or ethnicity (McGrew & Evans, 2004), and also by their socio-economic status. Poverty may influence both how and when educators charged with preparing students for the possibility of higher education provide those students and their parents with needed information about access and opportunity (Madaus, Grigal, & Hughes, 2014).

To exit high school and successfully transition into a college or university, long-term planning and preparation are the ideal. Often this preparation begins with conversations about college during the middle school years, to begin to build a student's awareness of postsecondary education options available to them. As students age, these conversations become more personalized and specific, and their results more tangible, impacting the courses students take in high school, the clubs and activities they join, and their discussions with families, teachers and counselors about next steps.

Brand, Valent, and Danielson (2013) state that while students with disabilities have transition plans, "many plans lack depth, breadth, and personalization; spell out low expectations; do not include plans for postsecondary education; and do not map out how the K–12 education system should connect to other systems, such as postsecondary, vocational rehabilitation, workforce training, or independent services. As a result, many students with disabilities leave high school with amorphous and generic plans that fail to address their individual circumstances or interests" (p. 12).

This lack of specificity is exacerbated by the exclusion of students with disability from many of the college-planning activities that exist in secondary education. Too often students with disabilities do not have access to high school counselors who could provide them with information about college fairs, financial aid, and college applications; but instead work with transition specialists, who have little training or knowledge about guiding students on choosing the right higher education path. Teachers and transition professionals may unintentionally set the bar too low, not based upon a desire to limit students, but instead based upon their own lack of understanding of the various paths to and through college that are available to students with disabilities and their families.

Impact of Services and Activities on Graduation

It is up to the student to self-disclose a disability and subsequently access services at the college level. Interestingly, only 35 percent of students with disabilities who received services in high school later self-disclosed in college (Newman & Madaus, 2015). There are a variety of reasons why students chose to not self-disclose, including a lack of knowledge about rights and available services, fear of stigma or negative experiences with faculty and staff, a desire to jettison the disability label, and accurate or inaccurate personal judgment about progress (Getzel & Thoma, 2008; Kurth & Mellard, 2006; Lightner et al. 2012; Martin, 2010; Megivern, 2002; Salzer, Wick, & Rogers, 2008). For those who self-disclose, the most common accommodation received is extended test time (Mamisheishvili & Koch, 2011).

Research is now looking at the impact of accommodations on student success. Lightner et al. (2012) found that those students who self-disclosed at the very outset of their college careers had higher grade point averages (nearly a half point higher) and six more credits earned than students who disclosed following their freshman year. Another study (Mamisheishvili & Koch, 2011) found that the use of course substitutions, readers, note takers, and scribes impacted persistence from year one to year two of college. There is also great variation of accommodation use by disability type, with students with more visible disabilities and students who received transition education in high school being more likely to receive services than students with learning disabilities (Newman & Madaus, 2015). Recent research also indicates that those students with disabilities who access services that are available to the general student population (e.g., tutors, writing centers) are more likely to be successful in college (Newman, Madaus, & Javitz, 2016). Although these studies used different data sets and methodologies, an important common theme is that self-disclosure, accommodation receipt, and receipt of supports in college is an individualized decision, and is one that can be impacted by careful transition planning and education at the secondary level.

An Overview of the Book

This book is structured in four sections as described below. **Section One** is comprised of Chapters 1 and 2, and focuses on students' lived experiences and professional expectations, thus offering a foundation for educators to reflect on their assumptions and experiences in helping students navigate college with a disability. **Section Two** is comprised of four chapters. Chapters 3 and 4 focus on practical strategies around planning for successful transition to college, along with the foundation skills needed to be successful. Chapters 5 and 6 provide information about the many college pathways, and addresses the impact of disability on application processes. **Section Three** contains Chapters 7 and 8, offering strategies for effective partnerships and structural supports that can assist educators in their pursuit of college-ready students with disability. **Section Four** – "Resources for Students" – contains practical advice for high school students with disability, along with a "top ten" list, an additional checklist, and recommended websites and books for families and students with disability to use as they explore college.

Section 1: Student Experiences and Professional Expectations

In Chapter 1, Kim Elmore, Hetsie Veitch, and Wendy Harbour share the perspectives of nine current and recently graduated college students with disabilities. Based upon interviews with the profiled students, these authors explore their lived experience as they prepared for and enrolled in college. These students' "lessons learned" reflect the complexity and diversity of the college experience for youth with disabilities. It also supports the premise that each student's experience, traditional and non-traditional, matriculating and non-matriculating, is equally legitimate, leading to desired outcomes and meaningful goals for students with disabilities. The chapter concludes with a range of online and print resources that will be helpful for parents, students, and educators who are supporting students with disabilities in the pursuit of a college education.

How do you engender student interest in college attendance? How can educators' expectations impact college as choice? In Chapter 2, Clare Papay and Meg Grigal explore perhaps the most important aspect of preparing for college: the expectation that it will happen. Research has demonstrated that the power of expectation often determines what students with disabilities do after high school. The chapter spells out the importance of school professionals expanding their personal knowledge regarding how students with disabilities can access and succeed in college. Strategies such as incorporating college prep activities in the IEP, visiting colleges, and understanding the different paths to college are discussed. In addition, the importance of middle and high school college preparation expectations, goal-setting skills, and accessing adult learning opportunities in the community, are described.

Section 2: College Preparation and Application

In Chapter 3, Zachary Walker, Elizabeth Getzel, Lyman L. Dukes, and Joseph Madaus address an array of academic and non-academic skills that typically result in a successful college experience. Information about how to learn about postsecondary education options, and how to cultivate a support system are shared, as is information on how to access disability services to seek appropriate accommodations with the proper documentation, which can sometimes be challenging and overwhelming.

In Chapter 4, Debra Hart, Molly Boyle, and Melissa Jones address the need for students to cultivate social and "soft" skills that best enable them to effectively navigate the new terrain of a college campus. These include academic and career habits, cultural know-how, balancing multiple roles, self-direction, communication, teamwork, and professionalism. A tool called the *Foundational Skills for College and Career Success* is presented that provides professionals with a system to develop student self-awareness and self-advocacy. Included are methods to cope with various social stressors and time management, as well as strategies to manage assignments and schedules, the creation of support networks including coaching and mentoring, participation in college success courses, and activities that promote a positive and empowering understanding of one's own disability. Lastly, strategies that can be used in the development of the individualized education program (IEP) are examined.

In Chapter 5, Judy Bass and Meg Grigal present the array of options available to students with disabilities. An overview of different kinds of colleges and profiles of the many types of programs available is presented, including some less traditional options such as comprehensive transition and support programs as well as programs for students with intellectual disabilities. The authors share descriptions of the levels of support available to students with disability as well as guidance regarding questions that families and students can ask when making a college decision.

Applying to college is a complex undertaking for all students. This process can be even more challenging when students have disabilities. In Chapter 6, Adam Lalor, Stefania Petcu, and Joseph Madaus provide a transition to college timeline, describe strategies to prepare for the application process, give guidance about applying for financial aid, and how and when to take any necessary testing (ACT, SAT). Understanding how to respond to different admission criteria, dealing with the dreaded essay, and framing high school experiences in the most positive light are also highlighted. Last, the chapter stresses the value of collaboration of the IEP team when preparing students for a successful application experience.

Section 3: Partnerships and Models for College Success

Chapter 7, by Danielle Roberts-Dahm, Lyman L. Dukes, and Debra Hart reviews a number of existing partnership models between school districts and institutes of higher education that use a range of supports intended to result in access to higher education for students with disabilities. This chapter shares secondary-level strategies and practices that have resulted in successful partnerships with disability service offices, other higher education units, and the adult service system. Suggestions designed to assist with replication are highlighted.

College and career readiness include a strong focus on academic preparation. Chapter 8, by Allison Lombardi, Mary Morningstar, and Laura Kern, provides an overview of some of the most common academic pitfalls that challenge students with disabilities, and strategies that can be used to support success. These include access to general education content, understanding and use of accommodations, and identifying the academic requirements for different types of college experiences. It examines transition through the lens of the college and career readiness framework as applied within a multi-tiered system of support approach in order to provide students with disabilities equitable access and support in secondary school settings.

Section 4: Resources for Students

This final section contains resources for high school students with disability that secondary educators, counselors, and transition personnel can use to facilitate exploration and planning discussions. The resource, "What I Wish I Knew" from Kim Elmore, Hetsie Veitch, and Wendy S. Harbour provides advice from current or recent college students with disabilities to high school students. This resource provides reflections and suggestions on how students can embrace disability history and culture, advocate for their needs, and build a network of personal supports that can help them achieve their desired goals. Our hope is that teachers will download this section of the book and provide copies of it to each student who may benefit from this advice. Additional downloadable materials include a "Top Ten List" of college advice, a college planning checklist, list of recommended organizations, and recommended books, the resource guide is on the product webpage: www.routledge.com/9781138934733. Ideally, copies of this section of the book will be provided to students and used to facilitate discussions about the importance of self-knowledge and self-advocacy when preparing for college.

Final Thoughts

It is our genuine hope and belief that all students, regardless of disability status, deserve the opportunity to determine their respective futures. It is the role of education professionals, whether in K–12 or college settings, to value, recognize, and teach toward maximizing student opportunities in adult life. It is, of course, often said education is an immutable right of children. Certainly, this includes young people with disabilities. All children merit the opportunity to choose college, if they so desire.

References

Blackorby, J., and Wagner, M. M. (1996). National post school outcomes of youth with disabilities: Findings from the National Longitudinal Transition Study. *Exceptional Children, 62,* 399–414.

Blosser, R. E. (1984). The roles and functions and the preparation of disabled student services directors in higher education (Doctoral dissertation, Southern Illinois University at Carbondale). *Dissertations Abstracts International, 45,* 2396A.

Boser, U., Wilhelm, M., and Hanna, R. (2014). *The power of the Pygmalion Effect: Teachers' expectations strongly predict college completion.* Washington, DC: The Center for American Progress: 1–7.

Brand, B., Valent, A., and Danielson, L. (2013). *Improving college and career readiness for students with disabilities.* Retrieved from www.ccrscenter.org/sites/default/files/Improving%20 College%20and%20Career%20Readiness%20for%20Students%20with%20Disabilities. pdf.

Condon, M. E. (1957). A survey of special facilities for the physically handicapped in the colleges. *Personnel and Guidance Journal, 35*(9), 579–583.

Getzel, E. E., and Thoma, C. A. (2008). Experiences of college students with disabilities and the importance of self-determination in higher education settings. *Career Development for Exceptional Individuals, 31,* 77–84.

Grigal, M., and Deschamps, A. (2012). Transition education for adolescents with intellectual disability. In M. L. Wehmeyer and K. W. Webb (Eds.). *Handbook of adolescent transition education for youth with disabilities* (pp. 398–416). New York: Routledge.

Grigal, M., and Hart, D. (2012). The power of expectations. *Journal of Policy and Practice in Intellectual Disabilities, 9*, 221–222.

Henderson, C. (1999). *College freshmen with disabilities: Statistical year 1998.* Washington, DC: American Council on Education.

Jarrow, J. (1993, Winter). Beyond ramps: New ways of viewing access. In S. Kroeger and J. Schuck (Eds.). *New directions for student services* (pp. 5–16). San Francisco: Jossey-Bass Publishers.

Kurth, N., and Mellard, D. (2006). Student perceptions of the accommodation process in postsecondary education. *Journal of Postsecondary Education and Disability, 19*, 71–84.

Lightner, K. L., Kipps-Vaughan, D., Schulte, T., and Trice, A. D. (2012). Reasons university students with a learning disability wait to seek disability services. *Journal of Postsecondary Education and Disability, 25*, 145–159.

Madaus, J. W. (1998). The effect of demographic characteristics on OSD administrators' perceptions of essential job functions. *Journal of Postsecondary Education and Disability, 13*(1), 3–22.

Madaus, J. W., Grigal, M., and Hughes, C. (2014). Promoting access to postsecondary education for low income students with disabilities. *Career Development and Transition for Exceptional Individuals, 37*, 50–59.

Mamiseisshvili, K., and Koch, L. C. (2011). First-to-second-year persistence of students with disabilities in postsecondary institutions in the United States. *Rehabilitation Counseling Bulletin, 54*(2), 93–105.

Martin, J. M. (2010). Stigma and student mental health in higher education. *Higher Education Research and Development, 29*, 259–274.

McGrew, K. S., and Evans, J. (2004). *Expectations for students with cognitive disabilities: Is the cup half empty or half full? Can the cup flow over?* (Synthesis Report 55). Minneapolis: University of Minnesota, National Center on Educational Outcomes. Retrieved January 18, 2009, from http://education.umn.edu/NCEO/OnlinePubs/Synthesis55.html.

McGregor, K. K., Langenfeld, N., Van Horne, S., Oleson, J., Anson, M., and Jacobson, W. (2016). The university experiences of students with learning disabilities. *Learning Disabilities Research and Practice, 31*(2), 90–102. doi: 10.111/ldrp.12102.

Megivern, D. (2002). Disability services and college students with psychiatric disabilities. *Journal of Social Work in Disability and Rehabilitation, 1*(3), 25–41.

Newman, L. (2005). *Family involvement in the educational development of youth with disabilities.* Menlo Park, CA: SRI International.

Newman, L. A., and Madaus, J. W. (2015). An analysis of factors related to receipt of accommodations and services by postsecondary students with disabilities. *Remedial and Special Education, 36*(4), 208–219.

Newman, L. A., Madaus, J. W., and Javitz, H. S. Effect of support receipt on postsecondary success of students with disabilities. (Manuscript under review)

Newman, L., Wagner, M., Knokey, A. M., Marder, C., Nagle, K., Shaver, D., and Wei, X. (2011). *The post-high school outcomes of young adults with disabilities up to 8 years after high school.* (NCSER 2011–3005). Menlo Park, CA: SRI International. Available at https://ies.ed.gov/ncser/pubs/20113005/pdf/20113005.pdf.

Raue, K., and Lewis, L. (2011). *Students with disabilities at degree-granting postsecondary institutions* (NCES 2011–018). U.S. Department of Education, National Center for Education Statistics. Washington, DC: U.S. Government Printing Office.

Rusalem, H. (1962). The physically handicapped student and the college faculty. *College and University, 37*(2), 161–167.

Salzer, M. S., Wick, L. C., and Rogers, J. A. (2008). Familiarity with and use of accommodations and supports among postsecondary students with mental illness. *Psychiatric Services, 59,* 370–375.

Scales, W. (1986, Winter). Postsecondary education for disabled students – written testimony. *AHSSPPE Bulletin, 4*(1), 20–32.

Wagner, M., Newman, L., Cameto, R., Levine, P., and Marder, C. (2007). *Perceptions and expectations of youth with disabilities. A special topic report of findings from the National Longitudinal Transition Study-2 (NLTS2).* (NCSER 2007–3006). Menlo Park, Ca: SRI International.

SECTION 1

Student Experiences and Professional Expectations

1

THE LIVED EXPERIENCES OF COLLEGE STUDENTS AND RECENT COLLEGE GRADUATES WITH DISABILITIES

Kim Elmore

TEXAS TECH UNIVERSITY

Hetsie Veitch

SYRACUSE UNIVERSITY

Wendy S. Harbour

ASSOCIATION ON HIGHER EDUCATION AND DISABILITY (AHEAD)

Contributors:

Nigel Abduh
Crystal Fike
Kings Floyd
Jason Harris
Ann Wai-Yee Kwong
Tara McFadden
Kate Pollack
Katie Roquemore
K Wheeler

Author and disability services professional Mary Lee Vance has written that every college student with a disability is a "first-generation college student," even if their parents went to college (Vance, 2007). Going to college with a disability is an incredibly unique experience, and it's rare for students with disabilities to have disabled parents, relatives, or friends who can guide and mentor them about what to expect. At the same time, prospective college students with disabilities face what Martha Minow calls "the dilemma of difference." If everyone focuses only on the disability and disability-related needs, then it becomes a transition process without the ups and downs of the college search process. If everyone focuses on the college search and ignores the disability, students may arrive on campus and realize it doesn't provide the services they need. The authors and contributors for this chapter understand that the "dilemma" for students with disabilities (and their friends, family, teachers, and others supporting them) is that they're both the same as and different from every other college student. Most of the students in this chapter convey that they needed to embrace the sameness and differences as they look back at what college taught them, focusing on the whole student experience and not only the part that relates to their disability.

At the National Center for College Students with Disabilities (NCCSD) (where the three co-authors were working when we wrote this chapter), we often encourage college students with disabilities to speak with other students with disabilities who have recently graduated or are in graduate school. When students are trying to get through the first years of college, they're having problems, or they're worried about the future, there's nothing quite like getting advice from someone who has been down the same road and really "gets it." The shared lived experiences of students with disabilities is the underpinning of this chapter.

There are several resources out there with advice about going to college, and we've included a list of our favorites at the end of this chapter. However, many of the resources are written by non-disabled professionals, or they are focused on parents, teachers, and disability services providers. In this chapter, the goal is to hear from students and recent graduates in their own words. As co-authors, we interviewed the contributors and made sure *their* stories were emphasized. We organized their thoughts and advice with students in mind – high school students thinking about college, current students in their first year on campus, and their support networks.

This chapter was prepared in close collaboration with the contributing students. With the permission of the contributors, we share a short biographical description of each student to provide some background and context to the stories they told us in March 2017:

- Nigel is a young African American musician, blogger, and college radio host who has almost finished a two-year certificate for students with intellectual disabilities (ID) at a private university in the suburban Northeast. Nigel plans to continue his college studies in English, communications, and music.

NIGEL

- Crystal, a black Hispanic student leader and blogger, will soon complete a two-year certificate program for students with ID at a public research university in a large northeastern city.

CRYSTAL

- Kings, a white writer and disability advocate with muscular dystrophy, worked for a year as the National Council on Independent Living Youth Transitions Fellow after graduating in English Language and Disability Studies from a private liberal arts college in the South. She has presented at the South by Southwest Conference and youth leadership summits.

KINGS

- Jason, a white man on the autism spectrum, is working on his Master's degree in Education and Disability Studies at a private research university in the Northeast. He founded Jason's Connection, an online community connecting disabled people to resources and each other, and interned with the National Disability Rights Network.

JASON

- Ann, a blind Chinese American doctoral student in Education and former Gates Millennium Scholar, attends a public research university in California. She co-founded the peer mentoring organization Survive or Thrive for students with disabilities and interned with the Institute of Educational Leadership.

ANN

- Tara is completing her Master of Social Work degree at the public liberal arts and professional studies institution where she received her Bachelor of Social Work. She lives with a congenital heart defect and learning disabilities.

TARA

- Kate is a Jewish and Irish Catholic disability rights blogger who identifies as culturally Deaf with learning and psychiatric disabilities. She is completing her Master of Science in Education and Disability Studies and works at one of the few college cultural centers for students with disabilities in the United States.

KATE

- Katie, a white woman with muscular dystrophy, is a former high school Rookie Teacher of the Year who taught English and Speech and Debate in North Carolina. She is working on her Ph.D. in Education and Disability Studies at a private research university in the Northeast.

KATIE

- K, who is a congenital amputee, is double-majoring in Law, Societies, and Justice and Disability Studies in the interdisciplinary honors program of a large Northwestern state university. K is Headmaster of the Harry Potter Club there and holds 3 world records in Paralympic swimming.

K

Some of the contributors will soon graduate, others are working, and others are in graduate school. They identify as having a disability, have been through college as a disabled student, and have had time to reflect about what worked for them or what could have been different during college.

If you are a student reading this, we hope you will feel like you're participating in a conversation with friendly mentors sharing their stories, and we hope it inspires you to find your own mentors and community of other students with disabilities. If you are a disability resources professional, teacher, or parent, we trust that you will find tools and information that will empower you to better guide and assist students in their journey to college.

Deciding to Go to College

Some of us always knew we would go to college. Jason is an example: "I always wanted to go to college. It was kind of expected because everybody was going to college. Everyone I knew, like my sister, went to college, so it wasn't a big deal."

K also always expected to go to college, and both parents shared this expectation although neither has a college degree. K explains:

> *I never thought that college wasn't an option. It was always on my master plan. Society has a general idea that everyone should go to college, and I had that mindset. I'm pretty good at academics, so my parents always had that expectation for me, especially during my junior and senior year of high school. And the careers I was looking at [doctor, lawyer] were all very academically intense.*

Like K, Kings and Katie both knew that "never going to college was not an option." Kings started thinking early about going to college because she and her parents knew accessibility would be an issue: "My mother started the conversation with my school in sixth or seventh grade. What does a college experience look like for me? How is it similar to and different from the experiences of my peers?" Both of Katie's parents went to college, and she was set on a college path by middle school with advanced classes. While Katie knew early that she wanted to be a teacher, Kings looked forward to college so she could "become more independent, make friends outside my bubble, and find out who I am."

For others, college was never on the horizon, or the idea of college was vague and uncertain even when expected. Some students receive mixed messages about their ability to go to college that makes them doubt themselves at times. Although Tara grew up with family and friends who expected that she would go to college just like they did, she wondered how she would succeed with her learning disability:

> *Everybody from my high school was going to college, and for most of them, but not all, college was the next step. I really had no fallback plan. Both of my parents went to college, and my mom wanted me to have a college experience. At the time, though, I was not really excited about college, because with a learning disability, I was not sure how the colleges would accommodate it. Teachers were always saying college would be much harder, and taking the ACT and SATs was going to be a struggle. I wasn't sure what I wanted to do, but at least I knew I wanted college. But the main message I got was that college was really difficult. I was never a strong writer, so that was an issue, and I worried about that going into college, trying to figure out how I would be able to crank out all the papers I'd have to write.*

With a lot of "very anxious" preparation and the right accommodations for the admission tests, Tara was able to demonstrate her academic skills and get into several four-year colleges in her region. Her next concern was to figure out, with the help of her mom, which of those college environments could best support her transition into higher education.

Jason, who also has a learning disability, found the high school message for students with disabilities who wanted to attend college discouraging:

> *The type of schools that I went to encouraged you to go on to the next level but there was a clear message that you would need a lot of support and would not be like a normal student. They told me that I would be different and not like the other students, so the focus was on the difference and there was a negative spin on it.*

Jason was also affected by his parents' anxiety about his ability to get into college, which required him to take SATs, and to succeed if he went. He felt these high-stakes standardized tests were his most difficult hurdle to getting into college:

> *It was hard for me to sit in a room and take the tests for almost a whole day because I wasn't that good at math. There were some things at the school that I was good at, but it was still very hard, the way that it is all set up. It was really hard work to get ready, to study before the time and prepare for it. I wish that there were other ways than these tests to show that you are ready for college.*

While Jason made the SAT scores to attend a Midwestern four-year liberal arts college with a strong support program for students with learning disabilities, Nigel and his family were initially stumped when he did not get the SAT scores he needed to attend college. After a couple of years of searching for the right opportunity, Nigel's father found a two-year college certificate program near his home that did not require standardized tests for admission and offered academic supports. So Nigel made the move from Atlanta to his father's home in the Northeast. There, he had a 30-minute bus ride from the college where he could "become a better learner, find myself as a mature man, and find my strengths and weaknesses."

In Kate's situation, growing up in a high-poverty area and skipping school meant college wasn't even a consideration for her. She described it in this way:

> *In high school, I hadn't thought about going to college at all. I had no accommodations at my crowded city school with drugs and crime everywhere. I skipped class and hung out in the streets and hadn't gone to school in a couple of years. I'd only thought I might become a drug addict or be in a rock band.*

College only became a possibility when Kate moved to a place where others insisted it was realistic. When Kate went to a new high school in a wealthy school district, which had a deaf program and sign language interpreters, her early love of school was rekindled. Students at this school expected to go to college, but

Kate would never have thought her family could afford it without specific guidance on how they might do so. One day at school, Kate got this guidance from a state vocational rehabilitation (VR) counselor with a disability:

> *Representatives from Gallaudet University came to give a presentation, and they said, "How many of you want to go to college?" and everyone raised their hands except me. I'm not in that demographic. I was a cashier after school and needed money for food, so it was a fantasy to think about going to college. Mom and Dad had no idea about anything academic; they were just not in that world. Somehow Access VR representative Kevin Shea also came to my high school with his service dog, and met me and my mother (and I think my resource teacher) and talked about how they would help pay for me to go to college, including tuition, books, and rent.*

Being part of a community that expected youth with disabilities to continue on to higher education, and meeting experienced individuals who could help with financial and accessibility planning made college possible for Kate.

For Ann, being an immigrant added an additional level of complexity to the prospect of attending college: "My family immigrated to the USA when I was eight years old. My parents didn't know about college. One of my parents completed part of high school in Hong Kong and the other one barely finished elementary school." Ann's parents expected that she would go to college, however, and take advantage of the greater opportunities that higher education could provide her. It wasn't until Ann began taking AP classes during her last two years of high school that she learned more about how to make her goal to attend a university in her home state a reality:

> *I only had a vague conception of college growing up. I started learning more during late middle school/early high school when representatives from universities would come in talking about college. But they would not go to the classes where students with disabilities were, like the resource room. My friend [who is also a blind Braille reader] and I didn't need to go to the special education resource room, and therefore lucked out and had access to the information provided about college. It was as if the disabled students in the resource room didn't need to hear about college and scholarships. Sometimes people will have lower expectations for you or worry about potential difficulties you might have if you go to college.*

Ann found that these lower expectations for students with disabilities at school were reinforced by her first VR counselor, who was "pretty against" her goal to attend a state university, quoting statistics that said students who are blind fail when they attempt to earn a bachelor's degree.

> *She told me to think about attending a community college, independent living skills center, or maybe a factory making plastic fruit decorations (which really stayed with*

me). The counselor further said it might be difficult to provide me with equipment, lessons and other support if I decided to go to a four-year college. She told me that she was giving this advice to protect me and save me from heartache, saying, "This is the route that we think would be best suited for you instead of college."

Even Ann's parents questioned the wisdom of Ann's decision to go to a state university that was six hours away. They worried about "what would happen if I got lost or in an accident while forgetting that the same thing could happen for everybody else that goes away to college." Ann not only needed to challenge herself to leave her comfort zone, she also had to contend with pushing her family out of their own comfort zone.

Although K and family and friends expected K would go to college, there were concerns from others that disability would prevent K from leaving home:

Some people questioned the logistics of living alone and the physical challenges that I might encounter. I feel very privileged that there was an expectation that I would or could go to college since I'm aware that isn't the case for all disabled students.

Through DO-IT at the University of Washington, K attended a ten-day on-campus summer program for college-bound high school students with disabilities that "really helped wrap my brain around" the logistics of on-campus living. But K recognized ableism in the way students with disabilities were treated differently by the professionals who most influence college decision-making in high school:

When nondisabled students don't want to go to college and they think it's not for them, they will be pushed, and teachers and counselors will try to convince them to go. When a disabled student thinks the same way, they are discouraged to even try. [Teachers and counselors] automatically assume because they have a 504 Plan or an IEP that they will not be able to go to college even though they have just as much ability and right to go.

While some of her classmates went to job corps, Crystal always knew that she "wanted to get a better learning experience, learning computer technology and how to work on computers." So when high school guidance "counselors tried to say college wasn't for me, [that] made me push even more," Crystal recalls. Crystal had a supportive parent who helped her explore all the college options that exist, including college-based transition programs or taking courses even if you aren't able to get into a degree program: "When I was getting ready to go to college, my mom said, 'Keep trying. Don't let anybody stop you.'" So when her guidance counselor continued to discourage Crystal from attending college, Crystal "realized you can get into some parts of colleges sometimes even if you can't get into a [four-year degree] program."

To some degree, all students receive mixed messages about continuing on to college, but disabilities should not be used to discourage or prevent anyone pursuing higher education. Ultimately, students with disabilities have to decide how to act on the mixed messages they receive and their own hopes and fears about attending college. Once the decision is made, strong support from parents, teachers, and counselors can empower students to make the preparations to attend college, knowing that they are not alone on their journey.

Preparing for College

As Kings stated, the process of students with disabilities applying to college is remarkably "similar to everyone else." The college search involves a long process of taking classes to prepare for college, preparing for SAT and ACT tests, selecting which schools to apply to, and completing their application processes. But as K noted, "disability does play a role" while searching for a college. As a Paralympic swimmer for Team USA, K wanted to stay close to the team and coach, but still did college tours like many other students:

> I did a college tour with my mom. My best friend and her mom toured every college from [the state] where they lived. I only applied for two universities: [a small private liberal arts college and a large state university in the Northwest]. At the end, I got into the [state university] honors program. I was happy about that because it makes a huge campus seem smaller, since it's easier to fit in with small classes and address misconceptions of disability.

Kings also preferred a smaller, personally welcoming environment and selected a small private liberal arts university in the South. Many of the campus buildings had recent additions and so were ADA compliant with ramps and push-button doors for wheelchair users like Kings. Beyond compliance, Kings found, based upon her earliest weekend visits, that staff from several departments were ready to learn from her about the accommodations she needed in order to work together to provide them: "The head of accommodations, maintenance, security, and other key players met with me. They told me 'we really like you as a student' and 'we lack a little in accommodations,' so what changes need to be made? The openness of that conversation literally changed the next four years." K, who also uses a wheelchair, learned enough about on-campus and off-campus accessibility from college tour visits to make a decision:

> On Admitted Student Day at [the small liberal arts college] campus, one of the activities took friends and family to learn about local restaurants. None of the streets had curb cut-outs and I had to drive in the streets. There were whole blocks that I couldn't access, and I realized I would be trapped on campus or driving in the street

if I went to that university. This was a very important observation for me; it made the state university the only possibility for me.

Visiting colleges ahead of time also helped Katie learn about campus accessibility as well as attitudes toward access. As a finalist for a state teaching fellow scholarship, Katie visited several schools for interviews and discovered that visiting college campuses was sometimes a challenge: "I don't know if there was any thought about accessibility in the interview process or the assumption was that no one interviewing would have a mobility impairment." Although Katie, who has muscular dystrophy, was able to walk in high school, she knew that mobility was becoming more difficult for her. From her campus tours, Katie decided to get a motorized scooter to help her with longer distance mobility. She also decided to attend a residential college that offered additional supports to first-year students, including "residential learning communities" available in certain residence halls that had students take general education courses in their respective residence halls.

Role of Disability Services

Like Kings, several students mentioned the role of disability resource offices during their preparation for college and when choosing one college over another. For Tara, disability services became the deciding factor in not only choosing a college, but deciding between a medium-sized state university or a smaller liberal arts college: "It came down to accommodations when I was deciding between colleges. [At the liberal arts college] I got to speak to the office of special services and got a feel for what it would be like, and there was a lab just for people with learning disabilities." Tara felt fortunate to receive not just accommodations, but supports and mentoring from her Disability Resource Center (DRC) and professors from her very first day: "My [DRC] counselor was one of my first professors. She was a huge resource throughout my college career and suggested that social work be my major. The professors are great at understanding accommodations too."

Although discouraged in high school by the constant reminders to focus on disability services and supports at potential colleges, Jason also found strong support for students with learning disabilities at the private liberal arts college in the Midwest he chose to attend:

> *The school had a specialized office within the disability services that you could apply to, called Project EXCEL, specifically for students with learning disabilities. They provided the specialized services like tutors and other things for students with different learning disabilities, and they helped me to become more independent. They would support you maximally in the beginning but then less and less so that you*

can learn to be independent. I didn't feel different in the classroom because this took place outside the classroom. There might have been someone anonymously taking notes and I took some tests outside of the classroom, but I was not treated differently in the class with the other students.

Nigel, who also received support from tutors throughout his program, noted that while such resources were crucial to his success in college, so was his willingness to seek and accept help:

From the first day I started I was successful. I got tutors to go through assignments with us and take our questions. That helped the most. Before, I didn't go to anyone for help, but now I was open to letting people help. It was hard to learn in high school, but [these resources] helped me begin the learning process, learning techniques like how to take notes and answer questions the best I can.

Touring colleges and visiting disability resources offices early in the process of college preparation was very important to successful students with disabilities. Students benefitted from searching out a campus environment that would support learning development from their first year, both in first-year programs open to all students and through services available to students with disabilities.

Accessibility on and off Campus: Transportation

Many students with disabilities need to consider on- and off-campus resources for people with disabilities as well as academic accommodations through the on-campus disability resources office when preparing for college. As Ann explained:

I wanted to be sure they had a larger or established disability services office on campus, but I was also concerned with the geographic location and the availability of public transportation. I would need access to buses and a system that would enable me to take advantage of opportunities, shop for groceries, and do internships. I was aware of the fact that not only did I need to figure out school, but also how to live there.

Nigel also needed the kind of public transportation available in a major city, not only to get him to and from school, but also to ensure access to activities on- and off-campus. While Nigel's commute to school was 30 minutes, Kate had a two-hour subway ride to and from her large urban campus, which left her little time to navigate the services she needed for academic success, and no time for extracurricular activities outside of work.

Access to on- and off-campus medical care, housing, and recreation is another important consideration when planning for college life. Although she lived just a few hours from home, Katie selected new doctors where she attended college as she needed specialized care on a regular basis. As Katie transitioned to using a wheelchair full-time in her last years of college, she was surprised by the inaccessibility of off-campus housing, restaurants, and recreation. While her campus and residence hall were accessible, Katie's friends had moved to off-campus apartments that were inaccessible: "Friends will go places you just can't go and learning to deal with that can be very isolating." Eventually, Katie found friends who were more interested in doing accessible activities together in smaller groups. Even school campuses that are relatively accessible will have problems with accessibility that can impact daily living. During their first years living on campus, both K and Katie struggled with laundry rooms that were not accessible. For K, this meant taking laundry back home because laundry facilities, as well as residence hall kitchens and lounges, were not considered necessities of daily living by the student housing services on K's large, generally accessible campus with its own disability cultural center for students. K argued with student housing services about her need to do laundry and cook in the common area kitchens for two years before moving out of student housing and into her own apartment.

Some students also needed to think through what kind of personal care support they would need and how to independently manage it. Disability resource offices rarely help students find personal care assistants (PCAs) who assist with daily living, like getting dressed, cooking, and hygiene. Although K had a PCA when attending an on-campus summer program for rising high school seniors with disabilities, K found that the assistance was not always needed and preferred not to have a PCA:

> *I was somewhat sure that I could navigate most of my personal care myself, but faced pushback from a lot of family, friends and acquaintances. They were urging me to have a PCA at college anyways, and then I could let them go if I didn't need them. But my mind was really set on not using one if I didn't need to, so I ended up not having one. I did have a friend that lived in the building right behind mine, and my friend agreed to help me until I found someone, should I need a PCA.*

Kings decided to employ female peers as her PCAs and found her greatest college challenge was "learning to manage friends as co-workers as well." While learning to manage her friends as PCAs was a hurdle, "it's still one of the best decisions I made because several are still best friends." For Kings and many other students with disabilities, "getting in [to college] wasn't the problem – it was what happened once I got in and dealing with disability accommodations."

Arriving at College

After all the mixed messages and despite the preparation, it's impossible to be completely prepared for college, but a welcoming campus climate can make all the difference. Nigel "prepared for the positives and negatives" of college but quickly discovered it a welcome change from high school:

College was way different from high school. People were nice, open, welcoming. One positive was all the diversity around campus, of religion, sex life, medical condition. I didn't know how people were going to be, and I didn't want to be around negative people. I've met none so far. But I had to come out of my comfort zone.

Kings also found her college campus welcoming, from the warmer Southern climate to the newly renovated, accessible buildings to the beautiful green grounds. For Kings, the friendly, curious, open "people invested in other people" were her school's greatest asset.

Some students quickly realized that because college was different than high school, they would need to adjust the strategies and coping mechanisms that had always worked for them. This was even true with social aspects of college and meeting people. For example, K had long been involved in competitive swimming but the campus didn't have a swim team, so it was necessary to "travel to a different pool to practice with my coach three times per week." K "definitely had good friends from swimming, but they were not on [my college] campus." By the third year of college, K had moved past swimming to new challenges and relationships, noting, "I also wanted to go to law school and had to start to focus on my studies more. I actually haven't touched a pool in over a year." Instead, K has become active as a student leader on campus, as a student representative from DO-IT and Headmaster of the Harry Potter Club, and off-campus, as a student advisory board member for Disability Rights, Education, Activism, and Mentoring (DREAM).

Ann's best experiences as an undergraduate involved "building community" with friends who shared her academic and professional interests or disability identity. For example, she helped create a student-led course at her university that paired the Paralympic team sport of goalball for blind or visually impaired players with content on disability sports and culture as "a way to communicate and learn more about each other." For Jason, social success was tied to academic success and supports that helped him fit in during class and become more independent. This confidence in himself helped him to join student organizations: "I joined clubs, different clubs of things that I find interesting, and looked for people and things that were familiar to me. I really enjoyed living on campus."

After a difficult undergraduate experience in which she felt very isolated as a deaf student with disabilities, Kate enjoys the disability community she has now through her graduate program and work. She is re-learning sign language with friends and mentors, and now coordinates the disability cultural center at her large Northeastern research university. She advises: "Meet other disabled people. It is great to be a disabled person: we have an identity and we have a lot to offer the world. I would also recommend taking a disability studies class or two." With time, students developed social circles both in- and out-side of the disability community that addressed different aspects of their identity as a student.

Compared with high school, college has a surprising amount of freedom, but many students with disabilities learn that the freedom requires a great deal of responsibility, including learning to take risks. Nigel thrived because that was part of why he went to college: "I thought that in college I'd be a better learner and I'd find out what I'm good at. High school wasn't a bad experience, but I was a teenager – I wanted to go somewhere to grow and mature." Jason and Tara realized during their first year of college that the greater freedom of college meant they had to improve their time management and organization skills to succeed. As Jason explained,

> I was surprised at how it all was organized and how organized I had to be. I guess that is two-fold: I had to do a lot of planning because of all the freedom that I had in college. It had less structure than in high school, so I had to do a lot of planning for myself. That took a bit of work to plan and stick to that, just to get through every day.

Tara felt she needed to learn more time management in high school to be better prepared for college, especially for writing papers:

> College is a whole change. Now you're on your own, not in school from 7–3 and your parents aren't there to remind you to do things. Nothing can really prepare you for that change and all the distractions you have as a freshman. But I had really good roommates who helped keep me on track. And I knew homework was a priority and that I needed to go to the writing center for help with my papers. Over time, I learned that I needed to go a day or two in advance to do well. Even to this day – and my writing has improved – I like to get a second pair of eyes to read my papers and work with friends and classmates to help me make sure I'm on track.

Crystal learned early that regularly going to her program's learning center to do homework and use the computers was important to her goals to further her education and get a receptionist job in a professional office. While she sometimes met others like her math tutors at the learning center, usually she went to get her homework done in a less distracting environment. Jason learned another important lesson early in his college career: failure is an important part of learning. He said, "In high school there was this big thing about failure and that you can't fail, but failure kind of comes with college [as you try new things and grow academically and socially]. There was this fear of failure in high school, but I never learned how to deal with failure until college."

Tara also emphasized the need to be your own advocate in college: "The biggest thing about having a learning disability is that you need to advocate for yourself because [teachers and disability resources counselors] have no idea how your brain works and how you process information." She would tell new college students,

> Don't be afraid to advocate for yourself, but I don't recommend doing it in the middle of class. After going over the syllabus during the first class of the semester, take your LOA (letter of accommodation) to your professor, talk about the syllabus, and explain the accommodations you need to succeed. If you don't advocate for yourself, you may not get the resources you need to make the class accessible to you.

Although "no stranger to self-advocacy" and "running my own 504 meetings by 8th grade," K did realize the need to be an even stronger self-advocate: "In college, some professors and disability services were big on knowing you better than you know yourself. I had to be way more forceful than I ever had to be in high school and develop a level of pushiness without being rude or expecting too much." From experience, K knew more than double-time was needed in math courses to physically work through the problems in writing and then have a scribe transfer K's solution legibly. Double-and-a-half time was given on the SAT and ACT. But K's request for more testing time in the math course than for other courses was originally denied until K could show the need for the extra time. This happened when K failed the first test.

Like many new college students with disabilities, Ann struggled to become an advocate for her own academic and independent living needs. Her struggle was intensified because she had to learn about all the systems of higher education as an immigrant and first-generation college student:

> I vaguely knew what accommodations I would need, but in public schools they [teachers] are responsible for providing accommodations by law and I didn't have to ask for it. At college, I knew I would have to be self-aware and know what I needed, because I needed to request accommodations, and I wasn't even sure how that might work. I visited the colleges that I was interested in because I knew even if they had disability services it didn't necessarily mean they served students with Braille or had an in-house embosser, so I asked about their alternative media department. I knew majoring in psychology I would need to take statistics and would need hard copies in Braille. All the vetting of services doesn't mean it will work. Even after I got to [college], I had some trouble convincing them to get equipment they needed to support me.

Katie needed more time to develop her self-advocacy skills. As academically prepared as she was for college, Katie had "no great conversations about transitioning from high school to college and what students with disabilities would need to be successful." Although Katie completed her education degree in four years and started teaching high school upon graduation, she feels that she didn't really develop the self-advocacy skills she needed until she was teaching her own students. During her first year or two of teaching, Katie began "reading Disability Studies blogs and scholarship and following those folks online." The only visibly disabled teacher at her school, Katie soon realized that "no one was talking about disability in the curriculum or in ways to make students with disabilities feel included." In her undergraduate teacher education courses, "no one challenged me to think about how my disability identity would interact and transform how I taught." She now advises high school students to look for a college with a disability services office they feel comfortable with and high school teachers and counselors to help students understand the very different process for getting accommodations in college.

Kate struggled with accessibility as an undergraduate. As one of a handful of deaf students at her large city university, Kate found the disability resources office not well equipped to help her receive accommodations and didn't follow up on needed paperwork. Kate, who was interested in historic preservation, was told that deaf and hard-of-hearing students don't major in art history. The office failed to send letters of accommodation to her instructors each term so that Kate had to tell them what she needed and advocate for those needs in class. Kate used hearing aids and worked really hard to read lips. When she had to remind professors that she could not understand classroom discussion when the lights were turned off or if the instructor did not use a microphone or when she could not sit in a reserved seat at the front of the room, she was often met with disbelief or criticism for requesting special treatment. With a lot of work, Kate maintained high grades, but the strain of college without a functional disability resources office and other deaf and disabled students she could talk to eventually took a toll on Kate's health and she needed additional years to recover and complete her degree requirements. Kate knew that she wanted to go on to graduate school, but she was very worried about getting the accommodations and supports she would need. Back in the northeastern town where she went to high school, Kate attended a public lecture by Gallaudet University History Professor Kirk VanGilder at the large research university there. The lecture was signed and live captioned, and Kate was excited that the lecture on disability identities was so accessible to her. She met Dr. VanGilder after the talk and became connected to the very active disability community at the university, where she decided to work on her master's degree. Kate discovered that pursuing disability studies in graduate school greatly improved her self-advocacy skills. Kate didn't take her first disability studies class until graduate school but found the experience transformational:

> *[In that class] on autism, I got a totally different take on disability than I had ever heard in my life: disability is to be celebrated as a part of diversity. No one had ever told me anything like that before. Deafness was an impairment, a deficit that scared parents who were hearing, and others try to ignore. I stopped going to school, stopped thinking about the future, because I didn't have access. This is a huge part of my identity that I had been suppressing for so long.*

With the encouragement of her professor and other culturally Deaf academics she met, Kate began the process of relearning sign language and incorporating disability in her education research. She found her academic and social needs far better supported by the people, services, programs, and activities at her graduate institution, which valued disability and diversity.

When students experienced discrimination, problems with services, and ableist attitudes of others, they needed to know their rights and fight for them, while also persisting in dealing with issues until they were satisfactorily addressed. Ann tried to think creatively when barriers arose, realizing she

> had to be competent, successful, and resilient. I was challenged and had to be willing to step out of my comfort zone and be uncomfortable. There will always be naysayers who say blind people can't learn Chinese for example. Sometimes "no" is just another opportunity for students to say, "Let me map out my plan using persuasive rhetoric and try again." A lot of blind students who have tried STEM have been discouraged because the field is so visual and there is a lot of naysaying about math. Many of the opportunities are in STEM, but the expectations aren't there. When blind students want to do physics or computer science, they are likely to be diverted. People should have the right to choose, not have choices made for them. "No" doesn't always mean "no." So students may just need to propose a different strategy.

K also learned that creative problem-solving and persistence is necessary when trying to engage other campus offices to be responsive to the needs of a person with a disability. When K followed the school's guidelines to request that a math final exam be rescheduled in order to represent TEAM USA at an international swim competition, the request was denied. While an able-bodied student competing for TEAM USA would be granted a date change to compete internationally, student services had to be convinced that a student with a physical disability would have such a need, and that this request was appropriate and legitimate.

Ann and Katie both had to be creative in order to navigate others' access concerns and determine for themselves what accommodations would enable them to complete educational fieldwork expectations. Although Ann started working on a field placement before her upper division course on literacy began, her project was not approved by a supervising teacher, first because of safety concerns, and subsequently because of questions about how a Braille reader could be employed to teach literacy in a general education class. Ann vowed to take the course until she was allowed to complete her fieldwork before she was allowed to complete her project the second time around. She then received high praise from the school district and the supervising teacher. Ann said, "You have to be challenging in a professional and persistent manner, depending on how much you value the opportunity." Knowing she had both internship and student teaching to complete senior year, Katie began planning for the accommodations she would need during her junior year, especially transportation to and from her school placement. Katie's mobility needs had increased, and she anticipated using a wheelchair full time and no longer being able to drive by her senior year. When she wasn't able to carpool with a friend in the program, Katie worked out a new solution to use the city's paratransit bus system to get to a field placement within the city limits. Katie was ultimately hired by the school in which she completed student teaching.

The principal lesson from the students we talked to is that they are having a wide-ranging college experience like all other students, involved in courses, athletics, academics, student organizations, and so much more. Disability services played an important role, but it isn't the only resource or support. Like other students, they also grow and mature throughout college, changing the way they view themselves, self-advocate, and socialize.

Conclusion

The contributors to this chapter shared, in their own words, their lived experiences as disabled students at colleges in the US. While some are working now, and others are in graduate school, the similarities and differences in their college experiences can serve as a valuable resource to prospective and current undergraduate students, teachers, parents, and others. The value and importance of finding mentors and role models, building networks and learning to self-advocate, learning to leave your comfort zone and develop new skills was emphasized by several students. Furthermore, finding the balance between disability support services and faculty that can support them sufficiently and just being a "regular" student "like any other" remains a never-ending process of negotiation. The students in this chapter learned to embrace the sameness and differences to access the whole student experience rather than focusing solely on their disability.

We hope that this chapter provides high school students and others thinking about college education with inspiration to find their own mentors and community of other students with disabilities. It is also our hope that teachers, parents, and others who support students with disabilities will find tools and information in this chapter to empower them to guide and assist the students in their journey to college.

References

Minow, M. (1991). *Making all the difference: Inclusion, exclusion, and American law.* Ithaca, NY: Cornell University Press.

Vance, M. L. (2007). Taking risks. In M. L. Vance (Ed.) *Disabled faculty and staff in a disabling society: Multiple identities in higher education* (pp. 11–24). Huntersville, NC: Association on Higher Education And Disability (AHEAD).

Resources

In addition to the valuable advice provided by the contributors to this chapter, we recommend you look for additional resources by college students and recent graduates for high school and first-year college students. For example, disability activist and editor, Emily Ladau (2017, August 10) recently interviewed college graduates for the *Self* magazine article "12 Things I Wish I'd Known Before Going to College with a Disability or Chronic Illness," which we highly recommend. Students involved in DREAM: Disability Rights, Education, Activism, and Mentoring, a national online group for college students with disabilities,

---

TEN TIPS
FOR STUDENTS WITH DISABILITIES...
FROM STUDENTS WITH DISABILITIES

1. **Disability accommodations are rights, not special help.**
   Ask for what you need. Advocate for yourself.

2. **You are an important and valuable part of campus diversity.**
   Diversity includes disability.

3. **College disability services offices can be gatekeepers.**
   Most are good allies for students, but some are not. Demand professional, individualized, respectful services and file a complaint if you don't get them.

4. **Feed your soul and body.**
   Balance your valuable time, energy, and health.

5. **Stay focused on your career.**
   If it won't help you get a job or maintain your passion for college, don't bother.

6. **Find a community.**
   Never go it alone. Consider connecting with others who have disabilities.

7. **Universally design your own learning.**
   Learn how you learn best, and then use your strengths and unique learning style.

8. **Never apologize for your disability or your accommodations.**
   If you apologize, people may think you are ashamed.

9. **Fight oppression and bully in g in any form.**
   Ableism is just one "ism." If one of us is oppressed, all of us are oppressed.

10. **Learn disability history.**
    Learn about the people and movement that made it possible for you to be in college.

This is available in other formats upon request. Funding for NCCSD and DREAM is from the Fund for the improvement of Post secondary Education (FI PSE) at the US Dept. of Education (P116D150005).

FIGURE 1.1 Ten Tips for Students with Disabilities From Students with Disabilities

produced another list of top tips for college students that complements the recommendations in this chapter and Ladau's article.

A reproducible poster of Figure 1.1, "Top Ten List for College Students by
College Students," along with other resources for college students with disabilities and their allies, is available on the DREAM website (http://Dream
CollegeDisability.org). In addition, the National Center for College Students
with Disabilities (NCCSD), which sponsors DREAM, has a comprehensive list
of campus-based student disability organizations, and information about national
organizations working with students, including those working with students who
have specific types of disabilities (http://NCCSDonline.org). Below is a sample
of the organizations for college students with disabilities on the NCCSD website
as well as recommended books on transitioning to college.

National Organizations:

- The National Center for College Students with Disabilities (www.NCCS
  Donline.org):
  The NCCSD provides resources and technical assistance to all college students with disabilities, including undergraduate and graduate students. They
  have an online Clearinghouse where students can get resources for free
  (www.NCCSDClearinghouse.org) and DREAM, a national group run by
  college students for students (www.DREAMCollegeDisability.org).
- The National Deaf Center for Postsecondary Outcomes (www.National
  DeafCenter.org/)
  If you are a culturally Deaf student, deaf or hard-of-hearing, the NDC can
  help connect you to resources and information. They can also provide information about deafness, hearing loss, and common accommodations to any
  parents, high school teachers, college faculty, or disability services staff. For
  high school students, they also have an online training tool to help students
  plan goals and a path to college.
- Think College (www.ThinkCollege.net)
  Think College focuses on expanding college options for students with intellectual and developmental disabilities, who have typically not had many
  opportunities to get an education after high school. They have lists of campus-
  based transition programs across the country, for high school students aged
  18–21 who are still receiving special education services, as well as for students who have graduated but are exploring college options. Think College
  can also provide information about financial aid options, Medicaid waivers,
  and other resources.
- PACER Center (www.pacer.org/)
  PACER Center is actually designed for parents, who can find information
  about transition services required in high school, including documents in a

variety of languages. Students may find PACER's resources helpful, as well, and they can refer family members to PACER for support and networking with other families.

Books

- *Preparing Students with Disabilities for College Success: A Practical Guide to Transition Planning* by Stan F. Shaw, Joseph W. Madaus, and Lyman L. Dukes (Baltimore, MD: Brookes Publishing Company). While this was written for professionals, parents and students can find everything they need to know about getting ready for college, and what high schools should be doing during the transition process. It includes comprehensive information about the ADA and Section 504, and how college disability services offices work.
- *Learning Outside the Lines: Two Ivy League Students with Learning Disabilities and ADHD Give You the Tools for Academic Success and Educational Revolution* by Jonathan Mooney and David Cole (Touchstone. See www.amazon. com/Learning-Outside-Lines-Disabilities-Education/dp/068486598X). This book can help students with any type of disability consider how they learn best, and suggests practical strategies for dealing with college-level academics.
- *Empowering Leadership: A Systems Change Guide for Autistic Students and Those with Other Disabilities* by the Autistic Self-Advocacy Network. This handbook by and for disabled students helps develop leadership and organizing skills to foster change on campus. Students may also find the information helpful for dealing with administrators when problems occur.
- *Navigating College: A Handbook on Self Advocacy* by the Autistic Self-Advocacy Network. While written for autistic students, the information could easily apply to students with many other disabilities, including mental and emotional illnesses. With tips for academics, housing, social situations, and talking about disability with others, it covers practical information that most students could use during their first years of college.

2

EXPECTATIONS FOR COLLEGE

Meg Grigal

UNIVERSITY OF MASSACHUSETTS BOSTON

Clare Papay

UNIVERSITY OF MASSACHUSETTS BOSTON

> *We had to first and foremost listen to Micah's dream to go to college. He has always lived IN the community and participated in the same classes and activities as his peers. Thus, he internalized the same expectations as his peers had: that is, after high school you go to college. It is just what you do in our community! It never dawned on him that he wouldn't go to college. We also had to listen to [Micah's] dream initially without worrying about how we would make this happen. If we started with the barriers and the unlikelihood of his going to college, we would have stopped dead in our tracks. We had to always be guided by Micah's dream. Our mantra became, "It isn't if he would go to college, it is how he would go to college." This didn't mean that we knew what we were doing or how to make it happen. We really had no idea about the first steps to get Micah to college. But we had to create the vision and move toward it.*
>
> *(Janice Fialka, sharing her perspective on her son*
> *Micah's dream of going to college*[1]*)*

Micah Fialka Feldman wanted to go to college. His family and teachers supported this expectation, and helped him make that dream a reality. Micah also had an intellectual disability. And when he was preparing to leave high school, there were no college programs in his state that enrolled students with intellectual disability. Thus, Micah's path to college wasn't easy or traditional. But he succeeded in going to college, and taking classes that met his needs and interests. His success started with the simple expectation that he should be able to go.

How do you get students interested in going to college? How can educators' expectations impact college as a choice? This chapter explores the most important aspect of preparing for college: the expectation that it will happen.

Research has demonstrated that teacher and parent expectations often determine what students with disabilities do after high school. Teacher expectations are impacted both by teachers' knowledge about existing college programs and services, and their experience supporting students with diverse learning needs when accessing programs. Strategies such as incorporating college prep activities in the individualized education program (IEP), building knowledge about higher education, visiting colleges, and understanding different paths to college are included in this chapter. Tools to support conversations about college priorities are provided, as well as disability-specific online resources.

The Impact of Expectations

College expectations permeate the academic and social experiences of college-bound youth throughout their K–12 education experiences (Grigal & Hart, 2012). Transition-aged students base their desired future plans largely upon what they have been told is and is not possible by their family and their teachers. Higher expectations for academic and career success have been found to relate to better high school completion rates and higher postsecondary school attendance rates (Grigal & Deschamps, 2012; Boser, Wilhelm, & Hanna, 2014; Wagner, Newman, Cameto, Levine, & Marder, 2007). Teacher expectations may be directly or indirectly influenced by the type or severity of a student's disability (Newman, 2005), their race, or ethnicity (McGrew & Evans, 2004), and also by their socio-economic status. Poverty may influence both how and when school personnel charged with educating students provide those students and their parents with needed information about higher education access and opportunity (Madaus, Grigal, & Hughes, 2014).

To exit high school and successfully transition into a college or university, long-term planning and preparation are needed. In the early elementary years, children are encouraged to recognize college as an option for their future. During the middle school years, conversations about college begin to build a student's awareness of postsecondary education options available to them. As students age, these conversations become more personalized and specific, and their results more tangible, impacting the courses students take in high school, the clubs and activities they join, and their discussions with family members, teachers, and counselors about next steps.

Brand, Valent, and Danielson (2013) state that, while students with disabilities have transition plans,

> many plans lack depth, breadth, and personalization; have low expectations for students with disabilities; do not include plans for postsecondary education; and do not map out how the K–12 education system should connect to other systems, such as postsecondary, vocational rehabilitation,

workforce training, or independent services. As a result, many students with disabilities leave high school with amorphous and generic plans that fail to address their individual circumstances or interests.

(p. 12)

This lack of specificity is exacerbated by the exclusion of students with disabilities from many of the college-planning activities that exist in secondary education. Too often, students with disabilities do not have access to high school counselors who could provide them with information about college fairs, financial aid, and college applications. Instead, they often work with transition specialists, who have little training or knowledge about guiding students to choose an appropriate path to higher education. Teachers and transition professionals may unintentionally set the bar too low. This is not because they wish to limit students, but because they lack understanding of the various paths to and through college that are available to students with disabilities and their families.

The overall focus of education in the United States centers upon preparing students to be college- and career-ready. There are a multitude of research entities (e.g., Community College Research Center, Educational Policy Improvement Center, College and Career Readiness Center) and corresponding reports (Barnett, 2016; Conley, 2007; Hein, Smerdon, & Sambolt, 2013) about how to support college readiness, how to connect the college experience to careers, and how to support access, retention, and graduation. These initiatives provide rich resources for college-going students. But they usually only target students without disabilities who are taking a standard path to and through college. These resources also presume that the student and his or her educational team are expecting the student to access higher education.

We suggest that the first step to becoming college- and career-ready is that school professionals believe that college is an option for a wide range of students. Expectations are the foundation upon which all future educational attainment rests. A teacher's beliefs and expectations can have as great an impact on a student going to college as that student's academic skills or performance (Gregory & Huang, 2013; Papageorge, Gershenson, & Kang, 2016).

This chapter begins with an exploration of who is "college material" and the myth of the perfect college student. Strategies for educators to change their own expectations about students' potential for college are provided, followed by strategies for educators to work with families to develop and support college expectations for students with disabilities.

Who is College Material?

Juan is a fifteen-year-old with an intellectual disability and attention deficit disorder who is in the tenth grade. He struggles with reading and has had detention a few times as he tends not to pay attention in class. He is very good with his hands, and enjoys building things and taking them apart. He doesn't speak up much in class, but during one-on-one he has talked about wishing he could get a good job and help his family.

- Is Juan college material?
- Should *all* students be expected to go to college?
- Does this include students with a range of disabilities?

The short answer to all of these questions is yes. Yes, all students with disabilities should be expected to go to college. That doesn't necessarily mean that all students with disabilities will choose to attend. Just like other students without disability, a student's path will reflect personal goals. But if the expectation for college is eliminated because of a student's disability label, that student is being shortchanged, and their future potential for success may be unnecessarily limited. So, if all students, even those with disabilities, are expected to go to college, how does that impact what we do every day? How does it impact our conversations with students, discussions with their families, and the educational services we provide?

How Do We Set Expectations?

The expectations of teachers are influenced by a variety of factors, including experience with previous students and exposure to knowledge and resources about available options. Teachers' experience and knowledge may be constricted to the content area they teach, and therefore they may not be aware of emerging support programs that help students with diverse support needs access and achieve success in college.

In order to set high expectations for college, it is essential that from the earliest grades teachers, parents, and students believe that it is possible, and that there is continuity in this belief across a student's educational career. How do you help people believe in something if their current frame of reference doesn't demonstrate that it is possible?

The Myth of the Perfect College Student

When talking about college expectations, it is necessary to address the pervasive myth of the perfect college student. This is the student who is quintessentially "college material." She has good grades throughout middle and high school, and has participated in athletics and school clubs, as well as other extracurricular activities. She applied for early admission to a four-year university to attain a bachelor's degree and graduated with that degree four years later. This tends to be a mythical path, as the majority of students do not fit this description.

Based on the latest data (from fall 2014), of the 17.3 million undergraduate students in the United States, 38 percent study part time, 39 percent are enrolled at two-year institutions, and nearly a quarter take distance education courses (NCES, 2016a). Fewer than half of all students at a postsecondary institution are enrolled in a bachelor's degree program. A substantial portion are enrolled in either an associate degree or occupational certificate program, or are simply participating in college classes (NCES, 2016b). Although most students at two-year and four-year public and nonprofit institutions are under age 25, the majority of students attending private for-profit institutions are 25 or older (NCES, 2016c).

Going to college does not mean that an individual cannot also work. Of college students aged 16 to 24 enrolled in fall 2014, 41 percent of full-time and 80 percent of part-time students worked (NCES, 2016c). A college degree can take longer than four years to complete, even for full-time students. Of first-time college students who were seeking a bachelor's degree or its equivalent and attending a four-year institution full time beginning in 2007, 39 percent finished within four years, 55 percent within five years, and 59 percent within six years.

Overcoming the perfect student myth can be very difficult for students with disabilities. Even though the percentage of students with disabilities enrolling in postsecondary education has grown in the past 20 years (Wagner, Newman, Cameto, & Levine, 2005), many students still receive the message from their teachers that they are not "college material." Sometimes this is directly related to their disability. Sometimes it is related to other factors, such as grades and socioeconomic status (Madaus, Grigal, & Hughes, 2014). The educational expectations that individuals have for themselves change very little between ages 14 and 26 (Mello, 2009). Therefore, if teachers and parents set low expectations in adolescence, these low expectations are likely to persist into adulthood (Gregory & Huang, 2013).

Illustrating the Power of Expectations

Teacher expectations not only influence the expectations of students and their families, they also impact the resources and opportunities that ultimately determine a student's academic path. Below we offer two examples of the academic path for Juan determined by perspectives and expectations of the educator involved.

One teacher's perspective

Mr. DiMaria, a secondary special educator who teaches a learning support class, has had students like Juan before. He finds them challenging in terms of both behavior and learning, and he expects that this student will not go to college after high school. He's not even sure Juan will graduate from high school.

At Juan's IEP meeting, Mr. DiMaria describes Juan's academic deficits and behavior problems, and when discussing his transition plan, informs Juan's family that there are services available for students like their son. Mr. DiMaria then shares some forms related to vocational rehabilitation eligibility, along with a transition checklist document, and tells the family about an upcoming transition resource fair. He states that this is where all of the local service providers that support sheltered work and day habilitation (Goodwill Industries, the Arc) describe their services.

Juan is placed into a segregated life skills class, where he learns how to make change, assemble kits in a makeshift assembly line, and engage in "functional academics." He is not exposed to the general curricula, and his IEP goals are related to connecting him with service providers and exposing him to career exploration experiences. In-school jobs, such as cleaning the cafeteria tables and making copies in the office, are a part of his vocational training.

The expectation for Juan is that he will leave high school in seven years with a high school certificate, and possibly have a part-time job after leaving high school.

A different perspective

Ms. LeGrand, a high school transition specialist, has also worked with students like this before. Juan struggles academically, but given the right supports and opportunities, she knows that he can succeed in high school and continue his education in college afterward.

Before Juan's IEP meeting, Ms. LeGrand meets with Juan and asks him about what his goals are for after high school. Juan says he'd like to build or fix things like his uncle, but doesn't think his grades are good enough for him to go to a technology school.

At his IEP meeting, Ms. LeGrand describes a few different paths that Juan could take to get into a vocational and technical college. She knows that Juan would be the first member of his family to attend college, so she makes sure to explain the different kinds of programs available and the types of financial assistance they could access.

College visits and a college fair are listed as activities in Juan's IEP for this year. Ms. LeGrand plans to hold an informational evening session for families to explain the support available to students with disabilities in college. She works with Juan's school counselor to help Juan enroll in a career academy course in HVAC, and plans to talk with him about getting an internship in his senior year with a local business.

In her advisory period, Ms. LeGrand creates lessons, group work, and projects that allow students with and without disabilities to explore what college looks like and identify things that they can do today to prepare for college. She expects that Juan may take a little longer to be prepared to go to college, but knows that given the right supports, he can do it.

Ms. LeGrand provides opportunities for her students to learn about college students with differing disabilities. She also invites recent graduates, with and without disabilities, to share how they began their college journeys.

Mr. DiMaria's and Ms. LeGrand's expectations of Juan determine his access to academic content, his access to specific teachers and other professionals in and out of school, and his parents' knowledge of area resources, supports, and future opportunities. The student in both of these scenarios is the same person: Juan. He has the same background, same disability, and same amount of potential. His educators' views of him, and their knowledge of future options, influence their response to his situation.

As an educator, transition specialist, or school counselor, you are setting the expectations of students with disabilities and their families about their potential for future learning. It may be that, through your interactions with families, you have indicated that college is not a realistic goal because of their child's learning or intellectual disability, their behaviors, or their lack of motivation or effort. It important to acknowledge the impact expectations have on both the short-term goals and long-term outcomes of students with disabilities. In the remainder of the chapter, we offer suggestions for changing one's expectations of students with disabilities, as well as strategies to support families and students with disabilities in setting and achieving the goal of college.

Changing the Expectations of School Professionals

Expectations are based upon two things: knowledge and experience. If one's knowledge of existing college programs is limited to the traditional two- or four-year matriculated path to an associate or bachelor's degree, it is likely that students who do not fit the "perfect college student" stereotype will be guided to a pursuit other than college. If one's experience is that most students with learning, mental health, intellectual, or mobility disabilities do not have the skills or abilities to go to college, it is likely that future students with these disabilities will not be expected to go to college. An important first step in changing the expectations for students with disabilities is to first expand one's own knowledge and experience.

How to Expand Knowledge

Sometimes it's easier to say something is not possible than trying to figure out all the ways it might be possible. School professionals may believe that a student with intellectual disability or autism is not capable of succeeding in college because they are unaware of existing pathways and programs for students with these disabilities to access higher education, or the supports that are available to help these students succeed in college. One way to expand knowledge of how students with disabilities access higher education is through watching videos. Examples of two videos that are available online and questions to consider while watching are shown in Figure 2.1. Reflecting on these questions is an important first step to understanding the expectations that one might inadvertently hold about students with disabilities.

A second step to increasing knowledge is to understand the supports that can help students with disabilities to succeed in higher education. It is not necessary

VIDEO TITLE	LINK	DESCRIPTION
Succeeding in College and Work: Students with Disabilities Tell Their Stories	www.newenglandada.org/videos	Video series produced by the New England ADA Center. A student with spina bifida, a student with learning disabilities, and a student with a visual impairment talk about their experiences in college.
Rethinking College	www.thinkcollege.net/ rethinking-college	Video produced by Think College that illustrates how students with intellectual disability are able to access college through innovative programs and supports.

Questions to ask yourself while watching these videos:
- How do low expectations and lack of opportunities impact students with disabilities?
- How have expectations and opportunities impacted your choices in life?
- How can you change your expectations to ensure that you are not limiting future possibilities for students with disabilities?

FIGURE 2.1 Videos to increase knowledge of students with disabilities attending college

to become an expert in college disability pathways to support the idea that every student can access college. A plethora of websites share disability-specific information around this topic. Some of these are highlighted in Figure 2.2. As you review these websites, ask yourself these questions:

- How does this change or add to what I know about how students with a particular disability can access college?
- How can I share this information with students, parents, or other educators?
- What knowledge do I still need to gain about how students with a particular disability can access college?

As an educator and counselor, your role is to encourage students and their families to gather this information. When you learn about a new resource, share it widely, and keep it in mind for future students and families.

How to Expand Experience

Unless a teacher or a teacher's family member has recently applied to college or is currently attending college, it might be difficult to draw upon current experience regarding supports and services available in college. Additionally, unless a teacher or a teacher's family member had a disability while attending college,

BLINDNESS	
www.accreditedschoolsonline.org/resources/helping-students-with-visual-impaiments/	A webpage from Accredited Schools Online that provides information on accommodations for students with visual impairment, tips for finding the right school, and links to resources and scholarships
http://ods.rutgers.edu/faculty/visual	A webpage for faculty at Rutgers University with information on accommodating students with visual impairment that may be useful for understanding the many strategies that can be used
DEAFNESS	
http://www.jsu.edu/dept/dss/nuts&bolts/introduction.pdf	A guide for students from Pepnet on college success for students who are deaf or hard of hearing
MENTAL HEALTH	
http://www.nami.org/collegeguide/	A downloadable guide for college students from the National Alliance on Mental Illness to begin the conversation about mental health issues during college
www.mentalhealthamerica.net/whats-your-plan-college-mental-health-disorder	A webpage from Mental Health America with information on planning for college for students with a mental health disorder
INTELLECTUAL DISABILITY	
www.thinkcollege.net	A website that provides information and resources on college for students with intellectual disability, including interviews and advice from college students
LEARNING DISABILITIES	
https://www.washington.edu/doit/sites/default/files/atoms/files/Academic-Accommodations-Learning-Disabilities.pdf	A guide from DO-IT on academic accommodations for students with learning disabilities
https://www.understood.org/en/school-learning/choosing-starting-school/leaving-high-school	A webpage from Understood.org that gives tips for families to ease the transition to college for students with learning disabilities
www.greatschools.org/gk/articles/college-planning/	A webpage from Great Schools that provides information for families to understand college for students with learning disabilities
ADHD	
https://add.org/college-students/	A list of resources for college students with ADHD from the Attention Deficit Disorder Association
https://www.additudemag.com/category/parenting-adhd-kids/school-learning/college/	A college survival guide from ADDitude magazine, with articles and tips for students and parents
MOBILITY	
www.usnews.com/education/best-colleges/articles/2011/12/05/4-tips-for-college-applicants-students-with-physical-disabilities	A list of tips for college applicants and students with physical disabilities from U.S. News and World Report
AUTISM	
www.navigatingcollege.org	A downloadable guide for autistic college students written by adults on the autism spectrum, with a focus on self-advocacy
CHRONIC HEALTH CONDITIONS	
www.onlinecolleges.net/for-students/chronic-health-issues/	A website by the Center for Online Education that provides information and resources on attending college for students with a chronic health condition

FIGURE 2.2 Disability-specific resources for college planning

he or she may also be lacking experience in navigating the process used to seek assistance from a disability services office, request and receive effective accommodations, or ensure services meet accessibility guidelines. Most high school teachers, unless they are involved in career academies or learning labs that are co-sponsored by colleges, may not have collaborated with college personnel since they themselves attended college.

If it has been a long time since you went to college or you attended college in a different state or region from where you currently teach, gather information about what is available for the students you serve in your state or region. Connect with the disability services office at your local colleges to ask about the supports that they provide to students. Visit local colleges to see support programs firsthand. If there are no nearby campuses, consider connecting via Skype or another video call platform. Invite representatives from the disability services office to speak to your class (either in person or virtually) to share with your students with and without disabilities the services that are available to support learning on their campus. Chapter 7 provides further information and suggestions on college visits.

Another important way to build your experience is by facilitating opportunities for your students to learn from current college students with a variety of disabilities about their experiences. Ask graduates who have gone on to college to visit your school to speak directly to your students, or visit college students at a local college. If it is not possible to visit a college nearby, there are a variety of online resources that allow you and your students to virtually tour college and university campuses. If it is not possible to arrange for in-person or virtual conversations with college students, ask graduates what helped them believe that they were capable of going to college, and share this information with your students.

Strategies to Ensure High Expectations for Students with Disabilities

Once you have expanded your own experience and knowledge of how students with disabilities can access and succeed in higher education, several strategies can ensure that students are encouraged and supported to aim for college.

Build college knowledge: "College knowledge" refers to all the skills that are necessary for knowing how to apply for and succeed in college. These skills include understanding the college admission and selection process, financial aid, academic expectations in college, and the cultural differences between high school and college (Hooker & Brand, 2010). Many students with disabilities, in particular those who will be the first in their family to go to college, lack college knowledge, and may have limited access to role models to help them gain knowledge (Brand et al., 2013). Educators can provide explicit instruction to build college knowledge and readiness skills. Resources that can be used to build college knowledge skills are shown in Figure 2.3.

RESOURCE	LINK	DESCRIPTION
Step by Step: College Awareness and Planning for Families, Counselors and Communities	https://www.nacacnet.org/advocacy—ethics/initiatives/steps/	Curriculum on college awareness by the National Association for College Admission Counseling with components for middle school, early high school, and late high school. Includes both learning activities for students and guides for leading parent workshops. A workshop on financial aid is also included.
KnowHow2Go	http://knowhow2go.acenet.edu	Website by the American Council for Education with resources to encourage primarily 8th to 10th grade students to prepare for college.
I'm First	www.imfirst.org	Online community for first-generation college students, including stores from college students and resources for finding colleges and getting answers to questions about going to college.

FIGURE 2.3 Resources to build college knowledge

Address disability needs as leadership: Too often in our schools, special education and disability have a stigma. This stigma manifests as an unwillingness by students to admit to having a disability, and can sometimes lead to depression, isolation, or behavior problems (Izzo & Horne, 2016). Disability stigma and corresponding shame may also prevent students from seeking help when they need it. Many students would rather struggle and ultimately fail than admit they need services, supports, or accommodations due to their disability. LeDerick Horne, a poet and disability advocate who was diagnosed as a child with a neurological disability, shared how the stigma of disability impacted his expectations for his future.

> My identity was at a crisis point by the time I reached high school. I had been in special education for years, but I still did not know exactly what my disability was or what was going to happen to me once I graduated. My academic skills were still way below my grade level, and as a result, I didn't think I was going to be able to go to college or have a career. I felt ashamed of my past, embarrassed by my present and completely frightened by my future. I knew that I was going to graduate from high school, I knew they would push me across that stage and hand me

a diploma. But then I had no idea what I was going to do. There was an abyss waiting for me on the other end of the graduation stage, and as the abyss grew closer, I was convinced that I didn't have the skills needed to successfully cross over to the adult world. Anxiety, depression, and nervousness became as constant as the air I breathed.[2]

LeDerick's experience reflects how deeply impacted students can be by their disability label and how academic struggles impacted his psychological and emotional well-being. He also illustrates how alone he felt during this time. Becoming comfortable with talking about disability can be a challenge for both students and teachers. Approaching disability supports in the context of self-determination and goal achievement can allow students to see themselves as a leader of the educational process, and their use of accommodations as just another tool to employ to achieve their goals. Teachers can establish a positive dynamic by helping students with disabilities learn and share what works for them. Given the current array of academic apps, study skills websites, and voice output software, it is no longer unusual to employ assistive technology to assist with academic tasks. Making this an expectation and providing positive feedback to students about not only how these strategies can be of benefit in high school, but also how they can contribute in college, will help to build students' expectations about their potential to succeed.

Support students in talking to parents/guardians: Many students with disabilities may find that the dream of going to college is not shared by parents/guardians or other important adults in their lives. They may be the first person in the family who plans to go to college, or their parents/guardians may have accepted the incorrect predictions of professionals who have deemed their child to be "not college material." These students will need support to begin the conversation with their parents/guardians. Figure 2.4 provides a list of strategies by the American Council for Education (ACE, 2014) for students to approach talking to their parents/guardians.

Educators can support students by first sharing these tips, and then supporting students in planning what they want to say to their parents. Educators can also help students with writing their ideas down and rehearsing, so that they are prepared to initiate the conversation with their parents.

Remember there is no "right way" to plan for college: As a busy educator, it can be tempting to offer a college preparation checklist to parents at an IEP meeting and consider the job of planning for college completed. For example, the checklist provided in Chapter 6 offers a detailed overview of the types of experiences that could facilitate college preparation for students between ninth and twelfth grade.

While these types of checklists serve a purpose, and provide some structure to the college-planning activities, they often present an "ideal" pathway to college. These checklists are not able to take into account each family's current priorities,

1. PLAN WHAT YOU WANT TO SAY.

Think about what you want your parents to know about your goal to attend college and why you need them to be on board.

2. BE DIRECT.

Tell them there is something you want to discuss and make sure you have their full attention.

3. PICK A GOOD TIME TO TALK.

Approach them at a time when they will be able to focus on the conversation. You can even set a time in advance, for example, "There's something I want to talk with you about. Can we make some time when we eat dinner tonight to talk about it?"

4. WRITE IT DOWN FIRST.

Write down your thoughts in a letter or email before your conversation. If you want to sent it, you can. Or, you can just use what you write to get ready and get your thoughts organized.

5. DISAGREE WITHOUT DISRESPECT.

Remember, you are challenging ideas that your parents have had for a long time. Be sure to use respectful language, listen to them, and stay calm.

FIGURE 2.4 Strategies for students to approach talking to parents/guardians

Source: American Council for Education (2014)

access, and resources. To complement this process and help facilitate conversations around these planning activities, we suggest that educators use the College Priority Mapping tool (see Figure 2.5 for a blank version and Figure 2.5b for an example of a completed tool).

This tool helps parents to reflect on the primary factors that may influence their child's path to college. It also acknowledges that a student's and a parent's thoughts about what college can offer may be different. Additionally, the tool presents a chance to discuss other important elements such as program availability, resources, and time management.

Productive conversations between parents and professionals about college cannot happen in a vacuum. These conversations must acknowledge that each decision takes place in the context of a family's current situation. In some cases, students may want to go to college, but may already have one or two siblings attending college. This may impact what their family can afford, where they go to college (e.g., a local community college instead of an out-of-state college), if they attend full or part-time, or if they are able to live in campus housing. Some families may be dealing with the care of an aging grandparent, health concerns of another family member, or unexpected unemployment. Other parents may be working multiple jobs or coping with the stresses of single parenting, and the idea of tackling college may be difficult.

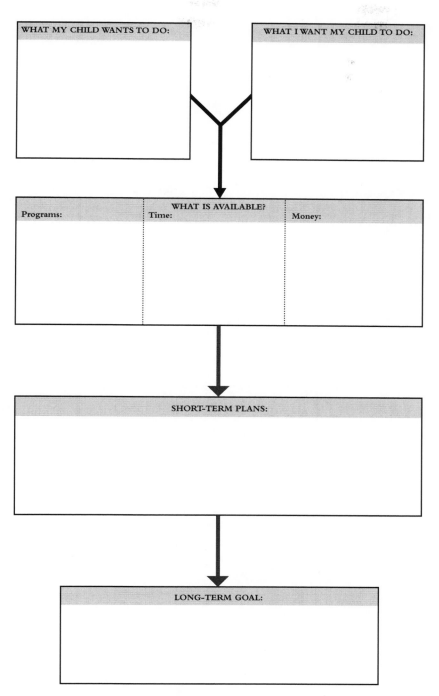

FIGURE 2.5 College Priority Mapping Tool

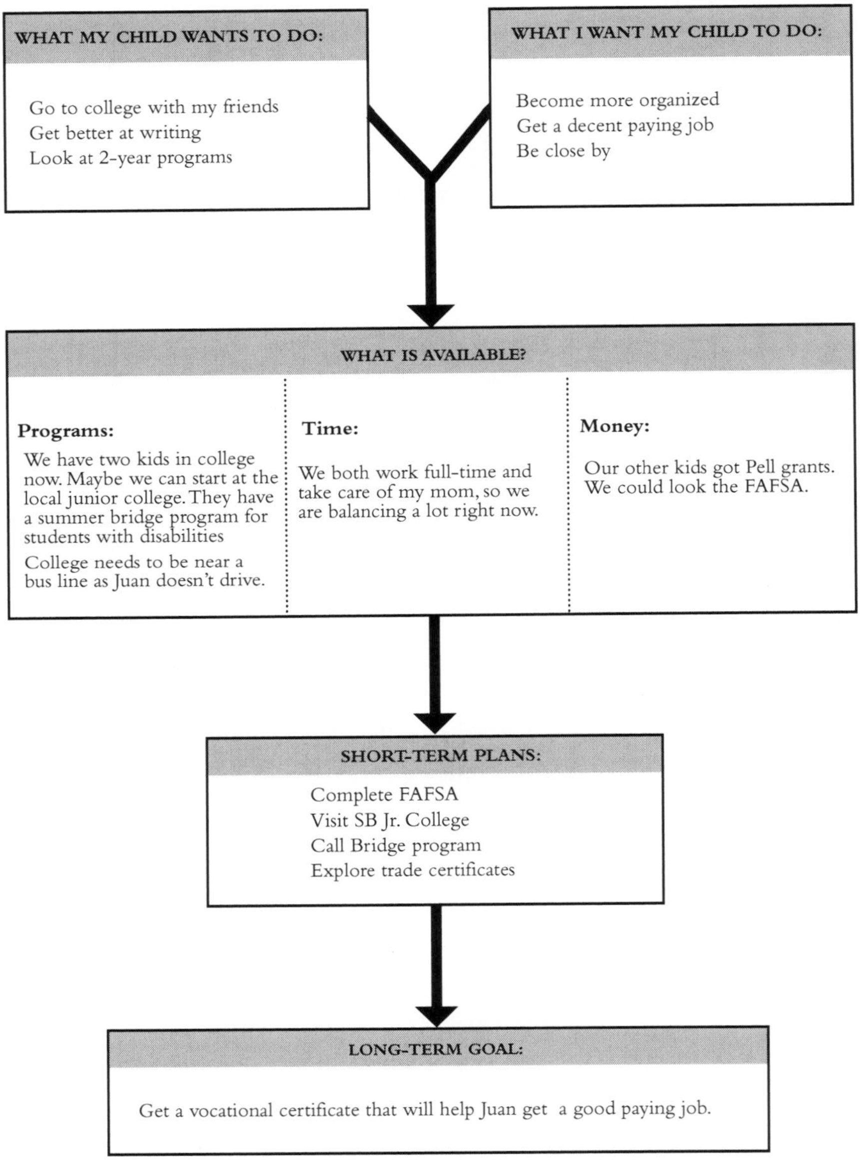

WHAT MY CHILD WANTS TO DO:

Go to college with my friends
Get better at writing
Look at 2-year programs

WHAT I WANT MY CHILD TO DO:

Become more organized
Get a decent paying job
Be close by

WHAT IS AVAILABLE?

Programs:

We have two kids in college now. Maybe we can start at the local junior college. They have a summer bridge program for students with disabilities

College needs to be near a bus line as Juan doesn't drive.

Time:

We both work full-time and take care of my mom, so we are balancing a lot right now.

Money:

Our other kids got Pell grants. We could look the FAFSA.

SHORT-TERM PLANS:

Complete FAFSA
Visit SB Jr. College
Call Bridge program
Explore trade certificates

LONG-TERM GOAL:

Get a vocational certificate that will help Juan get a good paying job.

FIGURE 2.5B   Example completed College Priority Mapping Tool

Family situations may impact the level of priority placed on college. Still, it is important to discuss with both students and families that even if an immediate plan for college might be difficult due to personal situations, discussing college options for the future should be a part of transition planning. Just because a student may not head directly to college after completing high school doesn't mean that that student can *never* go to college. Access to learning should be presented as a lifelong option.

For example, taking one evening course while working part time might be all that one student's family can commit to supporting. In another case, a student may want to live in a residence hall at a college, but family members may not believe she is ready to handle that level of independence yet, or they may not be able to afford housing. With some families, the college conversation may be about what kind of college program is a good match for right after a student leaves high school, for example attending a community college first and then a four-year school. With other families, the conversation might be establishing some short-term goals that would help lay a foundation for longer-term college goals that occur one or two years after leaving high school.

Another consideration is the availability of college and university programs that address specific disabilities. Although not all students with disabilities require specific types of programs, students who are deaf or hard of hearing, blind or visually impaired, or have an intellectual disability might desire a college or university program that has strategic services that meet their unique learning needs.

If there are few local options in your community for students with a specific disability, this should be acknowledged, but not used as a reason not to discuss the possibility of college access in the future. For example, in some states there are only one or two colleges and universities that enroll students with intellectual disability. However, talking with parents about what exists in other states, and providing students with information and experiences that could support future enrollment, are positive steps.

Overall, having honest and nonjudgmental conversations about the fiscal, time, and emotional resources needed to create college pathways allows for a parent–professional partnership in attaining those goals.

Support students in identifying champions: Educators can also help students identify other champions to support them in achieving their college dreams. Supporting students to identify college as a goal, engage in planning and preparation, and persist in achieving the goal is a team effort that requires the help of many adults.

As educators, you can support students in approaching and establishing relationships with school counselors in order to access the support for college preparation that is available to all students. You can also assist students in identifying other adults in their lives (e.g., other family members, parents of friends, coaches, spiritual leaders) who might provide encouragement and advice for the student throughout the process. To do this, teach a mini-lesson on what it means to have a mentor, and then have students brainstorm a list of adults they rely on for support. Have students rehearse initiating the conversation with an adult to ask them to be a mentor or champion in their college planning. You can also assist students by reaching out to certain adults to encourage them to provide support for the student's college planning. In cases where a student cannot identify any adults in their life who may be a champion, you could connect the student with local organizations that provide mentors. One example is the College Success Foundation (https://www.college successfoundation.org), which provides mentors to support students in Washington State and the District of Columbia as they apply for college.

Build college expectations into the IEP: The Individuals with Disabilities Education Act (IDEA, 2004) requires that transition planning be included as part of the IEP from age 16. However, many states and territories require transition planning to begin at an earlier age. For a student with a disability who is just beginning to explore the idea of going to college, the transition plan in the IEP can include goals, services, and activities to support the student in expanding their knowledge of their college options.

Figure 2.6 shows a sample postsecondary goal in the area of education and training for Juan, along with the corresponding IEP goal, services, and activities. The postsecondary goal is written in broad terms. It sets the expectation that the

---

Measurable Postsecondary Goal: Education and Training

After graduation, Juan will attend a college or university to pursue education in support of his chosen career path.

IEP goals

Using online resources, Juan will identify a minimum of three potential careers that match his interests and strengths, and will be able to state the educational requirements for those careers.

Transition Services and Activities

   Self-advocacy skills instruction
   Research and visit colleges and universities that have programs in areas
      that match potential careers
   Attend college fair
   Participate in extra-curricular activities
   Provide information on financial support for college
   Make a plan for paying for college

FIGURE 2.6   Sample Postsecondary Education and Training IEP Goals, Services, and Activities

student will attend postsecondary education, but allows for flexibility so that the goal can be refined as the student's desired program of study becomes clearer. It is better to set the goal for attending college and to begin providing supports towards achieving this goal than to have no goal for attending college.

The Connecticut State Department of Education Bureau of Special Education lists a variety of student IEP goals that support skill development, self-advocacy, college exploration, and college application goals (see Figure 2.7).

Goal:

Student will acquire the skills to successfully transition to a two-year or four-year college/university.

Objectives:

- Student will enroll in academic classes that will prepare them for the educational challenges of postsecondary education.
- Student will meet with guidance counselor/special education teacher to discuss academic requirements of pursuing a college degree.
- Student will demonstrate skill in developing a positive school profile and résumé that will be used in the college application process.
- Student will participate in at least one extracurricular activity in order to develop nonacademic aspects of learning.
- Student will describe their disability in terms of learning strengths and weaknesses.
- Student will attend postsecondary options fairs, events, and group sessions provided by the school.
- Student will participate in the traditional standardized tests necessary for acceptance to postsecondary institutions (PSATs, SATs, etc.).
- Student will complete the paperwork necessary to take the SATs with accommodations.
- Student will schedule a visit with the disability services coordinators of at least two colleges/universities to determine the levels of services available.
- Student will describe the accommodations/modifications available to them in postsecondary settings.
- Student will explain the difference between protection under special education law (IDEA) and Section 504 of the Rehabilitation Act and the Americans with Disabilities Act.

FIGURE 2.7   Sample Postsecondary Education IEP Goals

Source: Connecticut State Department of Education Bureau of Special Education

- Student will ensure that all evaluation data required by postsecondary institutions for documentation of disability has been conducted and is within three years of graduation.
- Student will receive direct skills training in becoming a positive self-advocate:

  - Learn whom to ask and when to ask for assistance.
  - Practice describing what is needed to become a successful student.
  - Develop and practice negotiation skills to get what is wanted/needed.
  - Develop strategies for seeking assistance.
  - Discuss disability needs in the context of seeking accommodations.

- Student will practice postsecondary education strategies:

  - Time management
  - Test preparation
  - Study partner/study group
  - Note-taking techniques
  - Special study locations
  - Stress reduction techniques
  - Text anxiety reduction activities

- Student will develop the skills to organize their work with efficiency.
- Student will develop strategies to enhance their study skills.
- Student will determine what testing and evaluation data is required by a postsecondary institution to receive needed accommodations.
- Student will research resources within and outside the college to find support:

  - Determine if they are eligible for vocational rehabilitation services.
  - Research private tutoring, if necessary.
  - Research personal care assistance services, if necessary.

- Student will submit a résumé and postsecondary list of options to their guidance counselor by September, Grade 12.
- Student will write a college admissions essay in the fall of Grade 12.
- Student will investigate availability of financial aid and complete paperwork.

FIGURE 2.7 (Continued)

Sharing these goals with parents and students and choosing goals that meet the needs of students can be done as part of the IEP process, or can be incorporated into work that the student is already doing via projects, internships, and college exploration activities.

Create access to counselors and private support for college searching: Meeting with a school counselor about postsecondary options is a strong predictor of students' plans to enroll in a bachelor's degree program after high school and taking steps to explore college options (Radford, Infill, & Lew, 2015). However, about half of school counselors in the United States report spending less than 20 percent of their time on college readiness, selection, and applications (Radford et al., 2015). In a study that looked at data from the High School Longitudinal Study of 2009, only 18 percent of ninth-grade students reported that they had spoken to a school counselor about college (Radford & Ifill, 2013). Given the impact that school counselors have on students' college aspirations, educators must ensure that students with disabilities are given access to this resource, for example by including college counseling in the transition plan in the IEP.

Students with disabilities may benefit from greater access to a guidance counselor than their school can provide. In situations that require greater expertise than the educator or family has, educators may want to suggest that the family look into the services that a private college counselor can provide. A private college counselor can provide individualized support throughout the college preparation and application process. Although the cost associated with a private college counselor may be prohibitive, it is an option that may be worth considering, in particular for students with more complex support needs.

A private college counselor can support students in the early stages of the college exploration process by identifying strengths and career interests, as well as later in the process of preparing and applying for college. Such a counselor can also recommend colleges that will be a good fit for the student's strengths and support needs.

Include students with disabilities in college-going culture: The College Board's National Office for School Counselor Advocacy (NOSCA, 2012) states, "School communities that intentionally encourage high aspirations for all students are more likely to help them gain the academic preparation necessary to graduate college and career ready" (p. 4). It is important that *all* students, including students with disabilities, are included in efforts to build a college-going school community.

Educators can ensure that students with disabilities are on the radar of school administrators when planning and delivering information about going to college. Students with disabilities should be invited to college fairs and other information events that are held for students and their families. It is important for students with disabilities to "see people who look like them" when they are learning about going to college. Educators can ensure that the school actively invites college students with disabilities to talk about their experiences, along with other college students who are invited to present.

Educators can also ensure that students with disabilities are included in measures that a school may use to track college readiness. These may include measures of attendance, grades, missing assignments, and basic academic skills. Using these college readiness measures increases the likelihood that resources will be devoted to ensuring that students with disabilities are on track toward accessing postsecondary education.

Summary

As an educator, your influence on the lives of students with disabilities—in particular, their access to higher learning—is profound. Your belief about your students' college potential will determine what they have the opportunity to learn, the professionals that they interact with, and the options and resources they see as available to them and their families. Accessing up-to-date information about college pathways and services is a critical element of building college expectations. Sharing this information with families and students builds a college-going culture into transition planning. The challenge in building expectations for college—for both families and teachers—is understanding the various options available, matching student and family priorities to those options, and creating plans that achieve desired outcomes, while reinforcing the expectation that all students, including those with disabilities, can be college material.

Notes

1 From J. Fialka (2016). *What matters: Reflections on disability, community and love.* Toronto, ON: Inclusion Press.
2 From M. V. Izzo & L. Horne (2016). *Empowering students with hidden disabilities: A path to pride and success.* Baltimore, MD: Brookes.

References

American Council for Education (2014). *Middle and high school students: Talk to an adult.* Retrieved from http://knowhow2go.acenet.edu.

Barnett, E. (2016). *Building student momentum from high school into college.* Community College Research Center series: Ready or not: It's time to rethink the 12th grade. Jobs for the Future. Retrieved from www.jff.org/sites/default/files/publications/materials/Building-Student-Momentum-112916.pdf.

Boser, U., Wilhelm, M., and Hanna, R. (2014). *The power of the Pygmalion effect: Teachers' expectations strongly predict college completion.* Washington, DC: The Center for American Progress. Retrieved from https://cdn.americanprogress.org/wp-content/uploads/2014/10/TeacherExpectations-brief10.8.pdf.

Brand, B., Valent, A., and Danielson, L. (2013). *Improving college and career readiness for students with disabilities.* American Institutes for Research. Retrieved from www.ccrscenter.org/sites/default/files/Improving%20College%20and%20Career%20Readiness%20for%20Students%20with%20Disabilities.pdf.

Conley, D. T. (2007). *Redefining college readiness* (prepared for the Bill and Melinda Gates Foundation). Eugene, OR: Educational Policy Improvement Center.

Connecticut State Department of Education Bureau of Special Education. (2007). *Writing transition goals and objectives.* Retrieved from www.sde.ct.gov/sde/lib/sde/PDF/DEPS/Special/Transition_GO.pdf.

Gregory, A., and Huang, F. (2013). It takes a village: The effects of 10th grade college-going expectations of students, parents, and teachers four years later. *American Journal of Community Psychology, 52*(1–2), 41–55. doi:http://dx.doi.org.ezproxy.lib.umb.edu/10.1007/s10464-013-9575-5.

Grigal, M., and Hart, D. (2012). The power of expectations. *Journal of Policy and Practice in Intellectual Disabilities, 9,* 221–222.

Grigal, M., and Deschamps, A. (2012). Transition education for adolescents with intellectual disability. In M. Wehmeyer and K. Webb (Eds.). *Handbook of adolescent transition education for youth with disabilities* (pp. 398–416). New York, NY: Routledge.

Hein, V., Smerdon, B., and Sambolt, M. (2013). *Predictors of postsecondary success.* Washington, DC: College and Career Readiness and Success Center. Retrieved from www.cde.state.co.us/postsecondary/americaninstitutes forresearchpredictorsofpostsecondarysuccess.

Hooker, S., and Brand, B. (2010). College knowledge: A critical component of college and career readiness. *New Directions for Youth Development, 127,* 75–85. doi:10.1002/yd.364.

Izzo, M. V., and Horne, L. (2016). *Empowering students with hidden disabilities: A path to pride and success.* Baltimore, MD: Brookes.

Madaus, J. W., Grigal, M., and Hughes, C. (2014). Promoting access to postsecondary education for low income students with disabilities. *Career Development and Transition for Exceptional Individuals, 37,* 50–59.

McGrew, K. S., and Evans, J. (2003). *Expectations for students with cognitive disabilities: Is the cup half empty or half full? Can the cup flow over?* (Synthesis Report 55). Minneapolis, MN: University of Minnesota, National Center on Educational Outcomes. Retrieved from http://education.umn.edu/NCEO/OnlinePubs/Synthesis55.html.

Mello, Z. R. (2009). Racial/ethnic group and socioeconomic status variation in educational and occupational expectations from adolescence to adulthood. *Journal of Applied Developmental Psychology, 30,* 494–504.

National Association for College Admission Counseling (2016). *Step by step: College awareness and planning for families, counselors and communities.* Arlington, VA. Retrieved from www.nacacnet.org/globalassets/documents/advocacyand-ethics/initiatives/steps/sbs_all.pdf.

National Center for Education Statistics (2016a). *The condition of education: Undergraduate enrollment.* Washington, DC. Retrieved from http://nces.ed.gov/programs/coe/indicator_cha.asp.

National Center for Education Statistics (2016b). *The condition of education: Differences in postsecondary enrollment among recent high school completers.* Washington, DC. Retrieved from http://nces.ed.gov/programs/coe/indicator_tpa.asp.

National Center for Education Statistics (2016c). *The condition of education: Undergraduate retention and graduation rates.* Washington, DC. Retrieved from http://nces.ed.gov/programs/coe/indicator_ctr.asp.

National Center for Education Statistics (2016d). *Digest of education statistics: 2014.* Washington, DC. Retrieved from https://nces.ed.gov/programs/digest/d14/ch_3.asp.

National Office for School Counselor Advocacy. (2012). Middle school counselor's guide: *NOSCA's eight components of college and career readiness counseling.* Retrieved from https://secure-media.collegeboard.org/digitalServices/pdf/advocacy/nosca/11b-4382_MS_Counselor_Guide_WEB_120213.pdf.

Newman, L. (2005). *Family involvement in the educational development of youth with disabilities.* Menlo Park, CA: SRI International.

Papageorge, N. W., Gershenson, S., and Kang, K. (2016). *Teacher expectations matter.* IZA Discussion Paper No. 10165. Bonn, Germany: Institute for the Study of Labor. Retrieved from http://ftp.iza.org/dp10165.pdf.

Radford, A. W., and Ifill, N. (2013). Preparing students for college: *What high schools are doing and how their actions influence ninth graders' college attitudes, aspirations and plans.* Arlington, VA: National Association for College Admission Counseling. Retrieved from www.nacacnet.org/globalassets/documents/publications/research/pub_hsls-_-preparing-students-for-college_.pdf.

Radford, A. W., Ifill, N., and Lew, T. (2015). *A national look at the high school counseling office: What is it doing and what role can it play in facilitating students' paths to college?* Arlington, VA: National Association for College Admission Counseling. Retrieved from https://www.nacacnet.org/globalassets/documents/publications/research/hsls_counseling.pdf.

Raue, K., and Lewis, L. (2011). *Students with disabilities at degree-granting postsecondary institutions.* (NCES 2011–018). U.S. Department of Education, National Center for Education Statistics. Washington, DC: U.S. Government Printing Office.

Wagner, M., Newman, L., Cameto, R., and Levine, P. (2005). *Changes over time in the postschool outcomes of youth with disabilities: A report of findings from the National Longitudinal Transition Study (NLTS) and the National Longitudinal Transition Study-2 (NLTS2).* Menlo Park, CA: SRI International. Retrieved from www.nlts2.org/reports/2005_06/nlts2_report_2005_06_complete.pdf.

Wagner, M., Newman, L., Cameto, R., Levine, P., and Marder, C. (2007). *Perceptions and expectations of youth with disabilities: A special topic report of findings from the National Longitudinal Transition Study-2 (NLTS2)* (NCSER 2007–3006). Menlo Park, Ca: SRI International.

SECTION 2

College Preparation and Application

3

PLANNING FOR A SUCCESSFUL TRANSITION TO COLLEGE

Zachary Walker

NATIONAL INSTITUTE OF EDUCATION, SINGAPORE

Elizabeth Evans Getzel

VIRGINIA COMMONWEALTH UNIVERSITY

Lyman L. Dukes III

UNIVERSITY OF SOUTH FLORIDA, ST. PETERSBURG

Joseph W. Madaus

UNIVERSITY OF CONNECTICUT

Harris, a high school student with disabilities nearing the completion of his freshman year, has heard both students and teachers talk more and more often about the importance of college. He's decided that he'd like to go as well, but he isn't sure what he needs to do in order to be college-ready. He has recently let his parents know of his college interest and they're excited but also unsure whether Harris can be successful. Frankly, many of his teachers have implied that he probably wouldn't succeed in a college setting. They are concerned, for example, that professors might not provide extra time for Harris to complete exams, and they also wonder if colleges have services like Individualized Education Plan (IEP) teams and guidance counseling for students with disabilities. The most immediate concern, however, is whether Harris has enough time to plan for college so that, once there, he can be successful. His parents decided to schedule an appointment with Harris's school counselor and also e-mail his case manager to request that the IEP team address his college interest at his upcoming IEP meeting.

Overview

Harris's interest in college is an important step forward as he ponders his adult life. It is projected that 65 percent of all jobs will require a college degree by 2020 (Carnevale, Smith, & Strohl, 2013). As with any significant life change, the transition to college will present students with novel environments and circumstances.

The transition to postsecondary education can include new living arrangements, navigating a new community, more economic independence, greater financial responsibilities, making new friends, the recognition and development of sexuality interests, and finding new ways to have fun (Wehman, 2006). Understanding and preparing for this next step will help students with disabilities equip themselves with the skills and strategies to both persist and succeed in this new environment, and a collaborative planning approach is critical to ensure student understanding and ownership of the planning experience. An appropriate place to begin learning about college expectations is to consider the academic and non-academic demands that students will face.

Academic Preparation

Preparing the Plan of Study

Considering college preparation four to five years prior to entry may seem daunting and even unrealistic to many adolescents, their families, and their secondary special education team members, but we should acknowledge that decisions made in eighth and ninth grade will have significant postsecondary implications (McGuire, 2010). A particularly important issue to consider is academic preparation and, specifically, the student's plan of study. Although the Individuals with Disabilities Education Act of 2004 (IDEA) requires transition planning that must result in a course of study aligned with the student's identified postsecondary goals (Eckes & Ochoa, 2005), individual states may determine policies related to diploma options, and, if required, high school exit exams. Some states provide multiple diploma options for students with disabilities, and alternate options have been described as being of questionable value (Hartwig & Sitlington, 2008). It is imperative that students and families understand the impact of the chosen diploma option. The Every Student Succeeds Act (ESSA), which was effective at the end of the 2015 calendar year, like the No Child Left Behind Act (NCLB) it replaced, allows states to continue to offer students the option of either a standard or alternate diploma. The standard diploma must be aligned with the state's respective academic content standards. Generally, the alternate assessment is the most appropriate diploma choice but only in cases where the student has significant cognitive disabilities. For more detailed information regarding the course of study and diploma options, readers are encouraged to also read Chapter 6.

The diploma decision will result in the determination of a plan of study for the student. Led by the student and family, in collaboration with other IEP team members, students should select appropriate concentrations and necessary course credits in English, foreign language, mathematics, science, and history courses (Getzel, 2005). Data from the National Longitudinal Transition Study-2 (NLTS-2) indicates that nationally, students with disabilities earned fewer general education and academic-based credits than their peers without disabilities. With the exception of English, students with disabilities earned fewer credits in all other subjects, and they earned more credits in basic mathematics than in mid-level or advanced math courses (Newman et al., 2011a).

Preparing for the Instructional Environment

Students can anticipate significant differences in the instructional climate between high school and college. The most evident contrast is the expectation that college students are expected to self-regulate their activities, and function more independently than in high school (McGuire, 2010). In college, formal instructional time happens less often and, generally, course attendance is not a requirement. Make-up work and late assignments are typically not options. Studying and seeking help about course assignments are the responsibility of the student. Therefore, it is important to provide students opportunities to develop and practice self-regulated behavior while in high school, as they are ready. High school is replete with opportunities to develop and practice such skills. For example, students can be taught to break a long-term assignment (e.g., science project or history project) into short-term goals; they can be taught to maintain a weekly study schedule and modify the schedule as needed; and they can be taught strategies for learning or making a determination for when she or he should seek assistance with a challenging academic or personal task. Note that some of these skills can be broken into smaller parts that the student completes as he or she is prepared, with additional elements added over time. Table 3.1 summarizes some of the key

TABLE 3.1 Differences between High School and College

Area	High School	College
Personal freedom	Less freedom – living at home with parents	More freedom – especially if students live on or off campus
Structure	More structure – school sets schedule	Less structure – student sets schedule
Classes	Predictable – typically 15 to 35 students	Less predictable – some classes can have 100 to 200 students or more
Teachers	Frequent contact – may see teachers every day	Less frequent contact – may only see professors one to three times a week
Study time	May be able to get studying done in a study hall or spend minimal time outside of class studying	Significant reading and independent work demands and may study two to four hours a day
Tests	More frequent tests on less information	May have only a few tests a semester and assessments may cover many chapters or be cumulative

(Continued)

TABLE 3.1 (Continued)

Area	High School	College
Grades	Course grade often based on many assignments	Course grade may be based on only a few assignments
Physical environment	Classes often held in one building	Classes may be held across a campus in many different buildings
Legal protection	IDEA: Entitled to a free appropriate public education	ADA and 504: Must be eligible for services and reasonable accommodations
Special education classes	Specialized instruction, classes, and resource room services for students with disabilities	Special education classes do not exist at the postsecondary level but supports do exist Some colleges may offer specialized programs, but often charge additional fees
Documentation	School evaluates the student and develops the individualized education program (IEP)	Student must provide disability documentation in order to receive accommodations Student's IEP or Summary of Performance (SOP) may not be considered sufficient documentation
Advocacy	Teacher and parent advocate for services	Student must advocate for services
Receiving accommodations	Accommodations determined as a part of the IEP process	Student must contact the person/office on campus responsible for providing accommodations

Source: www.going-to-college (Rehabilitation Research and Training Center, Virginia Commonwealth University).

differences between high school and college and emphasizes the necessary shift to increased student independence.

> *During the IEP meeting at the culmination of ninth grade, Harris and his parents added the post-high school goal of college attendance. The family and IEP team discussed the implications of his interest in college and agreed to the next steps including the following:*

- *The IEP team should carefully examine his course of study to ensure it's a match for his goal of college attendance and discuss his current skill deficits in order to ensure that they're eventually reflected in IEP goals.*
- *Harris and the IEP team agreed that he should prepare a transition portfolio, as part of the Summary of Performance (SOP), that includes documents and work samples relevant to college planning.*

- *The IEP team and school counselor should help Harris and his family complete a document titled, "The College Action Plan" (included as Appendix A), which is designed to help students detail the steps necessary to achieve their goal of postsecondary education.*

TRANSITION TIP

Consider having a recent high school graduate with disability who is attending college speak with high school students considering college attendance. Ask the college student to address topics such as differences in classroom instructional time, reading expectations, the amount of expected study time outside of class attendance, college teaching style, and class exams and projects.

Non-Academic Skills Preparation

To fully prepare students for postsecondary success, secondary schools should address skill areas that are sometimes underemphasized and nonacademic in nature (West et al., 2014). While academic preparation is undoubtedly important to college admission and later success in college, it is also necessary that non-academic skills, such as self-determination and self-advocacy, be developed as well. Without these, many students with disabilities may not receive needed accommodations and other supports available in college. Like the academic skills described on page 54, these skills can be taught using scaffolding methods and developed over time.

Self-Determination Skills

Research has established that the most persistent, self-disciplined, adaptable, and reliable students often outperform those with higher cognitive ability (Heckman & Krueger, 2005). In addition, self-determination and self-advocacy skills are especially important for students with disabilities in transition because of the significant changes in their legal status from high school to college, as was highlighted in Table 3.1. Field and Hoffman (1994) defined self-determination as "the ability to define and achieve goals based on a foundation of knowing and valuing oneself" (p. 136). It has several component skills including choice-making, problem-solving, self-advocacy, internal locus of control, self-awareness, and self-knowledge (Wehmeyer, Agran, and Hughes, 1998). College students with disabilities have also self-identified this skill as necessary for success in postsecondary education (Getzel & Thoma, 2008; Thoma & Getzel, 2005).

There are multiple ways that self-determination skill practice can be incorporated into students' daily activities. For example, students could be encouraged and supported to discuss classroom accommodations with their teachers, manage their daily academic and personal schedule, and maintain a leadership role in the IEP process. Whether at school or in the home setting, this preparation can include having students complete self-assessment surveys as a starting point for discussions about self-awareness, providing students opportunities to self-advocate, and, with guidance, encouraging students to make their own decisions. An especially valuable opportunity for training and practice of self-determination is to have students actively participate in the IEP/T meeting process. The Zarrow Center at the University of Oklahoma has developed an evidence-based instructional model for teaching students to lead their IEP meetings (see Appendix B).

> *The IEP team is aware that students who possess self-determination skills often perform better in college. Therefore, the team recommends that one of the first steps is to assess Harris's current level of self-determination. After conducting an online search, his case manager finds a number of available assessment batteries, some of which are available free of charge (e.g., AIR self-determination scale, Self-determination assessment battery). Based upon the assessment results, Harris, his family, and the IEP team decide that Harris needs improvement with regard to organizational, goal-setting, and time-management skills. Additionally, they decide to use the assessment battery annually to make decisions regarding where any needs remain and to note skills in which Harris has demonstrated growth.*

TRANSITION TIP

Give students opportunities to practice self-advocacy using role-play scenarios. For example, use a scenario in which a student meets with the Disability Services Office (DSO) to submit documentation and describe which accommodations have been helpful and why. You can also role-play a meeting with a professor in which the student shares a letter describing her/his accommodation needs.

Organizational Skills

Given the increased need for independence and self-management in a range of courses without the supports available in high school, students should practice the development of organizational skills (see also Chapter 4). These consist of competencies that facilitate the use of time and resources to meet chosen goals (Getzel, 2008). Examples of organizational tools include planners, color-coded notebooks for separate courses, various computer programs and applications for assignment completion, and using watches or electronic mobile devices as reminder tools. Students should identify and practice organization competencies before the transition to college, in collaboration with school professionals and family members, when possible.

As with the larger self-determination construct, it is important that students planning to attend college assess their organizational skills. Students can engage in various activities to determine what they are currently doing to organize themselves, particularly as it relates to their study habits (see www.collegesucessfoun dation.org). Feedback from teachers and family members is helpful to provide perspectives as to how they view a student's organizational strengths and areas for improvement. With practice and time, students can also learn to modify certain techniques to make them as effective and efficient as possible.

> *Based upon data gathered during the transition assessment process, Harris's family and IEP team determined that his organization skills merit attention. Given the importance of organization in college and the considerable practice necessary to learn to be well organized, the IEP team recommended that Harris do the following:*

- *Harris will maintain an electronic weekly calendar that is prepared each Sunday night or Monday morning. It will be updated daily to reflect changes in daily activities. It will be checked weekly by a teacher for at least the first half of the school year.*
- *Harris will use a detailed homework checklist for each course. The subject-by-subject checklist will allow him to "check off" whether he has gathered all necessary assignment materials, or whether there is no homework assignment for the subject. Additionally, the checklist will include a component for noting whether completed homework has been reviewed prior to submission.*
- *Harris finds organizing his thoughts difficult when writing. He will try out various electronic tools in order make connections and structure ideas for lengthy writing assignments (e.g., Inspiration, Mindomo) so that he can determine one or more that are effective for him.*

TRANSITION TIP

Teach students routines for organizing course materials in their high school courses. For example, guide students in the maintenance of binders for handouts and notes, and guide students in the development of organizational methods for maintaining an easy to navigate set of electronic folders on their personal computers and cloud storage systems.

Time Management

Although it may be hard for many secondary students to fully appreciate, they will have time outside of college classes that will need to be managed. This is a significant issue that students face in their transition to college (Getzel, 2008). Time management (also see Chapter 4) is comprised of both the planning and performance of time spent on an endeavor, and college requires that a student balance academic, personal and, sometimes, employment obligations. Organizational skills and time management go hand-in-hand in meeting academic and personal goals. As with organizational skills there are resources available to assist students to self-assess their time management strategies in order to determine what is working well and areas that need strengthening. Example activities include The Good Day Plan (www.imdetermined.org) and the Big Future tool (https//bigfuture.collegeboard.org) that provide tips and strategies for high school students as they prepare for college.

> *Ms. Smith, who teaches Social Studies, overheard Harris complaining to another classmate that he was going to be late, again, for his afternoon job. He also said he had to stop by his Math teacher's classroom to get a question answered before leaving school for work. Ms. Smith has heard other students in her class share similar problems regarding time management issues. She decided to set aside class time later in the week to discuss managing one's schedule. She began the lesson by asking the students whether they think they have enough time to meet obligations and, if not, why they believe that to be the case. Students shared concerns about not having enough time to study, see friends, or make it to work on time. She led the class in a time management discussion that included the following: 1) Judging what is important and what is not important, or in other words, what does one have to do versus what one may want to do? 2) Setting priorities and then setting aside enough time in the day or week to complete the priorities. She noted that those activities or tasks that are not important or not urgent should be scheduled around priorities. Studying, for example, is important and should be reflected in a schedule first, while social media time isn't an immediate need and can be done, for example, during study breaks or at another time. 3) Learning and practicing the preparation and maintenance of both daily and weekly schedules. Last, Ms. Smith led the students in a lesson in which they used MyLifeOrganized app (mylifeorganized.net), a tool for organizing daily "to do" activities.*

TRANSITION TIP

Have students complete "The Good Day Plan," a tool designed to help students visualize the day from beginning to end and assist in developing structures/routines that enable them to complete a series of activities. Middle and high school students are encouraged to include this as a component of the IEP process.

Goal Setting

In an educational context, goal-setting can be described as setting clear objectives for learning (Moeller, Theiler, & Wu, 2012). Students with disabilities often enter college lacking academic goal-setting skills; however, goal setting is critical to college success (Finn, Getzel, & McManus, 2008). In fact, students who participated in a goal-setting study showed significant gains in the ability to set long-term goals, break long-term goals down into manageable steps, stick to a plan, and match personal strengths to specific needs when making a plan (Finn et al. 2008). The *I'm Determined* website (imdetermined.org) provides a number of templates addressing goal-setting designed to help students practice these skills. For example, vocational goal examples are provided that include obtaining a part-time job or completing a vocational/technical course. Educational goals could include earning a chosen diploma, leading an IEP meeting, or earning a certain grade in a specific course. Community goals that students might identify are volunteering or visiting job sites to learn about different careers, and personal goals such as obtaining a driver's license, buying a car, or going to prom. Each goal can then be broken down into specific action steps and should include a time frame for goal achievement.

Another helpful goal-setting tool is the College Action Plan (See Appendix A); a tool designed to guide students in the development of a college preparation plan. The plan addresses areas such as career interests, in which students are asked to answer a few short questions about why a career is important to them, which type of postsecondary program is an appropriate personal match, the length of time it may take to earn a certificate or degree and, last, the identification of a postsecondary goal as well as steps necessary to complete the goal.

In sum, helping students set their own goals and also learn how to goal monitor is key. Setting goals that are specific, observable, and measurable make it easy for the student to determine whether they have prepared a road map for potential success. Like the other skills described, goal-setting is a skill that can be developed over time and modified to meet the student's preferences and comfort level.

Learning goal-setting skills is noted as one of the annual goals in Harris's current IEP. His teachers know that as students learn about goal-setting, it is prudent to provide scenarios that allow for the opportunity to brainstorm steps for goal development and achievement. Harris has indicated to his history teacher that his goal is to earn an A in the course. After a conversation with the teacher and his case manager, Harris decides to implement the following strategies in order to meet the goal: 1) Maintain detailed notes during class meetings (to be periodically reviewed by the teacher), 2) Choose a seat near the front of the classroom where there are few distractions, 3) Complete any history homework, including any reading by the due date, 4) Review class notes at least every other day and always begin studying for tests at least two days prior to the exam, and 5) Ask the teacher or a studious classmate for help if he does not understand a topic or if he incorrectly completed a homework task or test item and does not know why it's incorrect. Harris will check in weekly with his teacher to determine his grade status and also review his progress toward implementing the plan that he has prepared.

TRANSITION TIP

Teach students to use "The Goal Setting" template (www.imdetermined. org) as a visual representation of the steps necessary to achieve an identified goal. The student's goal is written in the center of the sun. On the template, each sunray represents an outcome resulting from goal attainment. In the box below the sun, the steps to reach the goal are noted.

Technology Skills

While academic preparation for college is typically addressed in the transition process, the application of learning technologies is more limited (Asselin, 2014). Understanding how technology can support learning in the classroom and applying that knowledge often results in improved academic performance for students with disabilities (Bolt, Decker, Lloyd, & Morlock, 2011). While online learning management platforms are generally commonplace and thus better understood, there are also personal technologies that can aid in academic goal achievement.

Mobile Devices

Mobile devices, such as smart phones, contain multiple built-in features that are useful to students. These features can generally be accessed utilizing the "Settings" menu on mobile phones or tablets. Examples include text-to-speech transcription for decoding text, larger typeface settings, subtitles, captioning, motion reduction tools, as well as voice memos and calendars. Interestingly, many of these tools can also be helpful for students learning to navigate campus environments. For example, map applications on some devices are quite detailed and provide students with photos in addition to directions for navigation. These applications can be very helpful when students are navigating campus or new communities. One way for secondary educators to prepare students for postsecondary education is to provide opportunities for responsible use of devices in the classroom setting. For example, encouraging the use of reminder apps that send text messages about assignment due dates, apps that help students review course content for upcoming exams, using devices as an in-class student response system, or even recording your class lectures for later review can all be quite beneficial to students.

Specialized Applications and Wearable Technologies

There are a number of specialized applications designed to help students with specific tasks. Examples include applications that provide real-time feedback to help students maintain awareness of activities such as breathing, augmented reality (AR) applications that provide detailed navigation data including specific

TABLE 3.2 Technology Tools for Success

Skill Area	Tools	Description	Notes
Academic Tools	Speech to Text Text to Speech Dictionary Text Magnifier Spell Checker Text Highlighter	These are built-in mobile device tools that read text aloud, transcribe speech into notes, provide word definitions, and magnify text.	Depending on the device that a student uses, these features may be called different things. However, you can usually find these in the device under the "settings" menu by searching for "accessibility" features.
	Adapted Pencils Reading FramesVelcro Highlighters Switches Portable word processors	These tools can be purchased or adapted for use from existing tools to assist a student with a disability.	These low-tech tools can be used in any academic setting. For more information on specific tools, search Assistive Technology on the web.
Organizational, Time Management, and Goal-Setting Tools	Calendars Text reminders Alarms Remember the Milk Evernote 30/30 Heart Rate Monitor Phillips Vital Signs Breathe2Relax Virtual Hope Box	These are features built into smartphones and other mobile devices. Downloadable apps and wearable technologies, for example, can help students do things such as read their vital signs, control breathing, and monitor thoughts.	There are additional apps and wearable devices that can support many of these same functions and include additional features. It is important to use these prior to college so students can learn how to best employ them.

directions and building identification, and applications that help students create to-do lists and specific reminders. These and other specialized applications can greatly enhance daily campus life. Table 3.2 presents some specific applications.

TRANSITION TIP

Use the College Readiness Assessment tool (See Appendix C for a reproducible copy) to help students to begin thinking more deeply about college preparation. The tool reviews student learning styles, strengths, preferences, and needs; types of postsecondary programs; their top three reasons for selecting a college; and technology designed to improve learning. At the culmination of the assessment, students begin the development of a college attendance plan.

Non-Disability Related Support Systems in College

In many cases, accessing college supports significantly impacts the likelihood of college completion. Interestingly, in one study, only 28 percent of students receiving special education in high school disclosed their disability in college, and just 19 percent reported the use of college accommodations and supports (Newman et al. 2011b). In fact, students who have not disclosed during the first academic year are 3.5 times less likely to complete a degree program (Hudson, 2013). Postsecondary support extends beyond the use of accommodations and typically includes establishing peer relationships, seeking out helpful campus support staff, getting to know faculty and academic advisors, participating in campus and community activities, and potential participation in support groups (Getzel & Thoma, 2008).

It is also important to learn about traditional college supports available to all students, including academic labs that offer tutoring, informal and formal study sessions, individual or small group meetings with faculty, campus ministry, academic advisors, and residence life advisors. Students may learn about these options through the student activity center or by speaking with residence hall directors, faculty members, and university staff. A support system in college can include a wide variety of people such as friends, faculty, learning specialists, health-related staff, and family. Support systems extend into the social sphere and can include participation in student organizations or utilizing gym facilities, thus, learning about and practicing the development and use of support systems at the secondary level is prudent. Transition specialists, school counselors, or teachers can assist in this process by working with students to identify individuals that make up their current support system and begin to discuss ways to establish these supports in college. The importance of these services was highlighted in a study of NLTS-2 data which found that students with disabilities who accessed such supports were more likely to complete college than students who did not (Newman, Madaus, and Javitz, 2016).

Harris, his family, and the IEP team recognize the value of participation in a variety of activities. Harris, like almost all students is very busy, so he and his family have carefully selected extracurricular and academic support activities that will not only help him practice the use of support systems, but also align with his college goals. Harris and the IEP team document that he will do the following:

- *The IEP team informed his parents of the new club focused upon robotics, which is one of his special interests. Harris and his family have arranged for a family friend to pick him up after school one day per week so that he can participate in the club.*
- *Harris learned from his teachers that before and after school tutoring is available in both math and science, two of his more difficult subjects. He will participate in before school tutoring for both courses at least twice per week.*
- *Harris enjoys working with animals and has developed a friendship with a veterinarian who works at the local humane society. He will volunteer there for approximately five to ten hours per week depending upon his availability.*

TRANSITION TIP

Download the "Comparing College Resources" chart (www.going-to-college.org) under the heading "Campus Life" and have students identify resources at three different colleges they are exploring.

The Legal Climate in Postsecondary Education

Many, but not all, students with disabilities in K–12 school settings are protected under the IDEA, which requires individually appropriate special education services, including modifications, when needed, for students with disabilities who are identified as requiring such services. Students, families, and school personnel should be made aware that the IDEA, and its required special education services, does not follow the student into college. Instead, qualified students with disabilities are protected under the Americans with Disabilities Act (ADA) and Subpart E of Section 504. ADA and Section 504 are civil rights laws, intended to protect people from discrimination based upon disability, and to ensure equal educational access to a postsecondary education. Thus, a student with a disability seeking support services in a postsecondary environment must be found eligible for services, and the first step is self-disclosure.

Self-Disclosure

Tied to the skills of self-determination is self-disclosure, that is, once a student enrolls in an institution, he or she must decide about self-disclosing to the campus DSO. As is the case when seeking accommodations for the SAT or ACT exam (see Chapter 6), the student is required to submit documentation of her or his disability. This documentation is used to verify that the student is a person with a disability, and to make determinations regarding what accommodations have been used in the past and whether they are appropriate in the college setting. Documentation may include student self-reports, diagnostic evaluations, an SOP, and a student's IEP. The student should be prepared to discuss accommodations provided in high school and how those accommodations were of benefit. Following a review of the student's disability records and any other relevant documentation, the DSO will determine if the student is eligible for accommodations. Secondary school personnel are encouraged to take a long-term approach to preparing the student for this reality. Students, with guidance from professionals, should maintain a portfolio of transition assessment data, including a checklist for what data remains to be gathered (Shaw, Madaus, & Dukes, 2012). Additionally, SOP data should be reviewed regularly, for example during annual IEP meetings, with the stated goal of helping students better understand the relationship of the data to their academic and other adult life goals.

> The IEP team recognizes the significance of the changes in legal status once Harris enters college and the importance it places upon self-determination skills. Therefore, as they engage in the process of backward planning in order to ensure subsequent IEPs will include the necessary college relevant activities, Harris and his family agree to the following:
>
> - By the sophomore year, Harris, with guidance from the IEP team, will develop an SOP portfolio, will annually update it, and report on its status at each annual IEP meeting.
> - By the junior year, Harris will practice explaining his disability to his teachers and also be prepared to describe which accommodations help him best learn and why.
> - By the senior year, Harris will contact colleges in which he has an interest in order to learn about the supports and services available.

Reasonable Accommodations

If it is determined that a student has a documented disability, he or she then may be eligible to receive academic accommodations under Section 504 and the ADA.

Accommodations are supports and services that allow students with disabilities to access the physical and instructional environment. Within the instructional environment, students must be provided access to academic content and the opportunity to demonstrate their understanding of this content, not the impact of the disability. Examples of common college-level accommodations include priority registration, exam modifications (e.g., extended time on tests, readers, scribes), testing in a room with limited distractions, interpreters, and the use of textbooks in an alternate format (Madaus, 2010).

It is important to note that simply because a student received an accommodation in high school it does not mean the student will be eligible for the same support in a postsecondary setting (Madaus, Faggella-Luby, & Dukes, 2011). Determination that one has a disability does not mean that the student is eligible for accommodations, which are determined on a case-by-case, course-by-course basis. Accommodations received in one college class may not be necessary, or in some cases, reasonable and appropriate in another college class, as the essential technical requirements of the course must be considered in making these decisions. For example, while it might be reasonable to not be penalized for spelling mistakes in a philosophy or history course, spelling may be an essential requirement of a course in pharmacy or nutrition.

If a particular accommodation is determined to be reasonable and appropriate, typically the student will be responsible for delivering a DSO-generated letter to each relevant instructor, which details the supports for which she is eligible, each semester. Students are obliged to monitor whether the accommodations are effective and communicate with the DSO to discuss any potential changes to the support plan. Table 3.3 illustrates a typical accommodation process and the roles and responsibilities of the DSO office, student, and faculty member. In particular, Table 3.3 clearly demonstrates the need for students to apply self-determination skills, including understanding their personal strengths and needs and being able to communicate with various campus personnel regarding their abilities and challenges.

TRANSITION TIP

Have students identify their Strengths, Preferences, Interests, and Needs (SPIN) in high school, and consider how these influence potential accommodations. This information can be culled from both formal and informal transition assessments that have been completed. Incorporate the information in the students' transition planning documentation and activities. See Appendix D for a reproducible form to document SPIN.

TABLE 3.3 Roles and Responsibilities

Roles and Responsibilities

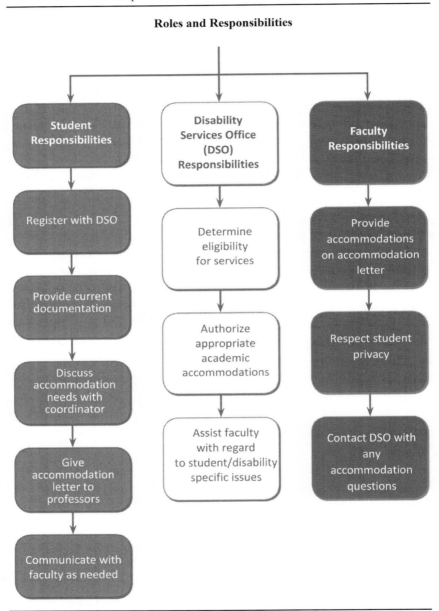

Source: www.going-to-college.org (Rehabilitation Research and Training Center, Virginia Commonwealth University).

Exploring Postsecondary Education Programs

Visiting Prospective Colleges and Universities

All students face a similar set of preparation needs and choices when considering postsecondary education options (see Chapter 6 for more information on college exploration). For example, every student should consider the size and location of a college, its programs and major degree offerings, extracurricular activities, the diversity of the student body, and available financial aid (Getzel & Wehman, 2005). Students with disabilities have additional considerations when determining an appropriate college or university including, but not limited to, the nature of support services available, health services, the degree of campus accessibility, and accessibility relevant policies and procedures. Students and families can arrange to visit colleges, participate in scheduled tours or gather information online through virtual tours. In fact, there are multiple sites that offer college-related advice for youth with disabilities (see Appendix B). Each resource provides information such as tips, college program recommendations, and advice from students and administrators.

Tying it All Together: The Campus Visit

An in-person campus visit can generally occur at any time; however, it is best to participate in an organized tour if possible. Summer can be a particularly good time given student and family schedules, and can offer an opportunity for extended conversations with available faculty and staff. Visits that take place during the fall and spring provide students and families with a realistic sense of the pace, character, and culture of a campus. If mobility and accessibility are potential issues, a campus visit in the winter can be helpful to experience the campus when it may be snowy and icy. Scheduled visits can include informational sessions and campus tours and are led by guides who are often currently matriculating students. Prospective students should maintain contact with tour guides, if possible, as they can act as mentors during the transition to college, particularly during the first year (Schmulsky, Gobbo, and Donahue, 2015). Also keep in mind that many colleges and universities offer virtual tours that are useful when determining potential colleges to visit or in lieu of an actual in-person visit.

> *Harris and his family are preparing to visit a local university. His case manager has requested that Harris and his family complete the College Readiness Assessment in advance of their visit. It will help to highlight some of the important considerations when planning for and entering college (See Appendix C). With help from his school counselor and his case manager he has prepared a college visitation plan. He has put together a daily schedule, identified a set of personnel, programs, and activities that will best help him make an informed college choice. In addition, he has prepared a*

series of questions, and also has a plan for documenting his experiences during his visit. Following his return, he will meet with his school counselor and case manager to dialogue about what he learned.

Where to Visit

Disability Services Office

Initiating contact with the campus DSO prior to a visit is prudent, as some will have students with disabilities with whom prospective students can meet. A visit to the DSO should be a priority as they provide an array of "features, supports, or assistance . . . for students with disabilities" (Newman & Madaus, 2015, p. 176). Some services are legally mandated while others may have an additional fee attached. Example services include access to learning specialists, academic counseling, priority registration, testing services, and counseling. Reasonable and appropriate accommodations are never subject to an additional fee. Prior to visiting a college, contact the DSO to see if a student with a disability can meet to discuss their experiences on campus. Hearing from students can provide insight about campus life such as campus accessibility, residence hall life, extracurricular activities, experience with faculty, and so on.

Questions Harris has for the DSO include, but are not limited to, the following:

- *Is the campus welcoming of students with disabilities?*
- *What documentation should I provide in order to be eligible for services?*
- *How often can I meet with staff from the DSO and what specific support services do you provide to eligible students? For example, what are the policies regarding priority registration, course load, waivers, or substitutions?*

Residence Halls

If a prospective student is considering living in a campus residence hall, it is worthwhile to visit and, if possible, meet one or more residential staff. Living in a shared space can be a challenge for all students and may be magnified for individuals with some types of disabilities. It is important to consider not only the readiness of the student but also the behavior of fellow residents, room cleanliness, the shared bathroom space, laundry facilities, and noise level (Schmulsky et al., 2015). Students should consider the following, depending on the nature of their disability: 1) Sensory load: What are the lighting, carpeting, and sound like in a space? Are students allowed to paint rooms? Is there natural light? What is the volume of outside noise? Is carpet allowed to reduce sound and improve sensory comfort? Can students have single rooms? 2) Roommate selection: How is roommate selection normally completed? It is important to consider whether it is possible for students to select roommates who will be sensitive to their condition. 3) Experience of residential staff: If possible, students should request assignment to a residence hall with staff that have experience with students with disabilities. Also, students and families may want to ask the staff the nature of the training they undergo as they prepare to oversee students and peers (Schmulsky et al., 2015).

Dining Hall

Many students will spend a good deal of time in campus dining halls, so it is worthwhile to become familiar with them. Consider the following during the visit: How crowded is it during peak hours? What are the seating arrangements? How loud is the noise when the space is crowded? How well do the dining options address special dietary needs?

Transportation

At some institutions, campus transportation is provided. If this is the case, students and their families could try routes between residential halls and classrooms, peruse transit schedules, and ask for information regarding any costs. Students should also consider if the transportation is accessible and locations that the public transportation serves. If students will need access to a pharmacy or local job site, they will want to check this out while visiting campus. In addition, some campuses do not allow freshman to have cars, so students and families will want to explore these policies as well. If transportation is not offered by the college and will be necessary for the student, it will be necessary to ask campus personnel, particularly DSO staff, about other campus or community support options for transportation.

Financial Aid

Many (40%) students have reported being unsure whether they can cover college costs (Novakovic & Ross, 2015). If not included as part of a campus tour, families should schedule appointments with financial aid staff to determine eligibility and subsequent options. Postsecondary institutions also typically have a plethora of aid information available online, thus it is an appropriate resource with which to begin. Chapter 6 contains more information about financial aid and scholarship opportunities.

Classrooms

When possible, students should sit in on both small and large lecture hall courses, even if only for a few minutes. This provides students an opportunity to ascertain differences in instructional format and student expectations regarding participation. Oftentimes, students with disabilities will want to be in smaller classes, which typically provide easier access to the instructor and more personalized attention. Smaller classrooms may also be less distracting for those with sensory disabilities. However, not all universities offer smaller classes, especially for freshman level courses, and it is important to discuss this with the college and/or program being explored.

Campus Events

Becoming an active member of the campus community improves the chances of college persistence. If possible, students and families may want to time their campus visits to coincide, for example, with a sporting event or a campus club activity in which the student may have interest. Certainly, it is prudent to not only ask questions about social activities but to also review the campus website for information regarding both institutional and community activities. These are all critical parts of the college experience and it is important that students and families get the full picture of campus life.

> *Harris and his family have been pleased with the guidance and support he has received from the high school team, including his case manager, classroom teachers, school counselor, and the other members of the IEP team. Harris is now at the point of making final decisions regarding which college he will attend. He and his family have narrowed it down to two possibilities, both in-state universities that offer the college majors Harris is considering and also have a well-staffed DSO that provides an array of services including learning specialists and individual counseling, if needed. Harris and his family are especially appreciative of the opportunity he had to facilitate his high school IEP meetings and discuss both his evaluation documentation and transition portfolio contents. Harris has a good understanding of his strengths and challenges as well as the accommodations that will best allow him to demonstrate his academic ability in college. He is looking forward to the opportunity to share his transition portfolio with the DSO and subsequently meeting with the university professors to discuss his strengths, challenges, and accommodation needs.*

Bridge Programs

Some colleges and universities offer "bridge" programs that are typically held in the summer and often coincide with the institution's new student orientation programming. These programs, generally speaking, are open to both students with and without disabilities and are fee-based. The primary goal is to provide students the opportunity to acclimate to the college setting prior to all students arriving to campus for the fall term. Bridge program content will typically include guidance regarding academic, independent living, and social acclimation instruction.

Program sessions are often led by college personnel affiliated with student academic success centers, residence halls, and student life (e.g., student organizations and student government). Sessions may address resources available on campus, roommate etiquette, time management, stress management, and organizational, study, test-taking, and learning strategy skills, to name a few. Students with disabilities who are living away from home for the first time should participate in programming of this nature, if possible.

Conclusion

Attending a college or university is an exciting time in any young person's life. It can be filled with new experiences, personal growth, and the opportunity to study a desired field or occupation. For secondary personnel, parents, families, and students, it is important to understand the differences in the laws governing secondary and postsecondary education. Choosing the right college or university and support program is also incredibly important as students develop the skills to learn and grow independently. Postsecondary education can also be overwhelming for students if they are not prepared academically, have not developed self-determination or self-advocacy skills, and do not know how to manage their lives both in and out of school. However, students with disabilities can succeed in postsecondary environments when prepared effectively and in a place that supports their personal and academic growth.

APPENDIX A: COLLEGE ACTION PLAN

Career interests

1. What is your top career choice that you are interested in pursuing after you leave high school?

2. Why is this career important to you?

Education and training

3. Which the type of education and training you will need for your career choice? (Check one):

    ☐ Participate in on the job training to acquire the skills required for the career
    ☐ Complete course work to earn certification
    ☐ Complete a vocational/technical training program
    ☐ Complete an apprenticeship program
    ☐ Earn a Bachelor's degree
    ☐ Earn a Master's degree
    ☐ Enlist in the military and complete a career training program

Time frame

4. What timeframe are you expecting to need in order to complete the above education/training?

    ☐ within 6 months of high school graduation
    ☐ within 1 year of high school graduation
    ☐ within 2 years of high school graduation
    ☐ within 4 years of high school graduation
    ☐ other, indicate timeframe

Postsecondary goals

Postsecondary goals are your desires for life **AFTER** high school and are included in your IEP and Academic and Career Plan. Develop postsecondary goals in the areas of employment and education/training. Remember to make these goals SMART.

5. **What is your postsecondary employment goal?**

   By (timeframe), I will be employed (full-time or part-time) as a (career title).

6. **What is your postsecondary education or training goal?**

   By (timeframe), I will complete (specific education and training needed) in the career field of (interest).

Action plan

Outline the steps you will need to take to achieve your postsecondary education or training goal. Use various resources to assist you with this section, which can include teachers, family members, the Internet, career services at your high school, and the "Getting Ready for College" checklist listed in the Expanding Your Knowledge section of this unit.

7. **What are the five to seven action steps you need to achieve your postsecondary education and training goal required for your career choice?**

Action to accomplish	Deadline	Will you need support?	This person can help me. (Family, friends, school counselor, coach, agency case manager, etc.)
1.			
2.			
3.			
4.			
5.			
6.			
7.			

The VCU Center on Transition Innovations is funded by the Virginia Department of Education, #881-62524-H027A15107. For further information about the Center on Transition Innovations, please visit our website www.centeron transition.org

APPENDIX B: ADDITIONAL RESOURCES

Going-to-College

www.going-to-college.org

This website provides information about living college life with a disability. It is designed for high school students and provides video clips, activities, and resources that can help get a head start in planning for college.

I'm Determined

www.imdetermined.org

This website provides direct instruction, models, and opportunities to practice skills associated with self-determined behavior.

Preparing for College: An Online Tutorial

www.washington.edu/doit/preparing-college-online-tuorial

Information on various aspects of college preparation is included.

Office of Civil Rights, U.S. Department of Education: Transition of Students with Disabilities to Postsecondary Education: A Guide for High School Educators

www2.ed.gov/about/offices/list/ocr/transitionguide.html

This document highlights significant differences between the rights and responsibilities of students with disabilities in the high school setting and their rights in the postsecondary education setting. Practical suggestions are provided that high school educators can share with students to facilitate their transition to college.

ThinkCollege

www.thinkcollege.net

Think College is a national organization dedicated to developing, expanding, and improving inclusive higher education options for people with intellectual disability.

American Association for People with Disabilities:

http:// aapd.com/wp-content/uploads/2016/03/Higher-Education—Getting-There.pdf

This document provides links on everything from applying, visiting, and choosing a college to gap-year programs.

Choicemaker Self-Determination Curriculum

http://www.ou.edu/content/education/centers-and-partnerships/zar
row/choicemaker-curriculum/self-directed-iep.html

The *Self-Directed IEP* contains 11 sequential lessons that typically take six to ten 45-minute sessions to teach. Over time students use their learned skills to lead their IEP meetings.

National Alliance for Secondary Education and Transition

http://www.nasetalliance.org/about/standards.htm

The National Alliance for Secondary Education and Transition (NASET) is a national voluntary coalition representing special education, general education, career and technical education, youth development, multicultural perspectives, and parents.

National Collaborative on Workforce and Disability Guideposts for Success

http://www.ncwd-youth.info/guideposts

NCWD/Youth is your source for information about employment and youth with disabilities. Their partners – experts in disability, education, employment, and workforce development – strive to ensure you will be provided with the highest quality, most relevant information available.

Teaching Self-Advocacy to Students

https://teachingselfadvocacy.wordpress.com/teaching-self-advocacy-skills/

Included here are useful tips and videos describing how to train students effectively in the use of self-advocacy skills.

Career Resources

Career One Stop
https://www.careeronestop.org/Toolkit/ACINet.aspx

A source for career exploration, training, and jobs.

Time Management

http://www.ldonline.org/article/23676?theme=print

A task analysis process designed as a starting point for teaching time management.

APPENDIX C: COLLEGE READINESS ASSESSMENT

Description & directions

This assignment will help you determine your present level of knowledge regarding some of the topics related to getting ready for college. **Please complete each section of this assignment as completely as possible without assistance from your family members, teachers, or classmates.**

About me

Learning styles
My two strongest learning styles:
List ways I can use my learning style to enhance my learning:

My strengths, preferences, interests, & needs

My strengths:
My preferences:
My interests:
My needs and weaknesses:

My college interests

Name the major types of colleges or higher education found in the United States? The ways I will pay for college include:

My top 3 college choices and my reasons for selecting each college:

College	Reasons for Interests
1.	
2.	
3.	

My technology

List pieces of technology than can enhance my learning:

My decision to disclose

Please review the statement and then type in whether the statement is true or false.

Statement	True or False
I can choose to tell or not tell the college I attend that I have a disability.	
I will have a special education teacher who can help me in college.	
Students can always use all of the accommodations they have in high school in college.	
Most colleges require more documentation than just your IEP or 504 plan to qualify for services in college.	
The only thing you need to do get accommodations in college is to sign up with the Disability Support Services Office.	

My plans

My postsecondary employment goal is:

My postsecondary education goal is:

The steps I need to take to reach my postsecondary goals include:

The VCU Center on Transition Innovations is funded by the Virginia Department of Education, #881-62524-H027A15107. For further information about the Center on Transition Innovations, please visit our website www.centeron transition.org

APPENDIX D: STUDENT STRENGTHS, PREFERENCES, INTERESTS, AND NEEDS

Name:

Address:

DOB:

i'm

de ter

m ine d

Date:

My Strengths

My Interests

My Preferences

My Needs

Resource provided by I'm Determined, a state-directed project funded by the Virginia Department of Education. © 2006–2018 I'm Determined. All rights reserved.

References

Asselin, S. B. (2014). Learning and assistive technologies for college transition. *Journal of Vocational Rehabilitation, 40*(3), 223–230.

Bolt, S. E., Decker, D. M., Lloyd, M., and Morlock, L. (2011). Students' perceptions of accommodations in high school and college. *Career Development for Exceptional Individuals, 33*, 80–94. doi: 0885728811415098.

Carnevale, A. P., Smith, N., and Strohl, J. (2013). *Recovery: Projections of jobs and education requirements through 2020*. Washington, DC: Center on Education and the Workforce.

Eckes, S.E. and Ochoa, T. A. (2005). Students with disabilities: Transitioning from high school to higher education. *American Secondary Education, 33*(3), 6–20.

Field, S., and Hoffman, A. (1994). Development of a model for self-determination. *Career Development for Exceptional Individuals, 17,* 159–169.

Finn, D., Getzel, E. E., and McManus, S. (2008). Adapting the self-determined learning model for instruction of college students with disabilities. *Career Development for Exceptional Individuals, 31*(2), 85–93.

Getzel, E. E. (2005). Preparing for college. In E. E. Getzel and P. Wehman (Eds.). *Going to college: Expanding opportunities for people with disabilities.* (pp. 69–87). Baltimore, MD: Brookes Publishing.

Getzel, E. E. (2008). Addressing the persistence and retention of students with disabilities in higher education: Incorporating key strategies and supports on campus. *Exceptionality: A Special Education Journal, 16*(4), 207–219.

Getzel, E. E., and Thoma, C. A. (2008). Experiences of college students with disabilities and the importance of self-determination in higher education settings. *Career Development for Exceptional Individuals,* 31(2), 77–84.

Getzel, E. E. and Wehman, P. (2005). *Going to college: Expanding opportunities for people with disabilities.* Baltimore, MD: Paul H. Brookes Publishing.

Hartwig, R., and Sitlington, P. L. (2008). Employer perspectives on high school diploma options for adolescents with disabilities. *Journal of Disability Policy Studies, 19*(1), 5–14.

Heckman, J. J., and Krueger, A. B. (2005). *Inequality in America: What role for human capital?* Cambridge, MA: MIT Press.

Hudson, R. (2013). *The effect of disability disclosure on the graduation rates of college students with disabilities* (Doctoral dissertation). Retrieved from https://vtechworks.lib.vt.edu/bitstream/handle/10919/24072/Hudson_RL_D_2013.pdf?sequence=1&isAllowed=y.

Madaus, J. W. (2010). Let's be reasonable: Accommodations at the college level. In S. F. Shaw, J. W. Madaus, and L. L. Dukes III (Eds.), *Preparing students with disabilities for college success: A practical guide to transition planning.* Baltimore, MD: Brookes Publishing.

Madaus, J. W., Faggella-Luby, M., and Dukes III, L. L. (2011). The role of non-academic factors in the academic success of college students with learning disabilities. *Learning Disabilities: A Multidisciplinary Journal, 17*(2), 77–82.

McGuire, J. (2010). Considerations for the transition to college. In S. F. Shaw, J. W. Madaus, and L. L. Dukes III (Eds.). *Preparing students with disabilities for college success: A practical guide to transition planning.* Baltimore, MD: Brookes Publishing.

Moeller, A. J., Theiler, J. M., and Wu, C. (2012). Goal setting and student achievement: A longitudinal study. *The Modern Language Journal, 96*(2), 153–170.

Newman, L., Wagner, M., Huang, T., Shaver, D., Knokey, A. M., Yu, J., Contreras, E., Ferguson, K., Greene, S., Nagle, K., and Cameto, R. (2011a). *Secondary school programs and performance of students with disabilities.* A Special Topic Report of Findings From the National Longitudinal Transition Study-2 (NLTS2) (NCSER 2012–3000). U.S. Department of Education. Washington, DC: National Center for Special Education Research. Menlo Park, CA: SRI International. Available at www.nlts2.org/reports/2011_11/nlts2_report_2011_11_rev30113_complete.pdf.

Newman, L., Wagner, M., Knokey, A. M., Marder, C., Nagle, K., Shaver, D., and Wei, X. (2011b). *The post-high school outcomes of young adults with disabilities up to 8 years after high school.* A report from the National Longitudinal Transition Study-2 (NLTS2). NCSER 2011–3005. National Center for Special Education Research.

Newman, L. A., and Madaus, J. W. (2015). Reported accommodations and supports provided to secondary and postsecondary students with disabilities: National perspective. *Career Development for Exceptional Individuals, 38*(3), 173–181.

Newman, L. A., Madaus, J. W., and Javitz, H. (2016). Effect of transition planning on postsecondary support receipt by students with disabilities. *Exceptional Children, 82*(4), 497–514. Advanced online publication. doi: 10.1177/0014402915615884.

Novakovic, A., and Ross, D. E. (2015). College student for a day: A transition program for high school students with disabilities. *Journal of Postsecondary Education and Disability, 28*(2), 229–234.

Schmulsky, S., Gobbo, K., and Donahue, A. (2015). Groundwork for success: Transition program for students with ASD. *Journal of Postsecondary Education and Disability, 28*(2), 235–241.

Shaw, S. F., Madaus, J. W., and Dukes III, L. L. (2012). Beyond compliance: Using the Summary of Performance to enhance transition planning. *TEACHING Exceptional Children, 44*(5), 6–12.

Thoma, C. A. and Getzel, E. E. (2005). "Self-determination is what it's all about": What post- secondary students with disabilities tell us are important considerations for success. *Education and Training in Developmental Disabilities*, 40, 217–233.

Wehman, P. (2006). *Life Beyond the classroom: Transition strategies for young people with disabilities*. Baltimore, MD: Brookes Publishing.

Wehmeyer, M. L., Agran, M., and Hughes, C. (1998). *Teaching self-determination to students with disabilities: Basic skills for successful transition*. Baltimore, MD: Brookes Publishing.

West, M. R., Kraft, M. A., Finn, A. S, Martin, R., Duckworth, A. L., Gabrieli, C. F. O., and Gabrieli, J. D. E. (2014). *Promise and paradox: Measuring students' non-cognitive skills and the impact of schooling*. Cambridge, MA: Harvard Graduate School of Education.

4

FOUNDATIONAL SKILLS FOR COLLEGE AND CAREER SUCCESS

Debra Hart

DIRECTOR, EDUCATION AND TRANSITION
INSTITUTE FOR COMMUNITY INCLUSION
UNIVERSITY OF MASSACHUSETTS, BOSTON

Molly Boyle

UNIVERSAL DESIGN FOR LEARNING & POSTSECONDARY EDUCATION SPECIALIST
INSTITUTE FOR COMMUNITY INCLUSION
UNIVERSITY OF MASSACHUSETTS, BOSTON

Melissa Jones

PROFESSOR, COLLEGE OF EDUCATION & HUMAN SERVICES
NORTHERN KENTUCKY UNIVERSITY

The Need for Foundational Skills

High school special education teachers and transition specialists know that it takes more than academics to succeed in college. In order to be successful college students and independent citizens or employees, young adults with disability also need to master skills that support continued success in a diverse and ever-changing society (Karp & Bork, 2012; NCWD/Y, 2016). These skills are what the chapter authors are calling *foundational skills*, because they are the skills upon which all others are built and include skills related to personal academic and career habits. These include skills such as punctuality, communication, cultural know-how, demonstrating respect toward others, a commitment toward a goal, and the ability to balance multiple roles through engagement with others, as well as independence and self-direction, including knowing and communicating one's needs through self-advocacy (see Table 4.1 for list of foundational skills). These skills also hold ramifications for the quality of one's personal life, affecting the ability to make and keep friends, find enjoyable ways to spend leisure time, and contribute to one's community in meaningful ways (NCWD, 2016).

Some educators refer to these skills as *soft skills*, because they are considered difficult to define and teach. However, without the ability to communicate, problem-solve, collaborate, and make decisions independently, young adults with disability are less likely to be successful in college or acquire or maintain employment. Students with disabilities are likely to need additional supports to learn about these skills, practice them, and incorporate them into their lives, but building these skills into a high school day can be difficult. Knowing what to focus on when there are so many competing messages and resources about foundational skills can feel overwhelming

One resource that teachers can use to help guide their approach to supporting students in these areas is a tool called the *Foundational Skills for College and Career Success*. The authors of this chapter designed this tool and based it on the work of Karp and Bork (2012) and Costa and Kallick (2000). Karp and Bork (2012) and Costa and Kallick (2000) surveyed a large number of students without disabilities who were not meeting with success, or at least persisting to completion in community college. In identifying the reason, they found that students lacked preparation for navigating the challenges of college and careers in skill areas such as social and performance behaviors. For example, knowing one needs help and how and where to go to get that help is critical; however, students did not possess those skills along with other executive function and social type skills. In order to address this need, it is imperative for high school teachers, transition specialists, students and family members to incorporate the teaching of these foundational skills across the high school curriculum, at home and in the community in naturally occurring settings, the goal being an effective, student-driven process, yielding much more positive student outcomes as students leave high school to enter adult life opportunities.

The Foundational Skills List

Table 4.1 presents a complete list of the foundational skills, including the four over-arching domains, a brief description of each domain, specific sub-skills that fall within each domain, and example characteristics. Each foundational skill is broad enough to encompass a variety of specific dimensions of social and performance behaviors, yet specific enough to provide students and their educational teams with direction for where to begin. The descriptions are written to be accessible to students in high school or post high school, are generalizable for use in high school or for preparation toward a career and/or postsecondary education, and are relatable to individuals across a variety of disabilities or to students who do not have a disability.

Understanding the foundational skills needed for adult success and independence is only the first step in planning. When used as part of a comprehensive transition planning process, as described in the next section, skill development in the various domains can be prioritized and achieved. The tools provided can be used to individually guide self-exploration and personal growth as students prepare for and engage in secondary and postsecondary experiences.

TABLE 4.1 Foundational Skills for College and Career Success

Domain	Description	Sub-Skills	Example Characteristics
Academic & Career Habits	Knowing and using strategies for approaching school and work-related learning. Students need to understand what will be expected of them and what steps they need to take to persist and complete their studies or continued learning in a profession.	Attendance & punctuality	Maintains current course & work schedules; Gets to class & work on time
		Use of resources	Is aware of educational supports (e.g. guidance counseling, library); Uses tutoring, coaching, mentoring, & other services as needed
		Communication	Communicates clearly and can make others understand their meaning; Checks for understanding such as asking clarifying questions; Communicates w/ teachers, supervisors, co-workers
		Quality of work	Plans ahead to manage assignments; Takes or knows how to get class notes; Organizes class or work materials; Maintains good study or work habits such as completing assignments or seeking help when needed
		Acceptance of direction & constructive criticism	Listens to and evaluates feedback from a variety of sources; Changes behavior as a result of assessments or feedback, if necessary; Accepts (OR understands) work performance assessments
		Technological know-how	Uses a computer; Uses office software (e.g., word processing & spreadsheets); Uses cell phone to make calls; Uses mobile device to text peers, co-workers, family as appropriate; Uses mobile device to manage and monitor calendar and assignments; Maintains social media accounts

(Continued)

TABLE 4.1 (Continued)

Domain	Description	Sub-Skills	Example Characteristics
Cultural Know-How	Understanding the institutional culture, expected etiquette and climate of a learning or work environment and its importance. Being able to apply that information to different educational and work settings.	Commitment	Attends class, job, and social activities; Follows through on assigned tasks to completion
		Respect	Adheres to context-specific rules & expectations; Demonstrates respect (as defined by culture/community); Manages conflict
		Flexible attitude (or flexible thinking)	Adapts to new & different perspectives & environments; Creates & seeks approaches to problems; Generates alternatives & considers options
		Responsible risk-taking	Considers ethical, safety, and societal factors in making decisions; Applies decision-making skills to deal responsibly with daily academic, employment, and social situations
		Interpersonal Skills	Maintains reciprocal relationships with friends and peers; Manages respectful interactions with teachers and employers
		Curiosity	Asks questions; Seeks out new information
Balancing Multiple Roles	Knowing how to balance personal independence with growing demands on an individual's time associated with the multiple roles as student, classmate, employee, volunteer, study partner, team member, and friend.	Persistence	Participates fully in academic task or project from initiation to completion; Problem solves when there are barriers
		Responsibility	Establishes and follows a daily/weekly schedule; Discovers key productivity places and times
		Collaboration	Coordinates with study/class/work partners; Contributes to group assignments; Performs a variety of roles within a group
		Independence	Completes familiar tasks at school or work without assistance; Navigates resources
		Engagement	Participates in a variety of organizations and/or groups related to interests; Motivated to learn; Demonstrates initiative in learning; Demonstrates initiative in getting involved in activities

Self-Direction	Having a sense of agency, decision-making and self-determination. Knowing when, where and how to seek help from available sources.	Communicates needs	Asks for help & clarification; Uses school & community resources
		Anticipates needs	Recognizes personal support needs; Uses external supports as needed; Learns from experiences; Anticipates problems or challenges; Takes initiative to solve problems
		Advocates for own needs	Knows of and uses school and workplace resources; Speaks up for self; Expresses desires; Articulates accommodation needs; Requests accommodations when necessary
		Accesses healthcare	Schedules preventative & emergency appointments; Manages prescription medication (as needed); Accesses school &/or fitness facilities
		Manages finances	Deposits & withdraws money (ATM, checking account); Pays bills on time; Budgets funds effectively

The Planning Process

The use of *the Foundational Skills for College and Career Success* involves a three-part process, with the student at the center of the planning. It is structured in such a way that students, with support, choose the skills on which they want to focus, set goals for their learning, and monitor their own progress toward those goals. The tool is divided into three distinct sections, with guiding steps throughout the planning, implementation, and evaluation phases of the process (see Figure 4.1).

Foundational Skills for College and Career Learning Plan

The Foundation Skills for the College and Career Learning Plan (CCLP) can be used to structure college experiences, including course work, employment, internships, on campus activities, volunteer and service learning experiences, and more. The CCLP is a goal setting and assessment tool designed to drive learning and productivity on campus, during internships and on the job. It can be used to structure the goal setting and to track and document the achievement of foundational skills. The CCLP may also be used as a planning document while developing the course of study, career goals, as a teaching tool for opening up conversations with students about the importance of foundation skills, and as an evaluation tool for providing ongoing evaluation and feedback on skill acquisition.

SECTION 1:

Foundation Skills identifies the skills common to college and career success. It is helpful to use this list of foundation skills as a guide when working with the student to develop their goals for the semester.

SECTION 2:

College & Career Characteristics Goal Setting provides and opportunity to identify characteristics specific to the college and work experience and to the student's personal development and transition goals.

SECTION 3:

Progress and Performance Review can be used to structure feedback and goal setting meetings regularly throughout the college and work experience, with the frequency of meetings to be decided by the faculty, staff, or supervisor with the student.

HOW TO USE THE COLLEGE AND CAREER LEARNING PLAN

STEP 1 Student should review the list of skills and characteristics in Section1 "Foundation Skillls" and identify 2-4 skills that they would like to work on in a semester. They should work with their advisors, mentors and coaches to identify both the skills and the environment where they can achieve these skills.

STEP 2 Student should meet with faculty advisor or supervisor to set specific plans for how they will learn that skill. Use Section 2 "College & Career Characteristics Goal Setting" of the CCLP to list those plans.

STEP 3 Student meet with their advisor at least 2 or more times each semester to review performance and progress and set new goals as needed. Students can use Section 3 "Progress and Performance Review" to record their progress. The first review meeting (Review 1) should take place during the first few weeks of the semester to assess the level of achievement and set goals. The next review (Review 2) should be scheduled at that meeting to review progress. Student and advisor should write comments and sign the CLLP at each of the reviews.

FIGURE 4.1 Foundational Skills College and Career Learning Plan

SAMPLE FOUNDATIONAL SKILLS FOR COLLEGE AND CAREER LEARNING PLAN

Name: _____ Advisor Name: _____

College: _____ Start Date: _____

Coach/Mentor Name: _____

SECTION 1: SPECIFIC COLLEGE AND CAREER SKILLS

Instructions: With the assistance of a coach, mentor, advisor, review the College and Career Skills that you want to focus on this semester, concentrating on skill areas that relate to your specific course of study and academic or career goals. Select at least 2 goals that you want to work on this semester. You may also add on an additional skill.

Academic and Career Habits

	Skill	Characteristics
	Attendance and punctuality	Maintains current course and work schedules Gets to class and work on time
	Use of resources	Is aware of college supports (e.g.. counseling, career, library) Uses tutoring, coaching, mentoring, disability services as needed
	Communication	Communicates clearly and can make others understand their meaning Checks for understanding such as asking clarifying questions Communicates w/ college faculty, supervisors, co-workers, residence hall staff
	Quality of work	Plans ahead to manage assignments Takes or knows how to get class notes Organizes class or work materials Maintains good study and work habits such as completing assignments, seeking help if needed
	Acceptance of direction and constructive criticism	Listens to and evaluates feedback from a variety of sources Changes behavior as a result of assessments or feedback, if necessary Accepts (OR understands) work performance assessments
	Technological know-how	Uses a computer Uses office software (e.g., word processing & spreadsheets) Uses cell phone to make calls Uses mobile device to text peers, co-workers, family as appropriate Uses mobile device to manage and monitor course schedule and assignments Maintains social media accounts Uses on-campus learning management systems

2 . Foundational Skills for College and Career Learning Plan

FIGURE 4.1 Continued

Cultural Know-how

Skill	Characteristics
Commitment	Attends class, job, and campus activities Follows through on assigned tasks to completion
Respect	Adheres to context-specific rules and expecations Demonstrates respect (as defined by culture/community) Manages conflict appropriately
Flexible attitude (or flexible thinking)	Adapts to new and different perspectives and environments Creates and seeks approaches to problems Can generate alternatives and consider options
Responsible risk-taking	Considers ethical, safety, and societal factors in making decisions Applies decision-making skills to deal responsibly with daily academic, employment, and social situations
Interpersonal skills	Maintains reciprocal relationships with friends and peers Manages respectful interactions with professors and employers
Curiosity	Asks questions Seeks out new information

FIGURE 4.1 Continued

Balance of Multiple Roles

	Skill	Characteristics
	Persistence	Participates fully in academic task or project from initiation to completion Problem-solves when there are barriers
	Responsibility	Establishes and follows a daily/weekly schedule Discovers key productivity places and times
	Collaboration	Coordinates with study/class/work partners Contributes to group assignments Performs a variety of roles within a group
	Independence	Completes familiar tasks at school or work without assistance Navigates resources
	Engagement	Participates in a variety of organizations and/or groups (on or off campus? Related to interests?) Is motivated to learn Demonstrates initiative in learning Demonstrates initiative in getting involved in activities

4 • Foundational Skills for College and Career Learning Plan

FIGURE 4.1 Continued

Self-Direction

Skill	Characteristics
Communicates needs	Asks for help, asks for clarification Uses campus and community resources
Anticipates needs	Recognizes personal support needs Uses external supports as needed Learns from experiences Anticipates problems or challenges Takes initiative to solve problems
Advocates for own needs	Knows of and uses campus and workplace resources Speaks up for self Expresses desires Articulates accommodation needs Requests accommodations when necessary
Accesses health care	Schedules preventative and emergency appointments Manages prescription medication Uses campus fitness centers
Manages personal finances	Deposits and withdraws funds (ATM, checking account) Pays bills on time Budgets funds effectively

FIGURE 4.1 Continued

SECTION 2: SPECIFIC COLLEGE AND CAREER SKILLS GOAL SETTING

Instructions: Choose the specific College and Career Skills that you want to focus on this semester, concentrating on skill areas that relate to your specific course of study and academic or career goals. With the help of a coach, mentor or supervisor, list those kills and identify how you will learn the characteristics associated with this skill. You may want to explain where you will learn this skill at either the college or in the workplace.

Specific College or Career Skills	How and where you will learn this skill
Skill #1	
Skill #2	
Skill #3	
Skill #4	

6 · Foundational Skills for College and Career Learning Plan

FIGURE 4.1 Continued

SECTION 3: EVALUATION OF PERFORMANCE AND PROGRESS

Instructions: Please meet with your advisor at least 2 or more times each semester to review performance and progress and set new goals as needed. The first review meeting (Review 1) should take place during the first few weeks of the semester to assess your level of achievement and set goals. The next review (Review 2) should be scheduled at that meeting to review progress.

Specific College or Career Skills From Section 1	Goals
Skill #1 Review #1 Date: Review #2 Date:	
Skill #2 Review #1 Date: Review #2 Date:	
Skill #3 Review #1 Date: Review #2 Date:	
Skill #4 Review #1 Date Review #2 Date:	

Foundational Skills for College and Career Learning Plan • 7

FIGURE 4.1 Continued

COMMENTS AND SIGNATURES

REVIEW #1

Student Signature _____ Date _____

Advisor Signature _____ Date _____

Coach/Mentor Signature _____ Date _____

REVIEW #2

Student Signature _____ Date _____

Advisor Signature _____ Date _____

Coach/Mentor Signature _____ Date _____

FIGURE 4.1 Continued

Using the Foundational Skills List: As previously described, the first step of the process is to determine the skills that will be prioritized. The *Foundational Skills List* (see Figure 4.1) is provided to help navigate the skill selection process. Use of the skills list ignites conversations with students about the importance of developing their personal skills along with academic skills and career, fostering ownership of their personal growth and development. Students are encouraged to reflect on their past successes and areas of difficulty, using this comprehensive list of skills as a guide. As an example, Grace lamented about not having any friends, but had been observed responding to peers in a negative manner on a consistent basis. Grace was then guided to review the list of skills to see if any might relate to her ability to make friends. After a review, Grace noted under the domain of cultural know-how, that she probably was not being respectful to her peers. With support from her teacher, she mapped out a plan to respond to peers in a respectful manner and agreed to practice with the teacher during group work situations in class. (See Figure 4.2) Facilitating the use of the foundational skill checklist for self-reflection can lead to student buy-in to the educational intervention, and promote personal commitment and growth.

The skill identification and planning process can be facilitated in a variety of settings, including during person-centered planning meetings, in preparation for IEP team meetings or transition planning meetings, graduation or career planning meetings, guidance sessions, and individual meetings with the student and teachers, parents, mentors, supervisors, or co-workers. The key is for the student to choose one to two skills on which she/he can focus. Beginning with the overarching areas of the tool, such as Academic and Career Habits, or Balancing Multiple Roles, students can then determine a specific skill to develop, making self-determined choices as to the priorities for growth. Skills may also be identified as a result of a challenge or obstacle experienced in high school, college or the workplace. The important point is that the student guides the process, with support from others as needed.

Some students may need additional explanation for understanding the skills included in the list, requiring scaffolding to support their understanding of the skills. Pairing each of the skills with an example or visual image is a helpful accommodation, as noted in Figure 4.1, providing students context for each of the skills listed.

Developing or enhancing the skill(s): Once a skill has been prioritized, the team moves to the second phase of the planning process, using the *College & Career Characteristics Goal Setting Grid* to guide their planning (see Figure 4.1). This grid provides students and team members with a graphic organizer to identify characteristics specific to the high school, college, and/or work experience desired and to the student's personal development transition goals. During this phase of the planning process, the student and her/his team determine the natural setting in which skill development can be supported, and structure experiences on either high school or college campuses, or in the

Specific College or Career Skills	How you will learn this skill
Skill #1 *Respect*	*I will practice speaking nicely to my friends. If a friend says that I hurt her feelings, I will say I am sorry. I will make a mark in my book each time I am not nice to a friend and be able to see my progress.*

Specific College or Career Skills From Section 1	Goals
Skill #1 *Respect* Review #1 Date: *9/12* Review #2 Date: *10/03*	*Goal: I will be nice toward my friends every day, saying nice things and being polite.* *Progress: I have been nice to my friends most of the time. I have said mean things 4 times, but I am trying. When Abbey tried to talk to me when I was mad, I listened instead of walking away, which is a good thing.*

Self-Monitoring Tool		
Grace's Goal: I will be nice toward my friends every day, saying nice things and being polite.		
Date	**Number of times I said things that were <u>not</u> nice.**	**Was I nice and polite to my friends**
Sept. 13	✓	Yes _____ No __X__
Sept. 14		Yes __X__ No _____
Sept. 17	✓ ✓	Yes _____ No __X__
Sept. 18		Yes __X__ No _____
Sept. 19		Yes __X__ No _____
Sept. 21	✓	Yes _____ No __X__
Sept. 22		Yes __X__ No _____
Sept. 25		Yes __X__ No _____
Sept. 26		Yes __X__ No _____

FIGURE 4.2 Example of completed plan & accompanying self-monitoring tool

workplace. As noted by the various skill domains, the planned experiences can focus on skills that specifically support learning in an academic environment, but can also extend beyond that to encompass employment opportunities, internships, social experiences, self-advocacy opportunities, and volunteer and service learning activities.

There are a few things to keep in mind when working with students and their families to address these foundational skills. First, these skills should be practiced in the environments in which they will be used. In order to do this, situations and environments would be identified in which it is likely for the skill to be needed and used. The skill would then be overtly practiced with the student during those situations. For example, Ed is a capable student, but experiences challenges when note-taking. He is very creative, and his mind often wanders during class lectures, causing him to frequently miss important information. After reviewing the skills list, Ed expressed a desire to do better in class, and wanted to improve the quality of his work, specifically related to note-taking, which is in the Academic and Career Habits domain. To address his need, Ed agreed to wear ear buds during History class, using an auditory beep provided every three minutes to prompt Ed to attend to what the teacher was saying. The device would need to be provided during each History class, with frequent review of Ed's History notes and periodic check-ins with Ed and his History teacher to determine the effectiveness of the strategy. Using naturally occurring opportunities within authentic environments to develop the prioritized skills increases the educational impact as students immediately recognize the relevance of each skill and are more readily able to apply and generalize the skill across a variety of situations and settings. This list of foundational skills provides competencies to incorporate across the general education curriculum and other activities where the skill can be used.

A second point to remember is that the structure of the foundational skills checklist and learning plan encourages student self-monitoring and self-assessment, as seen in the previous example, nurturing the development of skills ultimately needed for self-determination. The student can use a check-off sheet, an application on their phone or tablet to take notes, or any other appropriate tool to help her or him track skill development in practice.

This tool can be very motivating for students. Students take pride in recording their accomplishments, and understand that learning the skill can occur in a variety of settings, making the use of the skills checklist highly transferable. At the beginning of the school year, Abby, a sophomore student, was asked what her concerns were for starting the new school year and the rigorous demands of high school. Abby was unsure at first, until her teacher sat down with her and reviewed the foundational skills checklist. Through this activity, Abby identified a skill under the self-direction domain, explaining that when she does not understand something in class, she is reluctant to ask for assistance. She expressed an interest in being a stronger self-advocate, communicating her needs and asking for help. After rehearsing several scripts, she and her teacher devised a plan to self-monitor her self-advocacy attempts by recording in a daily journal her successes with requesting assistance. At the end of each month, Abby and her teacher reviewed the journal entries, counting the number of incidents of self-advocacy, discussing situations, and determining future strategies as needed. Abby not only self-monitored her behavior, but she also participated in a self-evaluation, assisting in determining future accommodation and support needs to help her reach her goal, which is the next step of the process.

Review of performance and progress: The third step of the process is the *Progress and Performance Review*. The graphic organizer provided in this section of the tool can be used to structure self-assessment, feedback, and future goal setting. It is here where planning meeting results and follow-up are recorded, and student outcomes are documented (see Figure 4.1). As noted in the previous example, the self-assessment process is meant to be an ongoing process with periodic opportunities for students to engage in a guided reflection of their successes and to make adjustments to goals or their learning plan as needed. Two suggested times for engaging in the formal review of student progress might be at the midpoint of a designated period (e.g., term/semester; grading period; employment quarter), and at the end of the designated time frame (e.g., term/semester, before an IEP meeting). To facilitate the performance review, the student should meet with a guidance counselor/peer mentor/supervisor/mentor / teacher to review personal progress and discuss if any benchmarks need to be refined and/or if additional skills are needed to help meet the goal. Any relevant information about the progress should be recorded on the learning plan in the comments section.

Consider the case of Tyrell. Tyrell often came to class unprepared to learn. He attended class regularly, but did not engage with his peers or teachers, offering little during class conversations or group work. He passively attended to his learning, making minimal efforts to engage with others. His teacher reviewed the foundational skills list with him and spent some time discussing items in the Balancing Multiple Roles domain. After the teacher provided Tyrell with several examples of how he sees Tyrell acting in class, Tyrell admitted that he is not engaged because he does not think he will ever graduate due to poor grades, so why try? After explaining to Tyrell that his teachers wanted him to be successful and were willing to help him, and that it was not too late for him to get the credits he needed to graduate, Tyrell agreed to consider some options.

Together, the teacher and Tyrell reviewed various characteristics on the Foundational Skills list, and pinpointed skills related to engagement. They identified specific actions Tyrell could take to address these skills and developed a progress-monitoring chart on which Tyrell and his teacher could document evidence of his efforts. The first week, Tyrell did very well engaging in class with his peers and the materials, but often gave up when assigned work he did not understand or found too challenging. Tyrell reviewed the skills list again with his teacher and realized his greatest issue was actually persistence, which was affected by his lack of self-advocacy. When he did not understand an assignment, he gave up instead of asking for clarification or assistance. Although Tyrell continued his plan for engagement, he added a component of the plan to increase the number of assignments he completed, asking for assistance when needed. At the end of the term, Tyrell was pleased with himself that he was able to pull his grade up to passing. As in this example, the performance review process is meant to be a component of a continuous learning process, and can be modified and enriched as necessary. When students have opportunities to practice the skills they are learning, there is a lasting effect on positive long-term student outcomes (Karp, Raugman, Efthimiou & Ritze, 2015).

Implications for IEP Development

Too often, adolescents with disabilities have few opportunities to make personal choices and indicate personal preferences (Chambers, Wehmeyer, Saito, Lida, Lee, & Singh, 2007). This is referred to as self-determination, and developing the skills needed to be a self-determined individual is crucial for adult independence. According to Loman, Vatland, Strickland-Cohen, Horner, & Walker, "promoting self-determination has become best practice in the education of students with intellectual and developmental disabilities" (2010, p. 1), and we know that to be true of any student, regardless of perceived ability or learning difference (Karp & Bork, 2012). Engaging in the Foundational Skills checklist review and planning process is one way to promote the development of overall skills related to self-determination. Embedding student identified goals in the IEP and transition planning process is one way to support the development of self-determination, meaningfully engaging the student in the IEP planning process as a result of the Foundational Skills activities. When IEP goals are written to focus solely on academic, social, behavioral, or adaptive behavior skill development, students with disabilities miss opportunities to develop and practice the foundational skills that will ultimately help determine their ability to be successful in competitive employment, live independently, and have a valued role in society.

This could mean helping students in younger grades, both with and without a disability to understand her/his strengths and weaknesses and learning style, or to choose what he or she wants to learn in the next grade. To foster the development of self-awareness and self-advocacy, students in early adolescence need to be aware of their learning styles and/or disability, as well as beneficial accommodations, supports, or tools. Students in secondary school can refine their skills in decision-making and problem-solving, and practice analyzing situations and determining the best response. Self-monitoring is an important priority throughout a student's school and career, honing these skills as the student matures and gains a better understanding of her/himself and others. The *Foundational Skills list and Learning Plan* provides teachers, students, and their families with a tool to support this process.

Role of Families and How to Support Their Child in Learning Foundational Skills

Empowering families to support and reinforce foundational skill acquisition is critical for all students, providing opportunities to learn these skills in natural settings across different environments in which students will need to use the skill. Unfortunately, research reveals that families often lack an overall awareness of what their son or daughter needs in order to be successful in college and future careers (Martinez, Conroy, & Cerreto, 2012; Hong & Ho, 2005). Educators can take a leading role in promoting awareness among parents and guardians of the need for the development of foundational skills (Figure 4.1).

The first step is to provide information to families about what foundational skills are and why they are so important to their child's future success. This should occur as early and often as possible, from kindergarten through secondary school and beyond. Once families are aware of the need for foundational skill development, the school can be more explicit with family members regarding how they can support their child in acquiring these skills in natural settings where the skill will be applied. Being cognizant that families come in all shapes, sizes, and ethnic, linguistic, and cultural backgrounds will help determine how this information is best conveyed (Greene, 2011).

Potential strategies for engaging and empowering families can include a myriad of activities during the K-12 school years, in adolescence prior to the postsecondary experience, and even during the inclusive postsecondary experience or on the job. Below are a few strategies that can be used to engage families in learning about the importance of foundational skills and how they can support their child in learning these skills:

- Identify existing high school family support services and integrate information on how families can support their child in learning foundational skills at home and in the community;
- Meet with families at home whenever possible to demonstrate how family members can support their child in learning foundational skills at home and in the community; and
- Identify community-based minority organizations, as they are typically trusted entities and are often gate-keepers to vital information, especially for families from diverse populations, and provide professional development on the importance of families supporting their children in learning foundational skills (Greene, 2011; Kochhar-Bryant, 2010).

Support for families does not have to be formal to be successful. For example, in one high school, transition personnel organized an annual Parent Café to help families of students with disabilities negotiate the transition from high school to the college experience. Pedro's family attended these events and appreciated that The Parent Café was a more personalized approach to support a specific population of students. The Parent Café was run and organized by veteran family members. Each year, an informal meeting and conversation was organized around coffee and snacks to discuss the postsecondary experience. Pedro's family was just learning about the transition process and had an opportunity to talk with experienced family members, discussing a range of topics from the importance of foundational skills, to class registration, to fears about safety on campus. Pedro's family, as well as other families, was invited to determine questions and discussion topics, as well as facilitate the ensuing conversation. High school transition staff were available to answer questions and provide input, but the focus was on fostering family discussions and learning from each other's experiences.

Conclusion

The importance of the need for all students, including those with disabilities, to learn foundational skills in addition to academic content is clear. In order for this learning to occur, services and supports must be provided in K-12 systems, higher education, and at home within the family structure. Whether students are planning to attend college or enter a career directly out of high school, regardless of perceived ability, each student should be given the opportunity to learn foundational skills, thus improving the chances of success in their future endeavors. This chapter sets forth a set of essential foundational skills that cut across student ages and ability levels, multiple disciplines, and systems. It establishes a common language for the foundational skills that can be used in K-12, higher education, and career services. Additionally, it offers a tool and process that is student centric, to assist professionals, students and families in teaching/learning the identified skills in naturally occurring inclusive settings.

References

Chambers, C., Wehmeyer, M., Saito, Y., Lida, K., Lee, Y., and Singh, V. (2007). Self-determination: What do we know? Where do we go? *Exceptionality, 15,* 3–15.

Costa, A. L. and Kallick, B. (2000). *Discovering and exploring: Habits of mind.* Alexandria: ASCD.

Greene, G. (2011). *Transition planning for culturally and linguistically diverse youth.* Baltimore, MD: Paul H. Brookes Publishing Co.

Hong, S., and Ho, H. (2005). Direct and indirect longitudinal effects of parental involvement on student achievement: Second-Order latent growth modeling across ethnic groups. *Journal of Educational Psychology, 97*(1).

Karp, M. M. and Bork, R. H. (2012). "They never told me what to expect, so I didn't know what to do": Defining and clarifying the role of a community college student.

College Ready Behaviors. CCRC Working Paper No. 49. New York: Columbia University, Teachers College, Community College Research Center.

Karp, M. M., Raufman, J., Efthimiou, C., and Ritze, N. (2015). Redesigning a student success course for sustained impact: Early outcomes findings, CCRC Working Paper No. 81. New York, NY: Columbia University, Teachers College, Community College Research Center.

Kochhar-Bryant, C. (2010). How secondary personnel can work with families to foster effective transition planning. In S. Shaw, J. Madaus, and L. Dukes (Eds.). *Preparing Students with Disabilities for College: A Practical Guide for Transition*. Baltimore, MD: Brookes Publishing Company.

Loman, S., Vatland, C., Strickland-Cohen, K., Horner, R., and Walker, H. (2010). *Promoting self-determination: A practice guide*. A National Gateway to Self-Determination. Retrieved from www.aucd.org/ngsd/template/index.cfm.

Martinez, D. C., Conroy, J. W., and Cerreto, M. C. (2012). Parent involvement in the transition process of children with intellectual disabilities: The influence of inclusion on parent desires and expectations for postsecondary education. *Journal of Policy and Practice in Intellectual Disabilities, 9*(4), 279–288.

National Collaborative on Workforce and Disability/Youth (2016). *Personal competencies for college & career success: What colleges can do*. Washington, DC: Institute for Educational Leadership, National Collaborative on Workforce and Disability for Youth.

5

COLLEGE PATHWAYS FOR STUDENTS WITH DISABILITIES

Meg Grigal

UNIVERSITY OF MASSACHUSETTS BOSTON

Judith S. Bass

BASS EDUCATIONAL SERVICES, LLC

The path to and through college looks different for every student, with or without a disability. However, the path for students with disabilities may include additional steps and considerations to ensure college choices meet student learning needs. Educators, counselors, therapists, and administrators in middle and high school are the first responders to students' and families' questions about college options, so it is critical that these individuals understand the range of options and types of supports and resources available to guide students with disabilities toward higher education. This chapter will explore the many postsecondary options for students with disabilities, including those options that are available to students who leave high school with an IEP diploma or high school certificate. These programs can be divided into several categories: career and technical colleges; residential colleges, post-graduate year programs ("PG year"); summer and postsecondary transition programs; community colleges; traditional four-year colleges; and specialized college programs. Each of these will be described and student experiences will be provided in order to best illustrate options available to students with disabilities.

Matching College Options to Student Goals

While not all students choose to go to college, for those who desire it, there are college opportunities for every student. It is important to note that the path to college will be impacted by many factors, not only a student's disability. All too often when the topic of college is raised, what comes to mind is the typical student leaving high school at 18 and applying to a four-year school to obtain a bachelor's degree. While this may be the archetypical college experience, it is not the experience of most college-bound students. Students who enroll in college full-time immediately after high school no longer represent the majority of postsecondary college students (Shapiro, Dundar, Wakhungu, Yuan, Nathan, & Hwang, 2015). Only one quarter of college students today attend residential colleges or universities with a full-time schedule. Forty-two percent of all undergraduate students attend community colleges and 38 percent of those attend part-time (Ma & Baum, 2016).

Finding the right college fit is crucial for college success. As described in Chapter 2, educators should help students and their families consider what their priorities are with regard to a postsecondary experience. If proximity or transportation is an issue, that will help guide the college search. Similarly, if the priority is obtaining employment rather than furthering specific academic pursuits, that goal will impact a student's college choice. It is important for educators to understand each student's college experience goals and subsequently identify resources available to the student.

WHAT ARE THE BEST COLLEGES FOR STUDENTS WITH (FILL IN THE BLANK)?

This is the wrong question. When deciding what colleges or universities are a good match for a student, it is critical to look at a student's *individual* needs as well as the type of accommodations and supports that are available. Just because a college or university is "well known" as one that is disability-friendly, it does not ensure that it will offer the right support for a particular student. For example, a student with dyslexia might need a college that has strong assistive technology available to provide audio books and/or programs to assist with reading and writing. A student with ADHD or poor executive functioning skills will likely need a college that offers weekly coaching to assist with time management and organization. It is important to note that not every college offers the same level of services or even the same services. As described in Chapter 1, it also may be helpful to talk to students with similar disabilities to hear about their experiences with requesting and receiving accommodations. Assessing the surrounding community is also important to ensure the college is a good fit for a student. If a student doesn't drive, is there adequate and accessible transportation in the town? If the student is living on campus, are the facilities in the dorms accessible? As described in Chapter 2, if a college does not have a lot of experience responding to a particular kind of disability, their resources may be technically adequate but not really optimal. Potential colleges should be chosen because they meet the specific needs of an individual student.

Certainly, decisions of this nature can be very difficult for students with disabilities who may also be contending with issues regarding their academic, social, and emotional well-being in high school. A good strategy is to offer information to students and their families in a variety of formats (in person, in writing, during back-to-school nights, parent–teacher conferences, college information nights) and to do so repeatedly in order to reinforce both the message that college is an option and that there are numerous paths to college.

College Experiences in High School

Dual enrollment is a college experience in which students can participate while still in high school. Dual enrollment is an increasingly common practice that permits high school students to be enrolled in high school and college simultaneously (Barnett & Stamm, 2010). Dual enrollment programs enable high school students to take college courses, either at the high school or on a college campus. Brand, Valent, & Browning (2013) suggest that these programs benefit students "by helping them learn about college, see themselves as college students, and experience college-level work in a supportive environment" (p. 12). Historically, dual enrollment experiences have been offered to high school students who have taken advanced placement courses, allowing them to seek high school and college credit simultaneously. Students with disabilities have the right to access any existing dual enrollment programs offered by their school district as long as they meet all of the same eligibility requirements and prerequisites for enrollment. Students with disabilities are held to the same financial obligations, academic performance expectations, and consequences for both success and failure as all other students.

Although students with disabilities may have access to dual enrollment programs, there are factors to consider in determining whether enrolling in such a program is in the best interest of a respective student. Factors that must be considered include:

- short-term and long-term funding options;
- how courses fit into the student's career and academic plan; and,
- accommodations and services available to the student, such as ongoing monitoring to support and develop the student's executive functioning skills (i.e., time management, organization, homework completion).

Most options require advance planning, so early conversations and decisions are both the ideal and preference. These matters should be addressed in collaboration with the high school counselor, special education providers, parents, and, most importantly, the student.

Dual Enrollment Programs for Students with Intellectual and Developmental Disability

The college campus can serve as a nexus for the transition experience, providing opportunities for personal growth and self-determination, access to adult learning and working environments, and new and expanded social networks (Grigal & Deschamp, 2012). A modified version of dual enrollment programs has demonstrated promise for students with intellectual and developmental disability (IDD), providing students the opportunity to receive community-based transition services on a college campus with same-age peers in lieu of remaining in high school (Grigal, Dwyre, Emmett, & Emmett, 2012; Hart, Zimbrich, & Parker, 2005; Kleinert, Jones, Sheppard-Jones, Harp, & Harrison, 2012). Dual enrollment programs (also known as concurrent enrollment or college-based transition programs) provide access to college courses, internships, and employment, as well as other campus activities for transition-aged youth with intellectual disability between the ages of 18 and 22 during their final two to three years of secondary education. Thirty percent of the higher education programs enrolling students with IDD throughout the US serve dually enrolled students (Think College, 2017).

Most dual enrollment programs serving students with IDD are operated and funded by school districts, though some have been initially established via federal or state grants (Papay & Bambara, 2011). One of the key purposes of dual enrollment experiences is offering access to learning that is not available in the high school; typically through enrollment in college coursework (Brand et al., 2013). The college catalog offers a wide array of credit and non-credit courses that could relate to students' career or personal development goals. However, dual enrollment programs for students with IDD vary in the amount of access students have to typical college classes. In some programs, students have access to a wide array of non-credit and credit-based college courses, and in others, there is minimal to no access to typical college courses. In a national survey of dual enrollment programs, Papay and Bambara (2011) found that only about one quarter of all students in PSE programs were participating in college classes and that course access was dependent on the type of program model, the location of the program, and the level of academic ability of the student. Limiting students' access to college courses might also limit the potential impact that a dual enrollment experience can have on a student's academic growth or future career plans.

Though offered in postsecondary settings, dual enrollment transition programs must also address issues related to the Individuals with Disabilities Education Act (IDEA). These include addressing IEP transition goals in a college setting, collaborating with secondary special education systems, dual funding structures, and schedule, staffing, and transportation issues. Chapter 7 offers additional information about dual enrollment transition services for students with IDD. The Think College website also provides a directory of dual enrollment programs offered in the United States at www.thinkcollege.net.

Another benefit of engaging in dual enrollment courses is that students may be able to take classes that help improve some academic skills during high school so that fewer remedial courses are necessary if the student chooses to enroll in college following high school. This may end up saving students and their families time and money, as tuition for most remedial courses is the same as it is for coursework that is credit-bearing. Because remedial coursework credit does not count toward a degree, it can take longer to complete a course of study and, as a result, cost more in tuition.

Career and Technology Education (CTE), Vocational and Trade Colleges

Other college options include technical, vocational, and trade colleges, all of which provide access to a more practical, hands-on approach to learning. Such colleges are often community-based and typically award one- or two-year post-secondary certificates and Associate's degrees. Postsecondary certificates are often occupationally focused and include awards from business, vocational, trade, and technical schools, as well as technical and non-degree awards from two- and four-year colleges (Carnevale, Rose, & Hanson, 2012).

In some states, community colleges also provide non-credit bearing courses through Continuing Education Program or credit-bearing courses through their one-year certificate programs for students with a specific vocational focus. This can be a good option for students who know that employment is their priority, as these pathways can provide short-term strategic coursework that can assist in building job skills.

Residential Vocational and Career Colleges

For students who are prepared to leave home and are more interested in learning a trade or technical skill, residential vocational and career colleges can be good options. Most have adequate disability support services and offer hands-on, experiential learning. Some two-year residential colleges offer certificate programs and Associate's degree programs. (Community college offerings will be discussed later in the chapter.) Students can study technical and vocational subjects that can lead them into the workforce without the need to obtain a Bachelor's degree. Certificate programs, and Associate of Applied Science (AAS) degrees are available in areas such as, but not limited to, Early Childhood Education, Heating and Ventilation, Automotive Technology, Graphic Design, Landscaping, Exercise Science, and Physical Therapy Assistant. Another benefit of this type of college is the ability to build on the certificate or AA degree. For example, if a student is not certain of her ability or interest in spending two years in school, she can take the certificate path. If she chooses to continue, then another year will earn her the AA degree. Once the student has the AA degree, she can either continue or return to school at a later date to build on the degree and earn a Bachelor's degree. For example, a student might earn an AA in Architectural Technology or Engineering Technology, and these two degrees could lead to a BA in Building Science and Sustainable Design or Construction Technology and Management. A student can also initially enter the workforce with the certificate, AA, or AAS degree which is a path that provides significant flexibility in terms of future credential attainment. According to a report by the Georgetown University Center on Education and the Workforce, certificates made up 22 percent of all college awards in 2012, up from 6 percent in 1980. Thirty-four percent of those who earn certificates also go on to earn Associate's and/or Bachelor's degrees (Carnevale et al., 2012).

Postgraduate Year Programs

Another non-traditional avenue to both college and greater independence that offers students an opportunity to bolster their chances of being successful in college is called a postgraduate (PG) year, where students attend a boarding school for an additional year following high school graduation. Kennedy (2017) suggests that students interested in a PG year may pursue the experience in order to address a variety of issues including: personal growth and maturity, college admissions, and athletic skills. Reasons for pursuing a postgraduate year vary, as does the timing of this decision. Some high school students with disability may know during their junior or senior year that they would like to pursue a postgraduate year and thus choose not to proceed with the college application process. Others may choose to apply to colleges, but maintain the PG year option as they determine next steps. In some cases, students may go through the college application process and then determine that they are not prepared for college. In this case, students can request a deferral from their selected college and pursue the PG year program to address needed skills.

Sometimes a PG year can help students develop a clearer vision of their college experience goals and refine the college search accordingly. Most PG programs

---

Understood.org

https://www.understood.org/en/school-learning/choosing-starting-school/leaving-high-school/15-college-programs-for-kids-with-learning-and-attention-issues

Admissions Quest

http://www.admissionsquest.com/~resources/showarticle.cfm/articleid/32/articletypeid/5/topic/post-graduate-year#

Boarding School Review

https://www.boardingschoolreview.com/post-graduate-boarding-schools

Internet Special Education Resources:
Gap Programs and Young Adult Transition Programs

http://iser.com/young-adult-transitions.html

FIGURE 5.1   Resources on Post Graduate (PG) Year Programs

are residential and offer a curriculum designed to improve and build the skills and abilities necessary for a successful collegiate experience. Because most of these programs are located at private schools, cost may be extensive. Counselors should work with families to explore potential scholarships and financial aid if a PG program is a good match for a student. Figure 5.1 includes a list of resources that can be used to identify Postgraduate Year programs.

> *Jason had been diagnosed with ASD as a young child and attended a small private high school with a great deal of one-on-one attention. He found it difficult to work with other students and sometimes was perceived as arrogant and overconfident. He seemed to be very rigid in his thinking and had a very specific career interest in the hospitality industry. He only wanted to study subjects that interested him, and did not understand the need for other subjects, such as English or math. Jason believed he would be fine in a traditional college dorm; however, his mother didn't agree. To address her concerns about Jason's social maturity and level of independence, Jason attended a PG Year at a boarding school for students with ASD and other social communication disorders. During the year, Jason acquired better self-awareness, improved his social skills, and began to develop his independent living skills. Above all, he spent the year learning how to be less rigid in his thinking and developed a more flexible outlook on his life. After his PG Year, Jason enrolled in a traditional four-year college with a strong Social Support Program, something he had refused to even consider the previous year.*

Summer Bridge and Postsecondary Transition Programs

Other experiences that can prepare students with disabilities for college life are summer bridge programs and postsecondary transition programs. These programs target independence and responsibility, self-advocacy, social issues, and organization and study skills, helping students develop the academic, social, and emotional skills they will need to succeed in college. For example, in Landmark College's Summer Transition Program, students are immersed in a living/learning experience that offers a real "taste" of college life, college-level work, and the challenges they will encounter when beginning a fall term. They develop a clear understanding of their personal learning strengths and needs, and discover how resources and self-advocacy can support their success in college.

> *Shira was a sweet, kind, and compassionate student. She loved everything about her high school: her teachers, her friends, and her drama program. Shira had been in on-grade level team-taught classes throughout high school, with a modified curriculum in math and science. Although her transcript showed a GPA of 3.5, her academic skill level was not adequate for many traditional college settings. Shira was hoping to study acting in college, but she needed to first develop the academic and social readiness to attend college as a full-time student. Shira attended a one-year transition program at a residential four-year college, taking developmental classes in reading, writing, and math. The program provided a separate housing facility on campus for*

the students in the program; however, the students were able to participate in many of the campus activities. Shira attended theater and sporting events on campus, ate in the cafeteria, and took one three-credit college class along with her college peers. All of Shira's social and academic support was provided through the transition program. At the end of the year, Shira successfully completed her transition program and remained at the college, matriculating as a freshman the following fall semester.

The Postsecondary Transition program differs from the Postgraduate (PG) year in that it is generally housed on a college campus, whereas the PG Year is a component of a high school program, which is, essentially, a "13th year." For students who are looking to be in a slightly more independent environment, the Postsecondary Transition program affords greater flexibility in academic offerings. Students often have the option of taking a freshman course on the college campus during their second semester if they are academically ready; this can further ease their transition to more challenging college-level work, while still having access to the level of support in a transition program. Some examples of summer transition programs are: College Internship Program (Summer@CIP); Beacon College (Summer For Success); Mercyhurst University (CREATE Summer Program). Transition Year programs include Thames Academy at Mitchell College and the CONNECT Program at Davis and Elkins College. Figure 5.2 includes college search resources for students with learning disabilities, ADHD, and Autism Spectrum Disorder.

Recommended Website

CollegeWebLD offers up-to-date, detailed information about the learning support services and programs available at over 400 colleges and universities in the U.S. There is a free version offering basic information as well as a fee-based version with more advanced search features and ratings. www.collegewebld.com

Recommended Book

The K&W Guide to College Programs and Services for Students with Learning Disabilities or Attention Deficit/Hyperactivity Disorder, 13th (2016) Edition by Princeton Review
This book provides a good starting point in researching the learning support services and programs at more than 350 colleges and universities in the U.S. (available at bookstores or online)

FIGURE 5.2 College Search Resources for Students with Learning Disabilities, ADHD and Autism Spectrum Disorders

Community Colleges

For a student who feels he would be more successful closer to home, attending community college can be a worthwhile experience. This option can be seen as a stepping stone, allowing the student to improve his academic skills and providing opportunities to navigate adult learning environments, while the student continues to live either with his or her family or close to home. Another benefit of attending a community college is that many community colleges have articulation agreements with four-year institutions of higher education. This offers students with disabilities who feel more academically and personally prepared after earning an AA degree to transfer to a four-year program. Counselors and educators should suggest that students ask about these options when visiting colleges so that they and their families are aware of any implications that impact the transfer of credit to other colleges.

Many community colleges offer a wide range of career-focused certificate programs, and as with two-year residential colleges, students can gain the skills they need to enter the workforce without the need for a two- or four-year degree.

> *Having a late November birthday, Jordan was the youngest in his class throughout school. He had been diagnosed with ADHD in early elementary school, and by high school demonstrated some lags in emotional maturity and social skills. Jordan became the proverbial class clown; he had a lot of friends who thought he was funny, but who did not take him seriously. Indeed, he did not take himself seriously either. Although he was very intelligent, he did the bare minimum to pass his subjects in school. He made a joke of "getting by" and acting like he didn't care about learning, while inside he was filled with anxiety because he knew he was smart but did not know how to show it. Fortunately, Jordan lived near a good, supportive community college and was able to create a schedule with fewer classes and access to ADHD coaching and subject tutoring. This approach provided Jordan with the supports and flexibility he needed to finally "launch" into independence and self-reliance. He was able to earn his AA degree in business, and after a year of working full time, Jordan proudly moved from his parents' home to his own apartment.*

Implications of Placement Testing and Remedial Courses

Community colleges can also vary in their responses to disability accommodations and academic requirements. Upon enrollment, students are typically required to take the ACCUPLACER, which consists of placement tests in math and English. These tests determine whether a student should begin higher education with college-level credit-bearing courses or non-credit bearing remedial courses. One issue faced by some students with disabilities is that community colleges typically will not allow a student to take credit-bearing classes without first passing the placement tests or, in some cases, until a student has passed the math and English remedial classes. If a student has a math-related disability, he or she might be required to retake the non-credit remedial math class two or three times. If the student does not pass this course, he cannot proceed to any credit coursework in that subject. This kind of experience can lead to frustration and can potentially cost more in tuition, as the tuition for non-credit remedial courses is not substantially different from that of credit-bearing courses.

If educators and families believe a student may need a remedial course, they could consider trying to access that course through a dual enrollment experience, thus better preparing the student prior to high school ending. If this is not possible, educators can help families consider the implications of placement testing policies on their short- and long-term higher education plans. Asking the college about their policies and whether or not there is flexibility in advance may help students avoid frustration in the future.

> *Mark, a community college student, had attended college part-time for six years, earning 58 credits, yet he was not on course to attain his Associate's degree. One barrier Mark faced was that he not permitted to take the one math class and two science classes he needed to graduate, because he had not passed the non-credit math class. This non-credit class was taught by computer module, self-paced, and only monitored by an instructor, and Mark's executive functioning skills prevented him from passing the class. This created a cycle of failure that was frustrating. Marc asked his advisor if he could retake the placement test so that he could remove this barrier to his attaining the needed courses. Fortunately, Mark was able to petition the school to retake the placement exam and was finally able to pass it. He was able to complete the three remaining courses and earn his Associate's Degree.*

In addition to being aware of placement test policies, it is also critical that students are empowered to advocate for themselves and seek out needed services. In the situation described above, Mark was not sure what to do to address his issue. Without guidance he might have decided to drop out. However, not all community colleges approach placement testing the same way. In other colleges, students that do not pass math placement tests may be advised to work with tutors to learn the material, or students may petition the college to waive the requirement and request a course substitution. Sometimes, even with good planning, a student can get stuck in a cycle of failure, and the best solution is to transfer to a different community college. Susana's story demonstrates how changing schools may open up pathways to continue learning.

> *Susana, a student with a specific learning disability in math, met with her college counselor after she had already failed the non-credit bearing math course three times. Susana felt hopeless and she was ready to drop out of college and go to work. After reviewing her options at her current college, Susana was advised to continue her education at a different college, one that had a more flexible policy toward remedial coursework. Fortunately, Susana lived near another local community college, and*

was able to transfer all of her credits there. Though it took two additional semesters, Susana was able to complete her studies and earned her Associate's degree. Achieving this goal allowed her to continue her education by pursuing and completing a four-year Bachelor's degree in Special Education.

For educators and counselors working with students with Specific Learning Disabilities or those with below-average academic ability in one or more subjects, it is important to review the policies of each institution to know in advance of student enrollment whether there is flexibility in the student's path to a degree. Had Susana not been provided with guidance and an alternate plan of action, her life could have turned out quite differently.

Traditional Four-Year Colleges and Universities

There are more than 3,000 degree-granting colleges and universities in the United States (National Center for Education Statistics 2016). Four-year colleges and universities provide pathways to Bachelor of Arts or Bachelor of Science degrees, and most offer residential options either on or near the campus. Four-year IHEs may have more rigorous admission requirements and may be more selective than some two-year colleges. These options offer a broad range of academic focal areas, and public state colleges and universities offer reduced rates for in-state students.

Educators have a wide array of search tools that they can use to assist students and their families to find the right four-year college or university. The National Center for Education Statistics offers the College Navigator website (https://nces.ed.gov/collegenavigator/), a comprehensive listing of college and university programs available in the United States. Other websites that may be more student-friendly include the College Board's Big Future website which offers a step-by-step online college search tool (https://bigfuture.collegeboard. org). It also provides a tool to allow students to compare certain college characteristics including location, type, campus life, admissions, cost, and financial aid. Other student-friendly search tools include College View (http://www.col legeview.com), which offers additional search categories, including quality of life issues such as "liberal-conservative," "party scene," "Greek life," and "great college towns," and information about schools with robust LGBT communities, and College Data, (https://www.collegedata.com/) which is a search tool that provides detailed information about financial aid offerings and receipt of merit aid, as well as representation level of students from particular backgrounds. These tools can help narrow down a student search to a manageable number of schools. Other websites can offer more specific information about a college or university's support services. For example, one search tool, CollegeWebLD (www.collegewebld.com) offers detailed information about the learning support services at more than 400 colleges and universities in the US. Students can take a short survey to create a success profile, which identifies the level of support and the type of learning environment best suited for that student. Figure 5.3 offers a sample of a student's search results. The student can use this learning profile to search for target schools that match his or her profile. ★

When considering a four-year program, students with disabilities should take into account the typical issues that other college students consider such as cost, proximity, available programs of study, available student aid, as well as campus size and culture. In addition, students with disabilities should also consider the accessibility of the campus and surrounding community, the culture of acceptance of all types of learners, and the level of responsiveness to disability in general. When gathering college choice information, students, families, and educators must have a clear understanding of the level and types of support available at the IHEs under consideration, regardless of the type of college.

KNOW BEFORE YOU GO

Did you know that families can and should meet with the college or university's Disabilities Services Office before a student enrolls? After the student has been accepted but before making the final decision to attend, the parents and student should request a meeting with the Director of Disability Services to determine whether the college will grant the accommodations and provide the services the student will need to be successful. Parents should send a copy of the student's most recent psychoeducational report to the Director ahead of time in order to have a productive meeting. Know before you go!

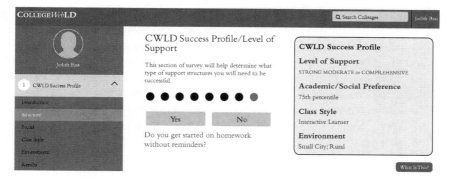

FIGURE 5.3   CollegeWebLD Student Success Profile Results from Online Survey★

★A free version allows the user to search for basic information on each college; the fee-based version contains more advanced search features and ratings.

Levels of Support in Higher Education

There are significant differences in the types and levels of support available to students with disabilities as well as the process through which these supports are accessed among IHEs. In accordance with Section 504 of the Rehabilitation Act of 1973 and the Americans with Disabilities Act Amendment of 2008 (ADAAA), colleges are required to provide reasonable accommodations for students with documented disabilities, a practice referred to as ADA Compliance. While all colleges must maintain ADA Compliance, some colleges may provide more supports than others. If we were to describe disability services in terms of levels or ranges, most disability services offered by colleges could be characterized as offering a moderate range of support services, which is sufficient to meet the needs of most students. There are some colleges whose supports would be characterized as more comprehensive, as they offer highly structured support programs for students with greater needs. Finally there are colleges whose supports would be characterized as basic, meeting only the minimal requirements under the ADA. Within these levels of support, colleges provide services and accommodations for a range of disabilities: students with Specific Learning Disabilities, ADHD, and/or Autism, as well as specialized support for students with visual, hearing, and intellectual disabilities. The following provides a description of four broad support categories: moderate support services, comprehensive or structured support programs, social support programs, and basic ADA compliance. Box 5.3 provides some questions that students and families can ask the Disability Services Office staff during a college visit.

QUESTIONS TO ASK THE DISABILITY SERVICES OFFICE DURING A COLLEGE VISIT

While often the first step in assessing a college is to visit the website, once a student narrows down her choices, nothing is better than actually visiting the college. There can be a marked difference among colleges in their culture of understanding and acceptance of students who learn differently. Some have college leadership that offers faculty workshops to support their understanding of students' learning styles and use of principles of universal design in their instruction, and others are less supportive and responsive to students who have disabilities. The only way to know how a college responds to these issues is to visit the campus and ask questions. In addition to attending a tour of the college or an Open House, students with disabilities and their families should be encouraged to visit the Disabilities Services Office on campus.

Questions to consider include:

- How welcoming and responsive are the staff people?
- Is the office located near the center of campus or far off on the edge of campus, where it might be harder to access?
- What is the minimum number of courses one can take to be considered a full-time student? You should take the minimum number of courses possible, especially the first year.
- Does the college offer a quiet place to take tests? Are you able to take essay tests on a computer?
- Does the college have a Writing Center? You will need a Writing Center to assist you in organizing written assignments, especially long-term research papers. Check the hours of operation and inquire whether it is professionally or peer staffed.
- Are organizational coaches available? You may need a coach to assist with staying on task with day-to-day and long-term assignments.
- Are note takers available? How are they selected? You want a note taker that is chosen by the professor or the learning specialist, who hands in notes to the learning specialist, where you can pick them up anonymously.
- Does the college offer priority registration? Being able to register early will help you manage your time better, have later start times, and schedule breaks between classes.
- Is there a contact person who will be able to assess if you are taking a balanced course load each semester? You should avoid having too many heavy reading classes in the same semester.

Reprinted with permission from Bass Educational Services, LLC ©2017

Moderate Support Services

Moderate support services comprise the largest of support categories, being offered by the majority of colleges across the country. These colleges offer services and accommodations above and beyond what is mandated by ADA and include a staff of professionals who can assist students with disabilities. The professionals on staff will typically help students learn to be self-advocates and might advocate for the student with professors if a student is initially unable to do so. While the Disability Services Office is typically administered by a professional with a background in disabilities, services such as tutoring might be conducted by peers, graduate students, and/or other professionals. Many colleges and universities offer a Learning Center where students can take exams in a distraction-reduced test environment, receive assistance in time management and organization, and meet with tutors and coaches one-on-one. Students do not apply separately for such services; these are provided as a civil right to all students with properly documented disabilities, once they request and are approved for such accommodations. Some examples of colleges and universities with moderate support services are Goucher College, College of Charleston, Florida A&M University, Tulane University, Beloit College, University of Puget Sound, St. Edward's University, and Howard University.

Comprehensive Support Programs

A comprehensive or structured support program is one that is designed specifically to ensure that students have access to advising and academic assistance. This type of program offers ongoing access to staff trained in specific disabilities, special orientation programs, assistance with advocacy, and academic monitoring and counseling. These programs are typically fee-based, in addition to tuition, room and board, and other student fees. Students often need to apply separately to the program when they apply to the college, and the application often requires an interview. The number of students accepted each year is limited in order to keep the student-to-professional ratio low and to ensure that adequate personal attention is available to students in the program. Students meet with learning specialists regularly, typically between one and three times a week. These programs assist students with some or all of the following: academic tutoring, remedial tutoring, ADHD coaching (assistance with time management, organization, scheduling), mentoring, and sometimes social skills support. These same colleges also offer moderate support services for students who do not need to be enrolled in a structured program. Some examples of colleges with comprehensive support programs are: Adelphi University, Lynn University, University of the Ozarks, Dean College, McDaniel College, Limestone College, DePaul University, and the University of Denver.

> *Aaron had always worked hard in high school, spending hours each night doing his homework. Because Aaron was diagnosed with a Specific Learning Disability in Reading, he used assistive technology to write his essays and listened to recorded books to complete his reading assignments. When Aaron entered his freshman year in college, he applied and was accepted into his college's comprehensive support program. There he found support for his academic needs, including individualized services and assistive technology. Aaron met with his learning specialist twice per week during his first semester and once per week in his second semester; he also received tutoring by professional tutors in English and History. Aaron appreciated the structure of these pre-scheduled appointments and felt that they were a major factor in his completing a successful freshman year. Now a second semester junior, Aaron is on target to graduate next year. He has chosen to use only disability support services during his senior year rather than remain in the program, because he has developed the skills to work more independently and is confident in his ability to succeed with less support.*

PROFILE OF THE PAL PROGRAM: A COMPREHENSIVE SUPPORT PROGRAM AT CURRY COLLEGE

The Program for Advancement of Learning (PAL) Program at Curry College is a structured support program designed for students who have a primary diagnosis of a language-based learning disability and/or ADHD and who have at least average to superior intellectual ability. Students are encouraged to become independent, self-directed learners.

For additional colleges with comprehensive support programs, go to www.collegewebld.com

Social Support Programs

Students with Autism Spectrum Disorder and other social communication disorders often have no trouble meeting the entrance criteria to the college of their choice, yet once enrolled, may have difficulty navigating the academic and social complexities inherent in the college experience. Many students lack the self-management skills needed to independently organize and integrate all aspects of college life. The stress of transition can inhibit a student's ability to know who and when to ask for help. Much like a comprehensive support program addresses a student's academic needs, the social support program addresses a student's social needs. Students are often paired with neurotypical mentors who accompany them on social outings or attend planned group activities. This type of program assists students in navigating campus life outside of the classroom and is effective in preventing students from feeling isolated on weekends. Some colleges that offer social support programs also offer comprehensive support programs. Colleges and universities with social support programs include: Rochester Institute of Technology, Mercyhurst University, Adelphi University, Davis and Elkins College, Marshall University, and Rutgers University.

Basic ADA Compliance

Some colleges and universities choose to adhere to the minimum standards required by law, providing basic accommodations, but not necessarily any enhanced services. In these IHEs, there may be a more decentralized approach to assisting students. Students receive accommodations through a Disability Services Office, but the administration of this office may not always be someone who has experience working with people with disabilities. Colleges and universities that could be characterized as meeting basic ADA compliance will usually have an academic support center available to all students, but they may not have a learning center specifically for students with disabilities. When necessary, students make arrangements directly with their professors for alternate exam locations; a distraction-reduced testing environment is not typically offered. It is the student's responsibility to find content or peer tutors available through each individual department. For students who are self-sufficient, who can advocate for themselves, and require minimal support, such a college environment may be sufficient. However, it is generally not adequate for the majority of students with learning differences. For students with disabilities who plan to attend a college providing minimal support services, there are some helpful online resources including: Beyond Booksmart (https://www.beyondbooksmart.com); New Frontiers in Learning (https://www.nfil.net); and Fairleigh Dickinson's LD Virtual Tutoring (http://view2.fdu.edu/campuses-and-centers/ldvirtualtutoring). Also, a good resource for finding a certified ADHD coach in your state or region is www.jstcoach.com.

Graham was an "A" student throughout middle school with little need for study. His earlier diagnoses of ADHD and dyslexia had never impacted his academic ability, because his natural intelligence was enough to allow him to coast through those years. However, the transition to high school really came as a shock to his executive functioning skills and his reading ability, and he began to feel overwhelmed with the increased workload. Graham had never learned how to study, so his mom began to help. She sat with him each night and made sure he completed his assignments. She read his books to him when he didn't have time to finish them. As a junior in high school, Graham was recognized as a National Merit Commended Scholar. He had a 4.0 unweighted GPA. He had taken six AP courses and scored 4s and 5s. He was accepted into his state's flagship university and invited to be part of the Honors Engineering Program. During the first semester, Graham became overwhelmed with the volume of work. He still did not know how to manage his time or how to study. Because his high school grades were good, his parents did not think it was necessary to request any accommodations or services at college, and now, Graham did not know where to go for help. Graham barely made it through the first semester with passing grades and was placed on academic probation. When he started the second semester, he applied for accommodations, but he found that his university didn't offer much. He had just learned about assistive technology and audio textbooks, but his school did not provide that; his school did not offer note takers. He was granted extended time, but there was no learning center that could provide him with a distraction-reduced setting to take exams. By mid-semester, Graham took a medical leave of absence; he had stopped going to classes, becoming depressed and staying in his room, until his parents decided that he needed some professional help. As sad as this part of the story is, the good news is that Graham was able to see what he needed to succeed and sought the right learning environment. After a short break to improve his mental health, Graham spent a semester at his local community college repairing his damaged GPA, and then transferred to a smaller, more supportive environment that could provide the accommodations and services

Graham needed to be a successful college student. He was able to graduate in 4.5 years, earning the Engineering degree he initially sought.

Specialized Higher Education Programs

Some college and university programs focus on responding to particular needs such as advancing independent living capacity for young adults or responding to students with disabilities underserved in higher education, such as students with intellectual or developmental disability. These specialized higher education programs may share some of the same features as the comprehensive support programs but may also focus on academic, employment, and independent living goals.

Independent Living Programs

For students who need to develop the skills to live independently, an Independent Living Skills Program can be a good postsecondary option. These residential programs provide training and education in skills of daily living, such as cooking, doing laundry, food shopping, money management, medication management, and good hygiene. Students also work on improving social skills through daily interactions and practice with mentors and peers. In addition, students may take college classes at a local college or enroll in a vocational training program. Some programs assist students as they move out into the community and enter the workforce, while maintaining the relationship through outreach to the student.

When Eric, a student with autism, first met with his college counselor, he indicated that he wanted to be an astrophysicist. When asked what he liked about the field, he responded that he liked science and space but didn't really understand what that career choice would entail. Additionally, his low GPA and attendance in mostly modified classes did not provide him with the academic background or study skills he would need to pursue the sciences in higher education. However, his parents were certain that Eric could handle college. Against the advice of professionals, Eric's parents allowed him to begin college at a traditional four-year university without any structured social support. His parents did not want to "break their son's heart" because he was so excited to go to college. Once Eric began his studies, he was overwhelmed by the level of independence and organization needed to succeed and he completely shut down emotionally. He was home by mid-November. Now, Eric's parents had to deal with his mental health issues before even considering his next options. They recognized that it would be advantageous for Eric to attend an independent living skills program to assist with his social anxiety and to support his ability to make good decisions and fit in socially. Many students also attend nearby colleges as part of their program, earning college credits towards a degree. Eric thrived in this environment; he learned to make eye contact with people, developed friendships, and even began to take care of his own needs. Over the three years Eric attended, he completed 21 college credits towards the Bachelor's degree he planned to earn, with a great deal of academic support and encouragement provided by the program.

When researching colleges for students with disabilities, educators, counselors, and families should be mindful of the broader connotation of the word "college." As mentioned earlier in this chapter, there is a college for everyone; one need only consider all the postsecondary avenues available to students with disabilities, and not focus solely on the traditional four-year college. Even without social readiness, students can take one or two college classes while attending an Independent Living Skills program; students who are not ready for the academic challenges of college-level work can take classes as part of a Certificate Program or non-credit classes to gain knowledge in an area of interest. Whether a student attends full-time or part-time, the college experience is one that can help students acquire the skills they need to develop into more confident and independent young adults.

College and University Programs for Students with Intellectual Disabilities

There are currently 268 colleges and universities that are providing access to students with intellectual disabilities (ID; Think College, 2018). Higher education options for students with ID have grown substantially since the passage of the Higher Education Opportunities Act in 2008 (Grigal, Hart, & Papay, in press). The legislation created new funding for program development and created or expanded options in 33 states in 88 colleges and universities (Think College, 2017). Since 2010, data has been collected on over 2,700 students with ID and other developmental disabilities who have accessed federally funded college programs.

Most higher education programs serve students who have exited from high school and are typically 18 years or older. At some IHEs, programs may be developed specifically to serve students with ID, offering specific application procedures, programs of study, and supports. At other IHEs, students with ID, often with the support of their families, access existing college or university programs that are not specialized to serve students with ID. Like the dual enrollment programs described earlier in this chapter, the focus of services provided to adult learners with ID includes academic access, career development and integrated paid employment, independent living, and campus membership. Higher education programs serving adults with ID vary significantly in their practices, including in their commitment to offering access to college courses or support for paid internships or employment (Grigal et al., 2016). One resource that educational professionals can use to help students and parents understand these options is the Think College program directory available at https://thinkcollege.net/college-search (see Figure 5.4).

FIGURE: 5.4

COLLEGE SEARCH TOOL FOR STUDENTS WITH INTELLECTUAL DISABILITY

Secondary educators and transition personnel should also be aware that students with ID attending certain approved college programs can now qualify to access forms of federal student aid. The college or university must be approved as a Comprehensive Transition Program[1] by the Office of Federal Student Aid. Previously, students with ID who did not have a high school diploma and those students who were not degree-seeking could not access Pell grants and other forms of aid. These limitations are no longer barriers for qualified students with ID seeking to attend college or university that offers an approved Comprehensive Transition Program. The Think College website offers more information about the options and resources that can be used to pay for college for students with intellectual disability. (https://thinkcollege. net/resources/innovation-exchange/paying-for-college)

To assist students with ID and their families to plan for college attendance, it is critical that secondary educators and professionals offer resources and guidance. One tool that could assist in college exploration is the tool, Conducting a College Search: Questions to Ask College Programs (Weir, 2017). This tool offers some basic considerations for starting the college search and includes key questions that families can ask staff from college programs, covering topics such as academics, employment and student supports, housing, financial aid, and the overall campus and community experience. As more colleges open their doors to students with intellectual disabilities and begin to see the benefits to these students as well as to their neurotypical peers, the hope is that these programs will expand and become ubiquitous. To learn more about these college programs for students with intellectual disabilities, check out Think College (www.thinkcollege.org).

Conclusion

The array of college options for students with disability explored in this chapter demonstrates that higher education can be responsive to students' traditional and nontraditional academic, employment, and social and emotional goals. To ensure that students' needs are met, the search process should include the full array of potential postsecondary options. In some cases these options can be seen as building blocks, allowing students to expand their knowledge and experience, and if desired, continue to the next stage of their higher education journey. Secondary educators and transition professionals can encourage college exploration activities, helping students and their families understand these options and how each may or may not meet a student's needs. Too often students with disabilities are dissuaded from pursuing college because they don't have the highest grades or because they may require supports to navigate adult learning and social environments. Assumptions about students' college potential should not be based upon their disability label or limited because they may require an alternate path to and through college. By building awareness and familiarity with existing college preparative experiences, as well as the many two- and four-year college and university options, educators can help families and students with disability see that there truly is a college option for all students with disability who desire it.

Note

1 As of November 2017, the Office of Federal Student Aid has approved has approved 69 IHEs as CTP programs in the U.S. (for current listing of approved institutions, see https://studentaid.ed.gov/sa/eligibility/intellectual-disabilities).

References

Barnett, E., and Stamm, L. (2010). *Dual enrollment: A strategy for educational advancement of all students.* Washington DC: The Blackboard Institute.

Brand, B., Valent, A., & Danielson, D. L. (2013). Improving College and Career Readiness for Students with Disabilities. American Institutes for Research. Washington, D.C.

Carnevale, A. P., Rose, S. J., and Hanson, A. R. (2012). *Certificates: Gateway to gainful employment and college degrees.* Washington DC: Georgetown University Center on Education and the Workforce.

Grigal, M., and Deschamps, A. (2012). Transition education for adolescents with intellectual disability. In M. L. Wehmeyer and K. W. Webb (Eds.). *Handbook of adolescent transition education for youth with disabilities*(pp. 398–416). New York: Routledge.

Grigal, M., Dwyre, A., Emmett, J., and Emmett, R. (2012). A program evaluation tool for dual enrollment transition programs. *Teaching Exceptional Children, 44,* 36–45.

Grigal, M., Hart, D., and Papay, C. (in press). Scope, challenges and outcomes of postsecondary education in the United States. In P. O'Brien, M. Bonati, F. Gadow, and R. Slee (Eds.). *Inclusion of students with intellectual disability in university settings.* Rotterdam, The Netherlands: Sense Publishing.

Grigal, M., Hart, D., Smith, F. A., Domin, D., Sulewski, J., Weir, C. (2016). *Think College National Coordinating Center: Annual report on the transition and postsecondary programs for students with intellectual disabilities.* (2014–2015). Boston, MA: University of Massachusetts Boston, Institute for Community Inclusion.

Hart, D., Zimbrich, K., and Parker, D. R. (2005). Dual enrollment as a postsecondary education option for students with intellectual disabilities. In E. E. Getzel and P. Wehman (Eds.). *Going to college* (pp. 253–267). Baltimore, MD: Paul H. Brookes.

Kennedy, R. (2017). *The benefits of a post-graduate year.* Retrieved from https://www.thoughtco.com/the-postgraduate-year-2774650.

Kleinert, H. L., Jones, M. M., Sheppard-Jones, K., Harp, B., and Harrison, E. M. (2012). Students with intellectual disabilities going to college? Absolutely! *TEACHING Exceptional Children, 44,* 26–35.

Ma, J. and Baum, S. (2016). *Trends in community colleges: Enrollment, prices, student debt, and completion.* New York: College Board Research Brief, April. Retrieved from https://trends.collegeboard.org/sites/default/files/trends-in-community-colleges-research-brief.pdf.

National Center for Education Statistics. (2016). *Digest of Education Statistics, 2014* (NCES 2016–006).

Papay, C., and Bambara, L. (2011). Postsecondary education for transition-age students with intellectual and other developmental disabilities: A national survey. *Education and Training in Autism and Developmental Disabilities, 46,* 78–93.

Shapiro, D., Dundar, A., Wakhungu, P. K., Yuan, X., Nathan, A., and Hwang, Y. (2015, November). *Completing college: A national view of student attainment rates – fall 2009 cohort* (Signature Report No. 10). Herndon, VA: National Student Clearinghouse Research Center.

Think College (2017). *College search program directory.* Institute for Community Inclusion, University of Massachusetts Boston. Retrieved August 21, 2017 from https://thinkcollege.net/college-search.

Weir, C. (2017). Conducting a College Search: Questions to Ask College Programs. How to Think College, Issue No. 1. Boston, MA: University of Massachusetts Boston, Institute for Community Inclusion.

6

APPLYING TO COLLEGE

Adam R. Lalor

LANDMARK COLLEGE

Stefania D. Petcu

UNIVERSITY OF NEW MEXICO

Joseph W. Madaus

UNIVERSITY OF CONNECTICUT

> *Jordan is 14 years old and starting the* ninth *grade at Mulberry High School. Like many students entering the ninth grade, Jordan is nervous about the transition to high school, especially about making friends in a new school and succeeding academically. Jordan is also diagnosed with dyslexia and ADHD, and he has difficulty with reading comprehension, time management, and organization. Despite this, Jordan is committed to his education and dreams of going to college. If he achieves this dream, he will be the first in his family to go to college.*

Jordan's goal of pursuing postsecondary education is shared by more than 80 percent of students with disabilities (Cameto, Levine, and Wagner, 2004). Unfortunately, this goal is not realized by all of these students, as only 60 percent of students with disabilities actually enrolled in postsecondary education within eight years of graduating from high school, a rate that is lower than their peers without disabilities (Newman et al., 2011). The transition from high school to college is a long and daunting process, filled with opportunities, challenges, and decisions, and so it is not surprising that many students, like Jordan, who aspire to enroll in postsecondary education never apply for admission (Roderick, Nagaoka, & Coca, 2009). Special education teachers and guidance/college counselors can play a central role in helping students with disabilities to engage in the college search and application process. However, some special education teachers may not know all of the specifics of the admission process, and guidance/college counselors might not be aware of the nuances of the process for students with disabilities. As this chapter will stress, the need for collaboration and communication among all members of the students' Individualized Education Program (IEP) team is critical to enhance the prospects of a successful application experience for students with disabilities.

This chapter will provide an overview of the application process and describe why it is important to start planning as early as possible. Key information and steps for the IEP team to consider are framed in an adaptable grade-by-grade timeline.

Grade-by-Grade: Preparing to Apply

Although the official application is submitted in the senior year of high school, the final college application is really a summary of the student's academic achievement and experiences from their freshman year on. Therefore, early planning and preparation is critical, and students with disabilities, their families, teachers, and counselors should begin thinking about college goals as early as possible. The next several sections of the chapter will examine important considerations for the completion and submission of an application employing a four-year timeline. Although this framework presents an ideal scenario (i.e., students making the decision to go to college in the ninth grade or earlier), it is not uncommon for students to make this decision later in high school, and clearly, there is more than one path to follow in the college application process. As such, it is recommended that team members modify this information on an individual basis to determine the best sequence of steps for a particular student to achieve their postsecondary education goals.

Pre-Ninth Grade and Ninth Grade

Like Jordan, many students transitioning to high school are focused on things such as social acceptance (i.e., "fitting in"), getting involved with sports and clubs, managing increased academic expectations, and navigating the daily schedule (Letrello & Miles, 2003). But many students and families may not yet be aware that decisions made at this time will also have implications for college readiness and their competitiveness for admission. For example, it is important that students understand grades earned beginning in ninth grade are reviewed by college admission counselors. And perhaps less apparent, but no less critical, is understanding the impact of which diploma path a student should pursue. As also noted in Chapter 3, states offer a variety of diploma options, including standard diplomas, certificates of attendance, and IEP diplomas (Erickson & Morningstar, 2009; Johnson, Thurlow, & Schuelka, 2012). This choice will drive decisions related to the student's plan of study and the educational rigor of the courses in which the student will participate (e.g., college preparation, honors, general). It may be apparent to students and families that this decision will impact the courses that the student will take in ninth grade, but it may be less apparent that these decisions also impact the courses for which students will be both eligible and prepared in subsequent grades. Therefore, collaboration between the middle and high school team is important in order to enhance the possibility that these options and their implications are examined during the eighth grade. Although circumstances may certainly change during the student's high school career, early collaborative decisions can minimize the possibility that students inadvertently limit their postsecondary options as a result of uninformed decisions that they make regarding ninth grade coursework and rigor.

DID YOU KNOW?

Decisions made in the eighth and ninth grade have lasting impact on graduation options and college application materials.

High School Plan of Study

The high school plan of study is a list of courses needed to achieve the requirements of the selected diploma track and the student's postsecondary education goal. The types of courses (e.g., art, business, foreign language, and math), level of rigor, and number of courses should be determined based upon the intersection of state standards, student goals/preferences, and student disability strengths/ needs. It is essential that all members of the team, including the family and student, understand that the initial plan of study can be modified. In fact, it should be reviewed and revised annually, based on the varying interests and needs of the student and their academic progress. All team members, including teachers, counselors, and family members, are critical sources of information that will help to make the plan a "living" document.

Most colleges list expectations for high school coursework, such as minimum foreign language and mathematics requirements for admission, and additional requirements for earning a degree from the institution. It is necessary to consider these expectations when developing the student's plan of study. For example, if the IEP team decides that Jordan should not take a foreign language in high school because of his reading disability, it may reduce the number of institutions for which he may be qualified for admission. Other institutions might accept him, but require that he complete a set of foreign language courses in order to graduate. Although many institutions provide a foreign language substitution as an accommodation, this is not available at all institutions, or in degree programs in which foreign language is considered an essential program requirement (e.g., international relations; Madaus, 2003).

Coursework sequence is also an important consideration because the eligibility to enroll and successfully participate in upper grade courses (e.g., Advanced Placement, International Baccalaureate, upper level elective courses) is typically contingent upon the successful completion of prerequisite courses. For example, if Jordan has the option of enrolling in a standard or honors level math course in ninth grade, he and the IEP team should consider the long-term implications of the decision. If he selects the standard course due to concerns about workload or difficulty, he may not be eligible to take more advanced courses later in high school, which may impact his qualification for admission to some colleges. Similarly, a decision to begin foreign language courses in the eleventh grade would result in Jordan not having the time necessary to complete three years of foreign language, which is expected by some colleges and universities.

Extracurricular activities: Admission counselors at many colleges look to see if a student balanced both academic and extracurricular demands, as this is an indicator that a student has potential to be an active participant both inside and outside of the classroom, and has developed time management and organization skills. Research suggests that students with disabilities engage in extracurricular activities at lower rates than their peers without disabilities (Coster et al., 2013). This is problematic for students when they apply for admission to postsecondary institutions and programs. While excellence in certain types of extracurricular activities can lead to scholarships and funding to attend college (e.g., athletics and arts) for some students, this is not the case for most students. However, involvement in these activities demonstrates desirable characteristics of college students, including engagement, service, leadership, and work ethic. Research also indicates that students with disabilities are more likely to persist from freshman to sophomore year in college if they become engaged in activities outside of the classroom (Mamiseishvili & Koch, 2011).

As Jordan makes his transition into high school and considers college, he and his family might ask how many activities and what type he should become involved in. There is no single answer to this question. The number and types of activities in which a student engages will depend upon the amount of student free time, their family commitments, employment, and academic load. In fact, admission officers frequently attempt to get a sense of a student's time commitments. For example, most admission officers recognize that students working part-time jobs have less time to engage in school sports, clubs, and activities. Additionally, being highly engaged in and holding leadership positions in a few activities, rather than holding membership in many activities with minimal engagement, is often preferred by admission counselors.

Self-advocacy and self-determination skills: As described in Chapters 3 and 4, in addition to academic preparation and extracurricular activities, high school students must begin to develop the key skills of self-advocacy and self-determination (Elksnin & Elksnin, 2010; Petcu, Van Horn, & Shogren, 2016). Although Jordan's high school teachers will set up necessary testing accommodations for him while he is in high school, his rights and responsibilities will change in college (see Chapter 3 for details), and he will need to be actively involved in both seeking out supports and requesting accommodations (Madaus, 2010; McGuire, 2010). Research is clear that self-advocacy and the use of available supports can enhance the college success of students with disabilities. For example, one study reported that students who disclosed their disability at the outset of college had higher grade point averages (GPA) and more credit hours earned by sophomore year than students who waited to self-disclose (Lightner, Kipps-Vaughan, Schulte, & Trice, 2012). However, national data indicates that only 35 percent of students who received special education services in high school later self-disclosed at the college level (Newman & Madaus, 2015). Other studies show that receipt of accommodations in college positively impacts both GPA and retention (Kim & Lee, 2015; Mamiseishvili & Koch, 2011), and that those who utilize supports that are available to the general student body (e.g., tutoring, writing centers) were more likely to complete college (Newman, Madaus, & Javitz, in review).

Clearly, students need help identifying and developing these skills, and the IEP team plays a foundational role in that process. For example, Jordan's teachers can help him understand the nature of his disability, how it impacts his academic achievement, and what supports are effective in helping him succeed. Jordan should also be aware of his strengths, and importantly, his preferences and goals, all of which should be used in developing transition related goals in his IEP. Jordan could be taught to request necessary accommodations, and when possible, be involved in the logistics of putting them in place. He could also move from being a passive participant at his IEP team meeting to becoming the leader of a portion or of the entire meeting as he develops the needed skills and confidence. Each of these activities may pay dividends for Jordan when he goes to college and requests accommodations and assistive technology support (Madaus, 2010). Table 6.1 summarizes some of the primary college-related activities in which Jordan can be involved during the ninth grade year.

Tenth Grade

At the outset of tenth grade, Jordan and the IEP team should examine his academic achievement and progress during the past year, and reevaluate and update his college goals based on grades earned, skills developed during ninth grade, and his new interests. The plan of study should be revised, as necessary, with an eye on postsecondary goals, while keeping in mind, as with ninth grade coursework, that the plan of study and grades earned will be reflected on the high school transcript reviewed by admission officers.

Course expectations and academic rigor will continue to increase throughout high school, and some students may need additional support adjusting to

TABLE 6.1 Mapping the Road to College: Ninth Grade

- Develop IEP goals, including postsecondary transition goals
- Choose diploma track
- Develop high school plan of study
- Engage in extracurricular activities
- Work on study skills and self-determination skills

increased demands. As outlined in Chapter 8, this may be offered in a multi-tiered system of support that is adjusted as the student faces new challenges, or as the student develops new skills and strategies for dealing with novel challenges. For example, all students should receive information about college expectations, and learn how to manage deadlines and about available supports in college. Some students might need more extensive instruction, such as support in developing and honing executive functioning skills, learning and study strategies, and skills to express understanding of academic content (e.g., writing, test taking). A smaller group of students might need even more intensive supports with respect to these skills (Madaus, Morningstar, & Test, 2014).

Employment: As Jordan reaches employment age, he and his family should consider looking into potential jobs. Admission officers recognize that some students work because they enjoy it, and like earning money, and that other students work because they need to help support their families. The National Association for College Admission Counseling (2015) states that employment experience exposes prospective students "to the process of earning, saving, and spending" and thus is considered important to navigating independent living on campus (p. 53). As such, employment experience can add to the overall "well-roundedness" of the applicant's credentials and speak to a candidate's work ethic and ability to balance multiple demands, which may be considered a plus in a candidate's application. Table 6.2 summarizes some of the primary college-related activities students might be involved in during the tenth grade.

Eleventh Grade

As Jordan moves into eleventh grade, the reevaluation of his progress, plan of study, and college goals should continue. But this year he will face more challenges, as eleventh grade is perhaps the most critical year for students planning to go to college. Coursework continues to become more advanced and, although twelfth grade courses and initial grades are typically listed on the transcript that is part of the application, the eleventh grade year is the last full year in which grades will be visible to admission officers. Table 6.3 presents a summary of the activities in which Jordan and other college-bound students may engage in during the eleventh grade year. Once again, it would be useful for the IEP team to look back

TABLE 6.2 Mapping the Road to College: Tenth Grade

- Revise high school plan of study, as needed
- Revise IEP goals, including postsecondary transition goals, as needed
- Engage in extracurricular activities
- Engage in paid/unpaid employment
- Work on study skills and self-determination skills
- Register for and take PSAT 10, and request accommodations if needed

TABLE 6.3 Mapping the Road to College: Eleventh Grade

- Revise high school plan of study, as needed
- Revise IEP goals, including postsecondary transition goals, as needed
- Engage in extracurricular activities
- Engage in paid/unpaid employment
- Work on study skills and self-determination skills
- Register for and take ACT and/or SAT, and request accommodations if needed
- Register for and take AP exams as appropriate, and request accommodations if needed
- Research/contact college(s) of interest
- Attend college fairs
- Visit colleges as possible, either in person or online
- Research/apply for pre-college enrichment programs, if appropriate

---

at the activities from ninth and tenth grade to evaluate the student's progress in building necessary fundamental skills.

The College Search

In addition to the advanced academic challenges that Jordan faces, the eleventh grade also brings the start of the college search process. This includes researching colleges; going on campus visits; and, in some cases, taking part in college interviews. The college search process is the process of examining and evaluating colleges and universities in order to determine which the student will apply to. With over 4,100 degree-granting colleges and universities and many non-degree-granting programs in the United States (McFarland et al., 2017), identifying which colleges and programs to apply to can be challenging. Chapters 3 and 5 discuss the college search in more detail and provide a variety of tools and ideas to help students, families and IEP teams navigate this process.

THE IMPORTANCE OF FAMILY INVOLVEMENT IN THE IEP

Students whose families are involved in the development of their Individualized Education Plan (IEP) and transition services are more likely to enroll in college (Mazzotti et al., 2015).

Though not part of the application process itself, identifying which colleges are the best "fit" for a student should be a precursor to any application process. The more a student knows and understands an institution and what an institution is looking for in applicants, the better able the student will be to articulate why they are a good "fit" for the institution. Besides taking into consideration common criteria for evaluating a college (e.g., major, location, cost of attendance, student life, athletics department), it is worthwhile for students with disabilities to consider the extent to which a college can provide the disability services and programs they need to succeed. Services for students with disabilities are available at nearly every college and university; however, the service offerings can vary from basic services (e.g., formal contact person and few established policies) to comprehensive support programs (e.g., full-time program director and full range of accommodations; Madaus, 2005). The HEATH Resource Center at the National Youth Transitions Center is a great resource for students with disabilities to start learning about Disability Support Services at college (https:// heath.gwu.edu/collegeuniversity-information-and-disability-support-services). Furthermore, some institutions offer campus support groups for students with disabilities (e.g., Eye-to-Eye; Disability Rights, Education Activism, and Mentoring [DREAM]), which may be valuable for some students, and not necessary for others.

Colleges frequently use a factor called "demonstrated interest" in evaluating a candidate's application. Demonstrated interest is the extent to which a prospective student indicates that they are enthusiastic about applying to or enrolling in a particular college, university, or program. Among the various ways in which students can demonstrate interest are:

- visiting a college, university, or program;
- meeting with an admission officer during a visit to a student's school;
- interviewing;
- visiting an institution's booth at a college fair; or
- completing online requests for more information.

This demonstrated interest is often used as one indicator of a student's likelihood of enrolling if offered admission, and therefore students often benefit from having frequent and multiple types of contact with schools that are of interest to them.

Standardized testing: In the junior year, Jordan will also begin to take standardized tests that will be part of his application (e.g., the ACT and/or SAT). Despite the increase in test-optional institutions in recent years, most colleges and universities still require the submission of standardized admission test scores (Belasco, Rosinger, & Hearn, 2015 National Center for Fair & Open Testing, 2016). Therefore, a decision to forgo standardized admission tests limits the number of institutions to which a student can successfully apply. For this reason, it will be important for students to pay close attention to the standardized testing admission policies of the institutions to which they wish to apply. Standardized testing can be a daunting process for some students with disabilities, and it might be tempting to decide to forgo them and simply apply only to colleges for which test scores are not required. However, this can needlessly leave out institutions that are a good match for a student. The planning tips offered below should be considered by students, families, and teams when making final decisions.

Registration deadlines: Standardized tests are offered on particular dates, and in particular locations throughout the year, therefore, test registration deadlines must be given consideration. Teachers can assist students to develop a schedule that spells out dates for gathering requisite materials, deadlines for accommodation applications (see Appendix A and Appendix B of this chapter), and deadlines for ACT and/or SAT registration.

Test preparation: Students can enroll in a preparation course and/or study independently. The benefit associated with preparation courses is inconclusive. Some research suggests that completing test preparation courses is beneficial (e.g., Buchmann, Condron, & Roscigno, 2010), whereas other work suggests that it is not (e.g., Allensworth, Correia, & Ponisciak, 2008). Despite differing views on test preparation, most researchers agree that, at a minimum, basic familiarity with the test (e.g., directions, major sections, etc.) is advisable (Allensworth et al., 2008). Test preparation courses may be offered by a student's high school at low or no cost, or they may be available through one of the many for-profit test preparation companies (e.g., Kaplan, Princeton Review, Sylvan Learning). In addition to the large, for-profit test preparation organizations, options have recently emerged that provide test preparation specifically tailored to the needs of students with disabilities. Students can also prepare and practice for standardized tests by taking the PSAT, a test available for students in the eighth and ninth grade (i.e., PSAT 8/9) and for students in the tenth and eleventh grade (i.e., PSAT 10). These versions of the SAT will also give students the opportunity to identify academic areas needing improvement prior to or early in high school.

Testing accommodations: Students with disabilities should be made aware that accommodations are available for standardized testing. Reasonable accommodations for the ACT and SAT are determined on a case-by-case review of documentation provided by students, and each testing agency lists the eligibility criteria on their websites (see Box below). It is important to note that documentation requirements frequently change based on interpretations of the Americans with Disabilties Act, and may change in the future based on new legislation. Teachers and students are therefore advised to check the websites of the proper testing agency.

DIRECTIONS FOR TESTING ACCOMMODATIONS ON THE ACT AND THE SAT

ACT: http://www.act.org/content/act/en/products-and-services/the-act/registration/accommodations.html
SAT: https://collegereadiness.collegeboard.org/sat/register/special-circumstances/students-with-disabilities

Jordan and his IEP team decide that it would be important to take the ACT and the SAT using accommodations that match those that he has been receiving in high school. His case manager goes to the website of both the College Board and the ACT and reviews the sections on testing accommodations. She notes that requesting accommodations requires the student to follow a process that includes working with the school, and must be completed in advance of the preferred test date. She begins to work with Jordan to identify his desired test dates early so that he has adequate time to prepare the required information and submit accommodation requests prior to the deadlines noted for that test date.

Frequently, students will retake either the ACT or the SAT during the twelfth grade, and some will take both. Students interested in applying for admission to a trade school will be required to take one of the standardized basic skills tests such as the COMPASS or Wonderlic. Exam scores can fluctuate from test-to-test, so students can discuss with parents and counselors the extent to which retaking the exam is worthwhile. If a student has already applied for and been granted accommodations on an exam (e.g., the SAT taken in the spring of the eleventh grade), they typically do not need to resubmit disability-related documentation in order to receive the same accommodations on subsequent exam administrations (e.g., the SAT taken in the fall of the twelfth-grade year). However, students must always notify the exam agency in advance of the need for accommodations.

Admission interviewing: Some colleges, universities, and programs may require an interview, while others encourage one, and others do not require one at all. College interviews may be conducted by admission officers as well as alumni and/or current students on behalf of an admissions office. Sometimes interviews are conducted on the institution's campus and sometimes they are offered closer to a student's home (e.g., in their high school, a coffee shop, a hotel lobby, an office). These interviews are opportunities for students to provide a bit more depth to an application and to share more about their personality, hopes, and dreams. Additionally, accommodations may be available if requested for students to participate in the interview process. For example, students needing sign language interpreters should contact the admission office a few weeks in advance of the interview in order to ensure that an interpreter is arranged by the respective institution (Brandeis University, 2016).

SHOULD A STUDENT DISCUSS A DISABILITY DURING AN INTERVIEW?

According to Shalini Uppu, Senior Associate Director of Admission, at Whitman College, "in an interview setting, students should be prepared to talk about their disability if the interviewer brings it up, but they should never feel compelled to share more information with their interviewer than they wish." Although Shalini stresses that students with disabilities do not have to disclose any disabilities, she notes that disclosing a disability provides colleges with an opportunity to discuss existing resources and services and better plan for a student's arrival to campus.

Twelfth Grade

As Jordan enters the fall of the twelfth grade, he will continue the college search process, interviewing as necessary, and preparing for and completing standardized examinations. In addition, this is when he will begin to work on his written application. Therefore, this is also the time where he must make final decisions regarding which institutions and programs to apply to. The number of institutions and programs to which a student applies will vary from student to student, based on a variety of factors including, but not limited to, time, interest, and cost associated with application fees. Table 6.4 presents a summary of the activities in which college-going students can engage during the twelfth grade year.

Application Types

College applications have changed dramatically in recent decades. Prospective students can now submit applications in a number of different ways, which can vary from one college or program to the next. As students narrow down their

TABLE 6.4 Mapping the Road to College: Twelfth Grade

- Revise IEP goals, including postsecondary transition goals, as needed
- Engage in extracurricular activities
- Engage in paid/unpaid employment
- Work on study skills and self-determination skills
- Register for and take ACT and/or SAT, and request accommodations if needed
- Register for and take AP exams as appropriate, and request accommodations if needed
- Research/contact college(s) of interest
- Attend college fairs
- Visit colleges as possible, either in person or online
- Narrow the list of colleges of interest
- Complete FAFSA if appropriate
- Apply to college(s)
- Submit enrollment form and deposit to the college of your choice

choices, it is important to be aware of the type of application requested by the college(s) of their choice. Until recently, there were two primary application types: The Common Application and the institution-specific application. In 2016, the Coalition for Access, Affordability, and Success put forth a new online college planning tool and application referred to as the Coalition Application. Another type of application, one specific for support programs for students with intellectual and developmental disabilities, may be less familiar to some special educators and guidance/college counselors. Some higher education programs will allow the student to choose between the Common Application, the Coalition Application, or one that is institution specific. Although completing an institution-specific application may not be a challenge for all students with disabilities, it can be more demanding for students with disabilities who have challenges with processing speed and/or executive functioning. Completing multiple applications increases the amount of time that a student must allocate to the process. Educators are encouraged to discuss with students the implications associated with completing institution-specific applications when other submission options are available. More information about each application type is provided below.

The Common Application (https://www.commonapp.org/)

The Common Application is likely the best known application type. It has been in existence for more than 40 years and is used by more than 600 colleges worldwide. The Common Application allows students to create one document that can be submitted to multiple colleges and universities. Although the Common Application only requires one essay and a letter of recommendation, colleges can customize the application by including college-specific questions and requirements. Frequently, these college-specific questions ask applicants to submit a supplemental essay and/or additional letters of recommendations. Access to the Common Application is free, but many colleges require a fee to process the application. All colleges using the Common Application accept College Board and National Association for College Admission Counselors (NACAC) fee waivers; however, students must request the fee waiver and demonstrate eligibility. Additional information about fee waivers and eligibility requirements can be obtained from the Common Application website. Educators and school counselors could provide support for students by informing them about the eligibility criteria for fee waivers and by helping them to create calendars with due dates for applying.

Institution Specific Applications

Some colleges and universities require that prospective students submit applications that are specific to their particular institution. All materials and requirements are presented together, and no supplemental questions are required. Whereas the Common Application and Coalition Application (discussed in detail below) allow students to complete information (e.g., contact information, demographics) once for several institutions, this information must be entered for each application that is institution specific.

The Coalition Application (http://www.coalitionforcollegeaccess.org/)

The Coalition Application, created by the Coalition for Access, Affordability, and Success, an alliance of more than 90 colleges and universities, is a new online platform that high school students can use to apply for college. The Coalition Application and its online planning and organization tools were launched in 2016. This application offers three unique features: (a) a student portfolio, (b) opportunities for students to interact with colleges and universities, and (c) a new application system. The main aim of the tool is to provide students the opportunity to engage in college planning as early as ninth grade. Instead of waiting until the senior year to begin gathering application content and preparing for the college application, the online platform, referred to as "the locker," allows students to add, organize, and revise content beginning in the ninth grade. For example, students can include examples of work or describe their extracurricular activities. When the time comes to submit application materials to institutions, students can choose their most representative work from the locker to be included in the final portfolio. Students also have the option of sharing all or part of their portfolio and ask colleges and universities to provide feedback on their progress as early as ninth grade. Similar to the Common Application, each college will be able to require institution specific expectations (e.g., additional essays) as part of the Coalition Application.

It is most likely that Jordan will select from the Common Application, the Coalition Application, and institution-specific applications. Teachers and guidance/college counselors can discuss with Jordan and his family the various types of applications. In particular, given Jordan's difficulties with time management and organization, teachers and counselors may wish to discuss the fact that it takes less time to complete multiple applications when using the Common Application or Coalition Application, instead of institution-specific applications. Additionally, teachers and counselors can work with Jordan to develop a detailed timeline for completing applications including goal deadlines and check in points.

Application Materials

Typical application elements include the student's high school transcript, the application form, standardized test scores, the counselor recommendation or high school report form, and recommendations. Students will need to gather necessary application materials and develop organizational systems for managing the materials. Parents, teachers, and guidance/college counselors, based on their knowledge of the student, can provide important support and direction during the collection and organization of application materials.

High school transcript: The grades earned (including GPA) and course-work rigor are considered by admission officers as the most important factors in the admission decision (Clinedinst, 2015). In addition to grades and coursework, if a student's school ranks students, information about rank-in-class may be presented on the transcript.

Application form: The application form is what many students think of when they envision the college application. Although the content and format of the application can vary (e.g., Common Application, institution/system-specific form) some content is fairly standard. The content usually includes the student's personal information (e.g., name, address, phone number), demographic information (e.g., race and ethnicity, gender), educational data (e.g., GPA, senior year courses, standardized test scores), parent/guardian information, activities and employment, essays, and the student's signature.

WAIVERS FOR APPLICATION AND REGISTRATION FEES

Colleges frequently charge an application fee of $30 to $60 that must be paid prior to the college reviewing a student's application. Standardized tests such as the SAT and the ACT also have a registration fee. Students coming from low-income families can apply to have test registration fees waived and, if received, they will also receive college application fees waived. Students should contact their guidance/college counselor to discuss how to obtain fee waivers.

DID YOU KNOW?

It is up to the student to decide if he or she wants to self-disclose a disability to a college, both during the application stage and after enrolling at the school.

The college essay (or essays) is also part of the application. Given that many students dread the college essay, it is not surprising that many how-to articles (e.g., *Writing the Common Application Essay* by Jeannie Borin and *Tip Sheet: An Admission Dean Offers Advice on Writing a College Essay* by Martha C. Merrill) and books (e.g., *On Writing the College Application Essay: The Key to Acceptance at the College of Your Choice* by Harry Bauld and *Conquering the College Admission Essay in 10 Easy Steps* by Alan Gelb) have been written on the topic. Although these guides offer sage advice, it is important to understand that there is no definitive guide to writing the college essay. College essays vary considerably in topic, organization, and creativity, and no two essays should be exactly the same. It is

SHOULD A STUDENT DISCLOSE AND DISCUSS A DISABILITY IN THE ESSAY?

According to Jessamyn Cox, Associate Director of Admissions at Kenyon College, "The essay is in fact meant to be a personal statement and there is more to the student than their disability!" Mentioning disability as a component of the essay may be necessary, but writing an essay solely about a disability provides admission officers with a limited picture of a student. Instead of devoting an entire personal statement to discussing a disability, Jessamyn suggests that students with disabilities use the "Additional Information" section in the Common Application. In this way, students can discuss their disability while devoting their essay to explaining more completely who they are as an applicant. Regardless of where a student discusses a disability in the application, they are encouraged to "reach out to their guidance or college counselor to plan how to discuss the student's disability in the application."

important that students remain aware of the fact that both the content of their essays and the mechanics (e.g., grammar, spelling, organization, structure) are likely to be evaluated by admission officers. Students with intellectual and development disabilities considering applying for one of the postsecondary education

WHAT TO DO WHEN SCORES AREN'T "GOOD"?

Sometimes, students may believe that their standardized test scores are not "good" or that they do not accurately reflect their ability. Here are some options for the student to consider:

- Retake the exam with different preparation methods (e.g., become more familiar with instructions; take a preparation course);
- Request accommodations (if not used before) and retake the exam;
- Request that the guidance/college counselor discusses the test scores as part of the counselor recommendation, describing how and why the scores do not accurately reflect the student's true ability;
- Choose not to submit test scores if they are not required by a particular institution.

ABOUT ENGLISH PROFICIENCY EXAMS

In addition to the ACT or SAT, non-native speakers of English may be required to submit scores from standardized tests that measure English language proficiency. The two primary English language proficiency tests are the Test of English as a Foreign Language (TOEFL; http://www.ets.org/toefl) and the International English Language Testing System (IELTS; http://www.ielts.org/). As with the ACT and SAT, it is important for students who are non-native speakers of English to understand the requirements and admission criteria for each college, university, and program to which they intend to apply. Students who need to submit scores from either the TOEFL or IELTS should take the exam during the spring of the eleventh grade or early in the twelfth-grade year to ensure that scores are available to admission offices by application deadlines. Testing accommodations are available for both the TOEFL and the IELTS, and non-native English speakers with disabilities should review each exam's website for information regarding applicable deadlines and documentation requirements.

---

programs are encouraged to check with the coordinator of the program of interest to ask if an essay is part of the admission criteria. If an essay is required by the program, students can follow the guidelines as outlined above.

Standardized testing: As noted earlier, students may take standardized tests multiple times, and he or she will need to formally release standardized test scores to colleges, universities, and programs as part of the application. Requests to release standardized test scores can be made by phone, mail, or online via the testing agency's website. Please note that processing fees are charged to release test scores.

Counselor recommendation or high school report form: A guidance/college counselor will typically include a letter of recommendation or high school report form with a student's college applications. In this document the counselor will detail information including the student's GPA, class rank (if calculated), twelfth grade courses, and whether the student has had any disciplinary violations. In addition, the counselor will frequently write a letter of recommendation for the student discussing their qualifications. Sometimes, these letters will refer to a student's disability, frequently in relation to the student's ability to overcome challenge. It is important for students to know that they are in control of whether a counselor discloses a disability. Students can be empowered and encouraged to have frank conversations with their counselor and parents/guardian regarding whether or not they want their disability disclosed through a letter of recommendation.

Letters of recommendation: In addition to the counselor recommendation or high school report form, colleges, universities, and programs frequently request letters of recommendation from individuals who know the student. Although a variety of individuals can offer recommendations, students need to think carefully about who writes on their behalf. Teachers should be the "go-to" individuals for recommendations as they can write about a student's academic ability and potential, and should be asked to prepare letters early in the twelfth grade in order to have sufficient time. Teachers might want to create a packet of materials that the student can compile and return to the teacher to assist in the process. This could include a cover or summary sheet that comprises, at a minimum, a list of the schools to which the student is applying along with respective deadlines and any specific procedures for submitting a letter to a given college. The student should also prepare a list of activities and achievements, and provide an overview of his or her academic history (e.g. GPA, grades received in the teacher's course).

A college, university, or program may set specific requirements for recommendations, but a good guideline is to include two teacher recommendations. Selected teachers, typically from tenth to twelfth grade, should know the student well, be able to write about the student from the classroom perspective, and be willing to prepare a positive recommendation. A teacher who knows the student from multiple courses or from both the classroom and extracurricular activities is typically the ideal. In addition to teacher recommendations, a coach, club advisor, mentor, or employer may be able to write an excellent recommendation that discusses a student's engagement outside of the classroom. Similar to the counselor recommendation, letters of recommendation will sometimes refer to a student's disability. For example, a teacher may refer to how well a student excelled "despite their learning disability" or an employer may discuss how the student "was the hardest worker that they ever had regardless of ability." Again, students can be empowered and encouraged to have frank conversations with individual letter writers regarding disability disclosure in letters of recommendation.

Students requiring letters of recommendation when applying for admission to postsecondary education programs for students with intellectual or developmental disabilities can follow the same recommendations with the exception of the disclosure of disability. As a diagnosis of a disability is one of the acceptance criteria, it is less critical to have a discussion with the letter preparer about disclosing or not disclosing the disability. However, these students still retain the right to ask counselors and teachers not to disclose their disabilities in the recommendation letter.

DID YOU KNOW?

Students have the right to decide if their disability is disclosed in a letter of recommendation.

Programs for Students with Intellectual and Developmental Disabilities

It is important to note that some students with disabilities have the right to extend their high school education up to age 21 (IDEA, 2004). Many of these students can now consider involvement in programs such as community-based high school transition programs or dual or concurrent enrollment programs. Students with intellectual and developmental disabilities now have increased access to postsecondary education. A list of postsecondary program options for students with intellectual and developmental disabilities in the United States can be found on the Think College website (http://www.thinkcollege.net). Some of these programs, approved by an external process, are called Comprehensive Transition Programs; while others are funded by the U.S. Department of Education and are called Transition and Postsecondary Programs for Students with Intellectual Disabilities (TIPSIDs). Additionally, other postsecondary education programs exist for students with intellectual and developmental disabilities beyond Comprehensive Transition Programs and TIPSIDs. Although these programs are usually affiliated with two-year, four-year, or vocational institutions, students who enroll in these programs do not typically complete the previously discussed applications. In fact, great variation exists in program admission processes and criteria. Usually, the admission of the students is based upon different criteria than that of the institution's general admission expectations. In much the same way that general admission criteria vary from institution-to-institution, admission criteria vary from program-to-program. Admission criteria for these programs may include, but are not limited to, a student's ability to follow a code of conduct, the ability to independently navigate campus, a high school certificate of attendance, documentation of a specific disability type, and/or a specified level of academic skills (Grigal, Hart, & Weir, 2012; McEathron, Beuhring, Maynard, & Mavis, 2013). It is best that students interested in applying contact a program associate at the college or university to discuss the admission criteria and process. Educators play an important part in assisting students as they prepare for and practice communicating with comprehensive transition program coordinators. For example, teachers and college/guidance counselors can rehearse phone call conversations using role play activities or assist students in drafting emails to program associates.

Financial Applications

Figuring out how to pay for college is an important consideration for many students, including Jordan. Although some families may have been planning for college costs, Jordan's family is confronting the issue for the first time and find the process confusing. Some means of help are described here.

Many families are eligible for financial assistance, if it is necessary (McFarland et al., 2017). Aid applications will need to be filed if a student is seeking financial support to attend college. The financial documents that students will need vary based on the particular application (e.g., Free Application for Federal Student Aid [FAFSA], CSS/Financial Aid PROFILE, college forms, or scholarship application). Documents required frequently include those that prove a student's identity (e.g., Social Security Number or Alien Registration Number for non-U.S. citizens) and those that describe the student/family's financial status (e.g., bank statements, investment records, or tax information). It is recommended that these financial documents be gathered as early as possible in the process of applying for financial support

Financial Aid

Although educators are encouraged to steer clear of engaging in discussions of family finances, they can assist families by discussing the process of applying for financial aid and tools available for college-related financial planning.

An important part of the college application process is to apply for financial aid. The first step in this process is for the students and their families to have an honest conversation about college cost and how much financial support the family can provide. For many families, these conversations can be difficult as personal information (e.g., salaries, retirement, debt) may be disclosed to a child for the first time. Communicating the importance of having these honest conversations will allow for informed decisions to be made by the student. Although finances are an important consideration, they should not be the sole criterion that limits students' dreams of going to college. A variety of options exist for financing higher education, and are worthy of exploration.

The second step in the process is to be familiar with the different types of financial aid along with their respective requirements and limitations. It is important to understand the difference between *merit-based* and *need-based aid*. Merit-based aid is offered based on students' accomplishments. Merit-based aid is offered directly by many higher education institutions (e.g., academic scholarship, football scholarship), but financial scholarships and awards are also offered through competitive processes by non-profit and for-profit organizations. A number of tools exist for identifying scholarships, and students are encouraged to talk with guidance counselors about scholarships offered by national, state, and local organizations. Colleges and universities also frequently offer information on their websites and through their financial aid office about scholarships available to prospective students. Need-based aid is determined based on a student's (i.e., the family's) finances and ability to pay. Financial aid is broken down into two major categories: money that must be paid back (i.e., loans) and money that does not need to be paid back (i.e., grants).

Students, or their parents, must fill out financial aid application forms in order to receive financial aid. As the forms needed may vary from institution to institution, students and families must check with each college to determine requirements. There are several common types of financial applications: the CSS/

Financial Aid PROFILE, the Free Application for Federal Student Aid (FAFSA), state forms, and institutional forms (College Board, 2016). PROFILE is an online application sponsored by the College Board, and is used by some colleges to determine to whom institutional aid (i.e., grants and scholarships offered by the higher education institution as opposed to the government) will be awarded. The PROFILE requires students submit detailed information about personal and family finances. Some states require in-state applicants to use their specific forms when applying for state financial aid, and colleges advise prospective students to use these forms. Some colleges also require an institutional form from students interested in financial aid; this information is generally provided on a college website or at the financial aid office. Advice for students who do not have a high school diploma or equivalent is shown in the Box below.

ABILITY TO BENEFIT TESTS AS A MEANS TO ACCESS FEDERAL FINANCIAL AID

Individuals who do not have a high school diploma or an equivalent are still able to benefit from federal financial aid if they can show that they are enrolled in an eligible career pathway program and they are college ready (Consolidated and Further Continuing Appropriations Act of 2015).

FAFSA is the most common type of financial aid application, as most of the colleges require this form; the main goal is to determine students' eligibility for federal, state, and institutional need-based aid. Usually a new FAFSA form is made available on October 1 on their website, and is offered at no cost. Students and parents can begin gathering the information needed to fill out the form well in advance.

Scholarships: Scholarships are one way students with disabilities can pay for college. As mentioned in the financial aid section of this chapter, students do not have to pay back scholarships. Obtaining a scholarship, however, is a complex process that involves steps similar to the college application. Although the documents needed to apply for scholarships vary, frequently required application materials include essays, letter(s) of recommendation, standardized forms, and information about a student's finances (College Board, 2016). The search to identify potential scholarships can be long and daunting as they can come from different sources: community organizations, federal and state governments, individual colleges and universities, private companies and foundations, and employers.

DID YOU KNOW?

Apply for as many scholarships as possible! Scholarships are gifts for your college and career that do not have to be paid back.

The best way to begin the scholarship search is to talk with high school guidance/college counselors, different community organizations to which students or their parents belong (e.g., churches, civic organizations), and the financial officers from the targeted colleges. Additionally, students can use one of the multitude of websites designed for scholarship searches (See Table 6.6), however, students and their parents must be aware of scholarship scams. In most cases, applying for and obtaining a scholarship does not include paying a fee.

Given the increasing number of students with Intellectual and Developmental Disabilities attending college, more and more funding opportunities are available for these students as well. Students enrolled in colleges and universities that have approved CTPs, now have the option to obtain funding for tuition or educational related expenses by applying for federal financial aid (e.g., Federal Pell Grants, Supplemental Educational Opportunity Grants, or Federal Work-Study). Other students may receive funding supports via Medicaid Waiver, State Vocational Rehabilitation (VR) Agencies, or Developmental Disability State Agencies. Several scholarship programs are also available but are mostly targeted for students with Down syndrome (e.g., Ruby's Rainbow). More detailed information about funding options for students with intellectual and developmental disabilities is

TABLE 6.5 Online Resources for Scholarships

Website	URL	Description
CollegeNET	https://www.collegenet.com/mach25/app	Allows students to identify scholarships by either using keywords or "profile search."
National Merit Scholarship Corporation	http://www.nationalmerit.org/	A non-profit organization offering support for students to identify scholarships.
Scholarship.com	https://www.scholarships.com/	Students can identify available scholarships as well as information about additional financial aid. Printable resources available.
Careeronestop	http://www.careerinfonet.org/scholarshipsearch/	Information about more than 7,000 scholarships, fellowships, and loans.
CollegeScholarships	http://www.collegescholarships.org/financial-aid/	Provides links to organizations that offer college scholarships.
OnlineSchools.org	http://www.onlineschools.org/financial-aid/disabilities/	Contains a section about financial aid/scholarships for students with disabilities.

provided on the Think College website (https://thinkcollege.net/resources/innovation-exchange/paying-for-college; Hart & Weir, 2013).

Summary

The benefits of postsecondary education for students with disabilities, including those with intellectual and developmental disabilities, are evident. For example, postsecondary education is associated with increased employment rates of students with disabilities (Newman et al., 2011; Smith, Grigal, & Sulewski, 2012), higher hourly wages, increased likelihood of financial independence, and better health and retirement benefits (College Board, 2004; Baum & Ma, 2007; Newman et al, 2011). Students with disabilities attending postsecondary education also have a higher level of community involvement (Komives, Lucas, & McMahon, 2009). However, students with disabilities enroll in postsecondary education programs at a lower rate compared to their peers without disabilities (Baer, Daviso III, McMahan Queen, & Dennis, 2013; Newman et al., 2011; Smith et al., 2012).

The process of preparing for college can be more complex for students with disabilities than for their peers without disabilities (Hitchings, Retish, & Horvath, 2005); thus, the support these students receive during their secondary programs and their early knowledge of what the college application process entails can be critical to ensuring a successful transition into college. As discussed, special educators and guidance/college counselors need to work with students with disabilities and their families as early as the end of middle school to increase their college-going expectations and educate them about the multi-year college application process. It is important that students have knowledge about different college application types and their requirements as well as how each year of high school has implications for the college application. Additionally, developing an understanding of the financial aid application process is an important aspect of college application activities.

Though it is encouraging to see the rapid increase in the number of postsecondary education programs for students with disabilities, there needs to be greater effort on the part of all stakeholders (e.g., teachers, school counselors, coordinators of postsecondary education programs) in spreading the word about college options and preparing students for the application process. With more than 4,100 colleges and universities across the country and at least 250 postsecondary education programs for students with intellectual and developmental disabilities, multiple opportunities are available for students with disabilities. Teachers play an essential role in helping students to begin the process early, and to be as prepared as possible. As the next chapter notes, this preparation must be both academic and non-academic, in areas such as self-determination and learning strategies. And perhaps most importantly, teachers play a crucial role in helping students to view postsecondary education as a viable option.

APPENDIX A: COLLEGE ADMISSION TIMELINE: 11TH GRADE MONTH BY MONTH

July	August	September	October
Standardized testing preparation	Review and revise the plan of study	ACT registration deadline (October Administration Date)	Take ACT
	Register for classes		SAT registration deadline (November Administration Date)
	Sign up for extra-curricular activities	Take ACT	Take SAT
	Identify self-determination skills to work on this year	SAT registration deadline (October Administration Date)	Standardized testing preparation
	ACT registration deadline (September Administration Date)	Request SAT accommodations	Attend college fair(s) and talk with admission officers
	Request ACT accommodations	Apply for SAT fee waiver	Research the colleges of interests and majors
		Standardized testing preparation	Research colleges and majors of interest
	Standardized testing preparation	Research colleges and majors of interest	
	Research colleges and majors of interest	Attend college fair(s) and talk with admission officers	
	Visit colleges	Sign up for extra-curricular activities	

November	December	January	February
ACT registration deadline (December Administration Date)	Take ACT	ACT registration deadline (February Administration Date)	Take ACT
SAT registration deadline (December Administration Date)	Take SAT		SAT registration deadline (March Administration Date)

November	December	January	February
Take SAT			
Attend college fair(s) and talk with admission officers	Email/contact the college(s) admission office and ask additional questions	Email/contact the college(s) admission office and ask additional questions	Meet with school counselor to discuss standardized scores, college of interests, and potential scholarships/financial aid
Research the colleges of interests and majors	Research for pre-college enrichment programs Visit colleges	Research and apply for pre-college enrichment programs Research and apply for pre-college enrichment programs Visit colleges	Discuss college financial resources with your parents Discuss your college interests during your IEP meeting★

March	April	May	June
ACT registration deadline (April Administration Date)	Take ACT	ACT registration deadline (June Administration Date)	Take ACT
Take SAT	SAT registration deadline (May Administration Date)	Take SAT	Take SAT
Develop a listing of colleges of interest	Research scholarships	SAT registration deadline (June Administration Date)	Contact colleges and request applications
For each college of interest make a list of their admission requirements	Attend college fair(s) and talk with admission officers	AP exams	Visit colleges of interest
Research scholarships	Visit colleges of interest	Call college admission offices to schedule official visits	Start applying for scholarships
Attend college fair(s) and talk with admission officers		Make a list of potential scholarships to apply for and required materials for each application	
Visit colleges of interest		Visit colleges of interest Attend college fair(s) and talk with admission officers	

Note: the month for this activity may vary based on the scheduled date for the students Individualized Education Program (IEP)

APPENDIX B: COLLEGE ADMISSION TIMELINE: 12TH GRADE MONTH BY MONTH

July	August	September	October
Visit colleges of interest	Visit colleges	ACT registration deadline (October Administration Date)	Take ACT
Continue searching and applying for scholarships	Register for classes	Request ACT accommodations	SAT registration deadline (November Administration Date)
Standardized testing preparation	Sign up for extra-curricular activities	Take ACT	Take SAT
	Identify self-determination skills to work on this year	SAT registration deadline (October Administration Date)	Request letters of recommendation
	ACT registration deadline (September Administration Date)	Request SAT accommodations	Attend college fair(s) and talk with an admission officers
	Request ACT accommodations	Apply for SAT fee waiver	Research colleges and majors of interest
	Standardized testing preparation	Standardized testing preparation	Early admission deadlines
	Mark all admisssion deadlines on your calendar	Start working on college application	Continue searching and applying for scholarships
		Start applying for scholarships	Visit colleges
		Discuss your college interests during your IEP meeting★	
		Visit colleges	

November	December	January	February
ACT registration deadline (December Administration Date)	Take ACT	SAT test	Continue searching and applying for scholarships

November	December	January	February
SAT registration deadline (December Administration Date)	Take SAT	Regular Decision application deadline for many colleges	Continue searching and applying for scholarships
Take SAT		Complete college applications	
Attend college fair(s) and talk with admission officers	Regular Decision application deadline for many colleges	Complete and apply FAFSA	
Research colleges and majors of interest	Complete college applications	Continue searching and applying for scholarships	
Early admission application deadlines	Continue searching and applying for scholarships		
Continue searching and applying for scholarships			
Visit colleges			

March	April	May	June
Continue searching and applying for scholarships	Apply for scholarships of interests	Take any AP exams	
Admission decisions and financial aid award letters are sent to students	Admission decisions and financial aid award letters are sent to students	Submit enrollment form and deposit to the college of your choice	
Compare college admission offers	Compare college admission offers		
	Choose one college		
	Visit college campus can help making a decision		
	Notify colleges that you will not attend		
	Apply for student loans if necessary		

* The month for this activity may vary based on the scheduled date for the students Individualized Education Program (IEP)

References

Allensworth, E., Correa, M., and Ponisciak, S. (2008). *From high school to the future: ACT preparation – Too much, too late. Why ACT scores are low in Chicago and what it means for schools*. Chicago, IL: Consortium on Chicago School Research.

Baer, R. M., Daviso III, A. W., McMahan Queen, R., and Dennis, L. (2013). *The Ohio Longitudinal Transition Study: Annual state report*. Retrieved from http://education.ohio.gov/getattachment/Topics/Special-Education/Resources-for-Parents-and-Teachers-of-Students-wit/Ohio-Longitudinal-Transition-Study-OLTS/2013-OLTS-Annual-State-Report.pdf.aspx.

Bauld, H. (2012). *On writing the college application essay*. New York, NY: HarperCollins.

Baum, S., and Ma, J. (2007). *Education pays 2007*. Washington, DC: The College Board. Retrieved from http://www.collegeboard.com/prod_downloads/about/news_info/cbsenior/yr2007/ed-pays-2007.pdf.

Belasco, A. S., Rosinger, K. O., and Hearn, J. C. (2015). The test-optional movement at America's selective liberal arts colleges: A boon for equity or something else? *Educational Evaluation and Policy Analysis, 37*(2), 206–223.

Borin, J. (2015). Writing the Common Application essay. *The Huffington Post*. Retrieved from http://www.huffingtonpost.com/jeannie-borin/writing-the-common-applic_b_7942260.html.

Brandeis University. (2016). *Visiting the campus*. Retrieved from http://www.brandeis.edu/admissions/visit/.

Buchmann, C., Condron, D. J., and Roscigno, V. J. (2010). Shadow education, American style: Test preparation, the SAT and college enrollment. *Social Forces, 89*(2), 435–461.

Cameto, R., Levine, P., and Wagner, M. (2004*). Transition planning for students with disabilities*. A Special Topic Report from the National Longitudinal Transition Study-2 (NLTS2). Menlo Park, CA: SRI International.

Clinedinst, M. (2015). *State of college admission*. Arlington, VA: National Association for College Admission Counseling. Retrieved from http://www.nxtbook.com/ygsreprints/NACAC/2014SoCA_nxtbk/#/0.

College Board (2004). *Education pays 2004: The benefits of higher education for individuals and society*. New York, NY: College Board.

The College Board (January 2016). *How to apply for a scholarship*. Retrieved from https://bigfuture.collegeboard.org/pay-for-college/grants-and-scholarships/how-to-apply-for-a-college-scholarship.

Consolidated and Further Continuing Appropriations Act, Public Law No: 113–235, (2015).

Coster, W., Law, M., Bedell, G., Liljenquist, K., Kao, Y. C., Khetani, M., and Teplicky, R. (2013). School participation, supports and barriers of students with and without disabilities. *Child: Care, Health and Development, 39*, 535–543. doi: 10.1111/cch.12046.

Elksnin, N., and Elksnin, L. K. (2010). The college search. In S. F. Shaw, J. W. Madaus, and L. L. Dukes III (Eds.). *Preparing students with disabilities for college success: A practical guide to transitioning planning* (pp. 203–228). Baltimore, MA: Paul H. Brookes.

Erickson, A. S. G., and Morningstar, M. E. (2009). The impact of alternate high school exit certificates on access to postsecondary education. *Exceptionality, 17*, 150–163.

Gelb, A. (2013). *Conquering the college admission essay in 10 easy steps*. Berkeley, CA: Ten Speed Press.

Grigal, M., Hart, D., and Weir, C. (2012). A survey of postsecondary education programs for students with intellectual disabilities in the United States. *Journal of Policy and Practice in Intellectual Disabilities, 9*, 223–233.

Hart, D., and Weir, C. (2013). *Financing higher education for students with intellectual disabilities*. Retrieved from http://www.thinkcollege.net/administrator/components/com_resdb/files/financing%20higher%20ed_F.pdf.

Hitchings, W. E., Retish, P., and Horvath, M. (2005). Academic preparation of adolescents with disabilities for postsecondary education. *Career Development for Exceptional Individuals, 28,* 26–35.

Individuals with Disabilities Education Act, 20 U.S.C. § 1400 (2004).

Johnson, D., Thurlow, M., and Schuelka, M. (2012*). Diploma options, graduation requirements, and exit exams for youth with disabilities: 2011 National Study*. University of Minnesota: NCEO Technical Report.

Kim, W. H., and Lee, J. (2015). The effect of accommodation on academic performance of college students with disabilities. *Rehabilitation Counseling Bulletin.* 1–11. doi:10.1177/0034355215605259.

Komives, S. R., Lucas, N., and McMahon, T. R. (2009). *Exploring leadership: For college students who want to make a difference.* San Francisco, CA: John Wiley & Sons.

Letrello, T. M., and Miles, D. D. (2003). The transition from middle school to high school: Students with and without learning disabilities share their perceptions. *The Clearing House, 76*(4), 212–214.

Lightner, K. L., Kipps-Vaughan, D., Schulte, T., and Trice, A. D. (2012). Reasons university students with a learning disability wait to seek disability services. *Journal of Postsecondary Education and Disability, 25,* 145–159.

Madaus, J. W. (2003). What high school students with learning disabilities need to know about college foreign language requirements. *TEACHING Exceptional Children, 36,* 2, 62–67.

Madaus J. W. (2005). Navigating the college transition maze: A guide for students with learning disabilities. *TEACHING Exceptional Children, 37,* 32–37.

Madaus, J. W. (2010). Let's be reasonable: Accommodations at the college level. In S. F. Shaw, J. W. Madaus, and L. L. Dukes III (Eds.). *Preparing students with disabilities for college success: A practical guide to transitioning planning* (pp. 37–64). Baltimore, MA: Paul H. Brookes Publishing Co.

Madaus, J. W., Morningstar, M. E., and Test, D. W. (2014, April). Multi-Tiered support systems in transition planning to promote college and career readiness. Invited Program Chair Presentation at the Council for Exceptional Children International Convention, Philadelphia, PA.

Mamiseishvili, K., and Koch, L. C. (2011). First-to-second-year persistence of students with disabilities in postsecondary institutions in the United States. *Rehabilitation Counseling Bulletin, 54*(2), 93–105. doi: 10.1177/0034355210382580.

Mazzotti, V. L., Rowe, D. A., Sinclair, J., Poppen, M., Woods, W. E., and Shearer, M. (2015). Predictors of post-school success: A systematic review of the NLTS2 secondary analyses. *Career Development and Transition for Exceptional Individuals, 39,* 196–215. doi:10.1177/2165143415588047.

McEathron, M. A., Beuhring, T., Maynard, A., and Mavis, A. (2013). Understanding the diversity: A taxonomy for postsecondary education programs and services for students with intellectual and developmental disabilities. *Journal of Postsecondary Education and Disability, 26*(4), 303–320.

McFarland, J., Hussar, B., de Brey, C., Snyder, T., Wang, X., Wilkinson-Flicker, S., Gebrekristos, S., Zhang, J., Rathbun, A., Barmer, A., Bullock Mann, F., and Hinz, S. (2017). *The condition of education 2017* (NCES 2017–144). U.S. Department of

Education. Washington, DC: National Center for Education Statistics. Retrieved from https://nces.ed.gov/pubsearch/pubsinfo.asp?pubid=2017144.

McGuire, J. M. (2010). Considerations for the transition to college. In S. F. Shaw, J. W. Madaus, and L. L. Dukes, III (Eds.). *Preparing students with disabilities for college success: A practical guide to transitioning planning* (pp. 7–36). Baltimore, MA: Paul H. Brookes.

Merrill, M. C. (2009). Tip sheet: An admission dean offers advice on writing a college essay. *The Choice* (Blog). Retrieved from http://thechoice.blogs.nytimes.com/2009/06/23/tip-sheet-essay/?_r=0.

National Association for College Admission Counseling (2015). *Guide to the college admission process*. Retrieved from http://www.nacacnet.org/research/Publications Resources/Marketplace/student/Documents/gcap.pdf.

National Center for Fair and Open Testing (2016). *Colleges and universities that do not use SAT/ACT scores for admitting substantial numbers of students into bachelor degree programs*. Retrieved from http://www.fairtest.org/university/optional.

National Collaborative on Workforce and Disability (2017). *Guideposts for success* (2nd ed.). Retrieved from http://www.ncwd-youth.info/sites/default/files/Guideposts-for-Success-(English).pdf.

Newman, L. A., and Madaus, J. W. (2015). Reported accommodations and supports provided to secondary and postsecondary students with disabilities: National perspective. Career Development and Transition for Exceptional Individuals, 30, 173–181. doi: 10.1177/2165143413518235.

Newman, L. A., Madaus, J. W., and Javitz, H. (in review). Effect of support receipt on postsecondary success of students with disabilities. *Career Development and Transition for Exceptional Individuals*.

Newman, L., Wagner, M., Knokey, A.-M., Marder, C., Nagle, K., Shaver, D., Wei, X., with Cameto, R., Contreras, E., Ferguson, K., Greene, S., and Schwarting, M. (2011). *The post-high school outcomes of young adults with disabilities up to 8 years after high school: A report from the National Longitudinal Transition Study-2 (NLTS2)* (NCSER 2011–3005). Menlo Park, CA: SRI International.

Petcu, S. D., Van Horn, M. L., and Shogren, K. A. (2016). Self-Determination and the enrollment in and completion of postsecondary education for students with disabilities. *Career Development and Transition for Exceptional Individuals*. Advanced online publication. doi: 10.1177/2165143416670135.

Roderick, M., Nagaoka, J., and Coca, V. (2009). College readiness for all: The challenge for urban high schools. *The Future of Children, 19*(1), 185–210.

Smith, F. A., Grigal, M., and Sulewski, J. (2012). *The impact of postsecondary education on employment outcomes for transition-age youth with and without disabilities: A secondary analysis of American community survey data*. Think College Insight Brief, Issue No. 15. Boston, MA: University of Massachusetts Boston, Institute for Community Inclusion.

SECTION 3

Partnerships and Models for College Success

7

COLLABORATION AND SUPPORT STRATEGIES TO CREATE COLLEGE ACCESS

L. Danielle Roberts-Dahm

UNIVERSITY OF SOUTH FLORIDA ST. PETERSBURG

Lyman L. Dukes III

UNIVERSITY OF SOUTH FLORIDA ST. PETERSBURG

Debra Hart

UNIVERSITY OF MASSACHUSETTS BOSTON

> *Tamara recently graduated from high school and, like many students with disabilities, is preparing for college. She has chosen to attend an inclusive postsecondary program for students with intellectual disabilities at a state university. She is proof that when multiple stakeholders in the educational system and community come together to support students, they can overcome great obstacles and achieve post-school success. Tamara is a kind-hearted teenager and, like her older sister, has worked hard to make college attendance a reality. Despite challenges, Tamara's mother regularly attended school events and meetings and encouraged her academic progress.*

Overview

This chapter addresses transition plans, as well as strategies and practices that have resulted in the development of collaborative models and operational partnerships among high school personnel, college disability service staff, other higher education professionals, and the adult service system. Finally, evidence-based methods, and practices that have helped improve the chances of college and career readiness for students with disabilities, such as utilizing technology and engaging students and families in the transition process, will be highlighted.

Engaging in Meaningful Transition Planning

Transition Assessment

The role of school personnel, students, and families: Transition assessment, a central component of the transition planning process, has been defined by Clark (2007) as follows: "Transition assessment is a process of obtaining, organizing and using information to assist all individuals with disabilities of all ages and their families in making all critical transitions in those individuals' lives both successful and satisfying" (Clark, 2007, p. 2). It is, by definition, a process designed for each individual.

The process should begin with identification of student preferences, interests, and adult life goals. Specifically, the student's goals should be identified in further education, employment, and, if appropriate, independent living (broadly defined here as including community participation and other related skills). Identification of the student's post-school interests and preferences help one determine the knowledge and skills areas to be assessed. For example, if a student indicates that he or she is interested in college attendance, one should consider assessing self-determination and self-advocacy skills, student rights and responsibilities in postsecondary settings, various learning and study strategy skills, and independent living and community participation skills (Dukes, 2010). Students may already possess some of these competences; therefore, the determination of which data should be gathered must be made on a case-by-case basis. Some data may already exist in student case files, while other data will need to be gathered.

Transition planning can and should include student participation to the greatest degree possible. In fact, because transition is a multi-year process, there are numerous meaningful options to provide students' leadership opportunities, as mentioned in the self-determination sections of the book. These include, but are not limited to, assisting with gathering and interpreting assessment data, learning how to and subsequently leading individualized education plan/individualized transition plan (IEP/ITP) meetings, maintaining a transition portfolio, and preparing the Summary of Performance (SOP) document. There are numerous tools, both free and for purchase, that are designed to teach students how to participate in the transition planning process. Figure 7.1 describes methods for increasing student participation in the assessment process.

The Transition Plan Process

Preparing a student for college entry should, ideally, begin no later than the freshman year of high school. This ensures that a course of study spread across a minimum of four years can be developed, implemented, and aligned with students' postsecondary goals, college admissions requirements and skills students need to be successful in college. It is certainly important to point out, however, that college remains a viable option for students even if they make the choice to

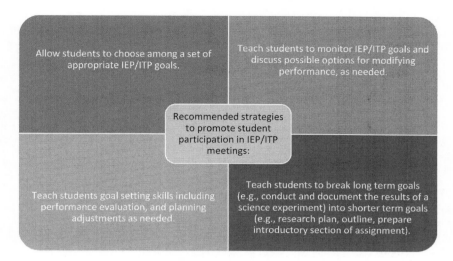

Recommended strategies to promote student participation in IEP/ITP meetings:

Allow students to choose among a set of appropriate IEP/ITP goals.

Teach students to monitor IEP/ITP goals and discuss possible options for modifying performance, as needed.

Teach students goal setting skills including performance evaluation, and planning adjustments as needed.

Teach students to break long term goals (e.g., conduct and document the results of a science experiment) into shorter term goals (e.g., research plan, outline, prepare introductory section of assignment).

FIGURE 7.1   Strategies to Promote Student IEP/ITP Participation

Dukes, 2010

attend at any time during high school. The National Collaborative on Workforce and Disability (NCWD) (2016) identified the following skills as essential for college students: self-awareness, decision-making, goal-setting and planning, self-advocacy, communication, problem-solving, self-management, and leadership, as well as competencies such as the ability to seek out and use assistance, develop supportive relationships, have confidence in one's abilities, and persevere against challenges. Chapter 4, "Foundational Skills for College and Career Success" provides a tool that students can use to identify the skills that they want to work on learning in naturally occurring settings. The identification of postsecondary goals in concert with gathering transition relevant assessment data from both formal and informal measures sets the stage for the selection of a high school course of study that is effectively aligned with the student's post-school goals. Additionally, these sources of information provide a road map for the identification of the student's annual IEP transition goals. In order to best position students' achievement of post-school goals, a four-year IEP transition planning process (see Table 7.1) can be prepared upon high school entry and modified annually depending upon student achievement of the previous year's IEP transition goals and whether the student's goals following high school remain the same or have changed.

> Tamara's case manager provided information about an inclusive higher education program which featured internships and independent living opportunities at an IEP meeting during her junior year. Once Tamara had a clear view of what she was working toward after graduation, her motivation skyrocketed.

TABLE 7.1 Map of Student Support for Success During High School: Guidelines by Year

Freshman Year – Setting the Stage for Transition
- Student Motivation/Interest
- Diploma Options/Graduation Policies
- Post-School Goals
- Access to the General Curriculum
- Course of Study
- First Year Transition Activities
- Peer Buddies in High School

Sophomore Year – Beginning the Transition
- Second Year Transition Activities
- High School Clubs
- Begin the College Search
- Implications depending upon disability, e.g., finding a college that provides interpreters for students who are deaf, note takers for students with learning disabilities

Junior Year – Continuing the Transition
- Investigate Financial Assistance/Scholarship Opportunities
- Third Year Transition Activities, e.g., visit local college/university & disability services office

Senior Year – Completing the Transition
- Fourth Year Transition Activities

Fifth Year and Beyond – Extending the Transition
Some students may benefit from remaining in high school for additional time to complete graduation requirements or to obtain additional services to develop additional skills (e.g., job readiness skills for the workplace; independent living skills, etc.).

The Summary of Performance (SOP)

According to IDEA (2004), local education agencies (LEAs) are required to develop an SOP for each child with a disability who no longer qualifies for public school services due to graduation or exceeding age-based eligibility. The federal mandate noted that the purpose of the SOP is to "provide the child with a summary of the child's academic achievement and functional performance, which shall include recommendations on how to assist the child in meeting the child's postsecondary goals" (IDEA, 2004, section 614 [c]5ii). The three core SOP requirements specified in IDEA 2004 are: (1) A statement of academic achievement, (2) A statement of functional performance, and (3) Recommendations on how to help the student meet postsecondary goals.

Martin, Van Dycke, D'Ottavio, and Nickerson (2007) created the student-directed SOP (SD-SOP) template, which included guidelines for practitioners to facilitate student-led development of the SD-SOP. The SD-SOP template, as it's name suggests, employs a student-driven approach, and includes sections in which students identify postsecondary goals, describe perceptions of their disability, and present relevant information including academic performance and evaluation results. Further information on SOP lessons, templates, and examples of student participation are included in the resources section (See Appendix A). The SOP should be implemented as part of the larger transition planning process and, when facilitated by students, provides the opportunity to gain knowledge about their interests, strengths, preferences, and needs and also provides an opportunity to practice self-determination (Shaw, Dukes, & Madaus, 2012).

> *Tamara's teachers set high expectations for her. They taught her to complete academic assignments, how to gather information on postsecondary options, and facilitated completion of career interest assessments. For example, they facilitated the development and practice of self-determination skills, especially in preparation for her IEP meeting by teaching her to develop a presentation to introduce those in attendance at the meeting, describe her strengths and needs, and describe her short- and long-term goals. Practices such as these ensured Tamara's authentic participation in the IEP meetings. In addition to the presentation, prior to the IEP meeting, Tamara and her family completed interest inventories and other self-discovery exercises. She was also active in the development of her SOP, which was completed with her goal of college going.*

TRANSITION TIP

Ensure that the SOP includes both subjective and objective information related to the student's strengths and needs. The goal is to provide a comprehensive learning profile that can be used by college personnel to guide educational decision-making (Hamblet, 2014). For example, the SOP should link the need for accommodations to a student's particular area of need. A well-developed SOP may improve the likelihood that students receive requested accommodations and supports. See Figure 7.2

---

 1. Review the SOP at regular intervals with the student.

TIP: Incorporate SOP during the annual IEP review meeting in order to promote understanding of educational growth over time and how that impacts future transition goals.

 2. Beginning in 9th grade and based upon postsecondary goals, develop and use an SOP portfolio that includes a checklist of anticipated necessary transition data, including a timeline for acquiring the information.

TIP: This information can be transferred annually to a working SOP document.

 3. When possible, have the student lead the discussion of the SOP during the IEP annual review in order to foster the practice of self-knowledge, self-advocacy, and self-determination.

TIP: Provide students with a template to guide completion but encourage them to personalize and be creative (use photos from real life or found online).

 4. Include multiple stakeholders in order to promote a team approach that provides the best chance of a comprehensive SOP document.

TIP: Include input from the student, family, school teachers, counselors, and psychologists, and others.

FIGURE 7.2   Suggestions for Employing the SOP as a Component of Ongoing Transition Planning

Dukes, Shaw, & Madaus, 2007

Shaw, Dukes, and Madaus, 2012

Engaging Students and Families in Transition

Person-Centered Planning

Transition planning is federally mandated to begin by age 16, and some states mandate that it begin earlier. It is recommended that planning begin at an age that is appropriate for each student (Sherron Targett & Wehman, 2011). In fact, teaching and assessing transition relevant skills can begin in the primary school years. However, documentation of adult life goals, or what are referred to in the IEP as measurable postsecondary goals, must occur based upon the state or federally mandated timeline. Person Centered Planning (PCP) is a practice that is student centered, empowers students to begin taking the lead in their lives, and lays a foundation for the transition assessment process.

PCP ensures that transition plans are developed based on an individual's goals and vision for their future. There are numerous types of PCP processes including, Whole Life Planning, PATH, McGill Action Planning (MAPs), and Five Bold Steps. The type of PCP process chosen should be based on how well a student has articulated their plans for post–high school life, as some methods are more elaborate and designed for students who are beginning the planning process, while others are more concise and designed to assist with finalizing post-school goals. Despite the process used, the goals that are established can be used to guide the focus of the transition assessment. PCPs each come with their own set of instructions or facilitator's guide, which includes details regarding appropriate participants and their respective roles.

Promoting Student and Family Involvement

Student and family involvement is critical for post–high school success. Effective inclusion strategies include acknowledging family perspectives and expectations, including them in transition planning, as well as understanding transition-relevant multicultural issues. Specifically, educators should discuss with students and families the need to develop self-determination and self-advocacy skills so that students are prepared to set goals, make choices, and function as independently as possible. This is especially important when preparing students to shift from the entitlement programs in the K-12 system to eligibility-based programs, such as those in postsecondary education and adult service agencies.

Natural Supports

Natural supports are available resources within a specific setting or environment that facilitate the purpose or goal of the situation. Natural supports can be almost anything – a person, a device, or a process (Corbière et al., 2014). Based on the unique situation and needs of those involved in a specific context, natural supports are typically individualized, informal, and reciprocal. Most people experience natural supports in the context of an environment, such as high school, college, or work. For example, a student who is adept at mathematics may assist a fellow student in understanding a mathematical concept. Research on natural supports indicates that support providers can help facilitate increased social interaction, length of employment, and also lessen the need for accommodations on the job (Corbière et al., 2014). Moreover, natural supports increase choice making and independence for individuals with disabilities.

Natural supports are helpful for meeting support needs following high school when they typically become less available. Students should be guided to build natural supports, including expanding their social network, as it will facilitate post-school success in college, career, and life. Most people are unaware of the natural supports they utilize, especially during life transitions like college or job entry, and people with disabilities, in particular, are often less likely to have many established natural supports. Moreover, there is no single method for developing a system of natural supports, thus practitioners should actively assist youth in their development. Teachers can help students identify the natural supports already in place in their lives by sharing personal examples, or examples of former students. As a follow-up activity, teachers can devise a lesson in which small groups or pairs of students review a scenario in which they would likely need to utilize natural support, such as when starting a new job. Students can be guided through the activity and determine how to identify and use natural supports to meet employment expectations. Another approach is to monitor the student's activities and note persons that step in to assist the student. Often, once the individual is established in the new environment, it is easier to determine who can best fulfill the natural support role. Ideally, this will be people who fit the support into their usual routine.

The first step when identifying appropriate natural supports is to know the individual in order to best ascertain their support needs, especially needs that are ongoing. An awareness of students' strengths and needs is particularly important. In high school, students should be encouraged to join clubs and organizations of interest, which often result in the development of friendships with like-minded students. When identifying supports, target students' neighborhood or work settings to learn how she or he spends the day. Gather information, for example, about neighborhood or work organizations and associations in which the person could participate. A support system can promote independence and growth in both individuals with disabilities and the person serving in the natural support role.

Tamara's transition teacher recognized that she had a personal interest in anime and also knew about a campus anime club. She provided the information to Tamara and encouraged her to attend. One concern was that Tamara would need transportation after any evening club meeting and her teacher suggested she ask a friend she'd made in the club about whether she could help her get home from evening meetings. Her friend was happy to provide Tamara a ride when meetings were in the evening and the downtown trolley was not running.

TRANSITION TIP

Teachers, para-educators, or other school personnel can observe the setting, or the student in the setting, where natural supports are sought. Through sharing observation data then brainstorming with others, the support team can develop ideas to best support students in the natural environment. The student should be a part of this brainstorming session and should also be given the opportunity to take the lead in establishing the natural support.

Mentoring

Mentoring programs can facilitate inclusive school experiences by connecting students with another student or adult. Established models for building mentor relationships include Best Buddies, Peer Buddies, Check & Connect, and 5000 Role Models. Within the Check & Connect model, for example, a mentor is trained to both *check on and connect with* a student, with the dual goals of reducing at-risk behavior and keeping students in school. Check & Connect, as well as other mentoring models, have the common component of facilitating a trusting and reciprocal relationship between the participants. The success of any mentor program rests upon the degree of training and ongoing support mentors receive prior to and during the experience. Vignette 1 provides an overview of the role of peer mentors in such programs.

Vignette 1. A dual enrollment high school/college program student mentorship structure

The students in STING RAY, a dual enrollment high school/college program, are supported by three mentor types – peer, academic, and community. Mentors can be used to help in almost all program areas, including the social, academic, and independent living components, as well as internship and employment experiences. Mentors may be volunteers, paid positions, or arrangements where course credit is earned for time spent mentoring.

Peer mentors help students become acclimated to the campus and help orient them to college social life. These mentors are important because they help students become involved in clubs and organizations that allow students to meet new people and develop friendships.

Academic mentors take a class alongside the student or have already taken the class in the past and have a strong command of the subject. This type of mentorship is structured to ensure time together is spent discussing course lectures, assignments, and projects.

Community mentors, who are persons that have demonstrated responsibility and leadership in some capacity, facilitate a series of independent living lessons with the student. They guide students in the program through lessons such as choosing a cell phone plan or apartment rental.

TRANSITION TIP

If there are limited traditional mentoring program options in your school or district, there are online mentoring options. The Ohio State University Nisonger Center Electronic Mentoring Program (EMP) is a career-focused curriculum that teaches 21st century literacy skills. This program guides students through the development of a Transition Portfolio, which can be used as a catalyst to facilitate student–mentor dialogue. (See Additional Resources in Appendix A).

Engaging College and Community Partners

Interagency Collaboration

Typically there is little collaboration between high schools and postsecondary institutions (Rippner, 2017), which has the potential to deleteriously impact student retention and college completion. School personnel can serve as connectors to bridge the lack of collaboration. In order for teachers and other school personnel to learn firsthand the expectations and requirements of postsecondary education, a professional "field trip" to a local institute of higher education (IHE) can be especially worthwhile. While time and existing classroom obligations may be a barrier to making such visits a reality, this type of meeting could take place, for example, during the afternoon of an in-service or training day. While on campus, school faculty can meet with the disability services personnel to find out about the requirements, procedures, and expectations for students with disabilities (Hamblet, 2014). If a campus program unique to students with intellectual disability and autism (ID/A) is offered, school professionals should meet with their staff and participants as well. In lieu of a site visit to an IHE, virtual tours that allow school personnel, families, and students to learn about a college and gather information about disability services as well as other campus support services should be considered. Information can be shared, for example, with students and families during IEP meetings or at other formal and informal school functions.

Interagency collaboration through transition fairs and interagency councils are an additional means by which the high school to college information gap can be improved. Interagency councils are district-wide or regional groups that include schools, community service providers, vocational rehabilitation (VR), and other agencies in order to collaboratively deliver services to students and families. Interagency councils often develop informational products such as brochures or websites to help students and their families connect with local agencies and services. Teachers can also inquire with their local interagency councils for transition-related suggestions and resources for their students. The purpose of transition fairs (which are also sometimes titled "parent night," "career fair," or "agency fest") is to connect students and families to post-high school resources. Fairs are typically hosted by school districts, at least annually, to bring together relevant community agencies and service providers related to education, employment, and the community, including colleges and universities. Teachers can encourage students and families to attend transition fairs and might also choose to attend as well, in order to learn and gather information. The chapter resource section (Appendix A) features the National Technical Assistance Center on Transition's (NTACT) Transition Fair Toolkit, which provides a comprehensive set of materials for planning or participating in a transition fair.

While in high school, Tamara's teachers shared information about post-high school resources, opportunities, and supports available. In addition, she was encouraged to attend the district interagency transition fair in order to learn more about agencies, services, and supports available. While at the transition fair, Tamara spoke with VR about support with employment and postsecondary training. Tamara had heard about VR from her case manager who provided her and her mother with an explanation of VR benefits, a brochure, and application at a recent IEP meeting. Meeting the VR counselor at the transition fair and learning about how VR helps students meet career goals prompted Tamara and her mother to complete and return the application in order to become a VR client.

Vocational rehabilitation partnerships: The 2014 Workforce Innovation and Opportunity Act (WIOA) increases access to high-quality workforce services and preparation for competitive integrated employment for individuals with disabilities. One focus of WIOA is to increase individuals with disabilities' access to

---

TRANSITION TIP

Teachers play a critical role in the transition fair. The following table describes transition fair activities that can be completed by school personnel.

Before Transition Fair	During Transition Fair	After Transition Fair
• Prepare a list of students attending • Ensure students have the nametags and/or other pertinent information (student ID, state-issued ID, etc.) • Talk to students and families about their questions and which agency might be best suited to answer those questions • Gather a list of participating organizations and provide suggestions to students and families about how to best use their time	• Collect transition brochures and related materials to share with those who could not attend • Encourage students to attend the fair and engage with agencies and other vendors • Encourage students to attend informational sessions	• Assist students with saving informational brochures by having them included in an IEP binder as transition documentation of direct contact with service providers • Send a follow-up email to families who attended to see if there are follow-up questions • Offer to host a smaller information session on a particular topic or with a community resource organization that many families will use

Adapted from NTACT's Transition Fair Toolkit (2014).

VR and workforce services in order to foster competitive integrated employment, which includes pre-employment transition services to youth in high school. VR agencies are now mandated to expend at least 15 percent of their budget on transition aged youth who are 16–21 years old. As a result, school personnel should consider partnerships with VR to support students with disabilities who have an interest in college attendance. Armed with background knowledge about VR, school professionals can effectively connect youth with disabilities to VR in order to facilitate positive post-school outcomes, including postsecondary education and employment. Information can be obtained online or through a local VR office. Some schools have an assigned VR counselor who can provide information about their employment-related services and are available to meet with students. Students and adults with a range of disabilities can access a myriad of support from VR.

Additionally, VR agencies can use federal, state, local, or private funding sources to coordinate with local educational agencies when providing pre-employment transition services. Such provisions are particularly beneficial as they have the potential to increase college- and career-readiness of students with disabilities. These activities can include: (1) career counseling; (2) work-based learning experiences (e.g., in-school or after school opportunities); (3) counseling on opportunities for enrollment in comprehensive transition or postsecondary educational programs at institutions of higher education; (4) workplace-readiness training to develop social skills; and (5) instruction in self-advocacy (including person-centered planning), which may include peer mentoring (Federal Partners in Transition [FPT], 2016).

College- and Career-Readiness

There are numerous organizations that promote College and Career Readiness (CCR), including the American Youth Policy Forum, National Collaborative on Workforce and Disability for Youth, and Ready by 21 (See Table 7.2 and the Appendix A for a comprehensive CCR list). CCR incorporates core academic and non-academic skills such as critical thinking, metacognition, self-monitoring, study skills (Farrington et al., 2012), student motivation and engagement (Savitz-Romer, 2012), and knowledge of postsecondary requirements (Conley & McGaughy, 2012). CCR efforts focus on ensuring that secondary and postsecondary expectations are synchronized so that students are prepared for college and careers. As such, it is imperative that students with disabilities are involved in existing CCR approaches or initiatives in place at the school, district, or state level so that they are afforded the same opportunities and exposure as all students. Table 7.2 features several examples of CCR models, including websites where readers can find additional information.

> *While in high school, Tamara participated in a two-week summer program at a community college near her house that shared detailed information about college attendance as well as careers currently in high demand. The program featured an opportunity to meet with the college's disability services office personnel as well as with other agencies within the community, including but not limited to VR, Career Source, and the Center for Independent Living. Tamara's summer program experience helped her realize that she was capable of going to college and living independently following high school.*

College and Career Pathway Systems

According to the National Center for College and Career Transitions (NC3T), a pathway system is a "coordinated collection of College-Career Pathways (CCP), connected with meaningful learning opportunities outside of the high school" (NC3T, n.d., p. 1). CCPs are collaborative in nature and work to connect school districts, IHEs, and employers whose goal is to ensure that students learn about a wide range of career options as well as core academics. CCPs are often operated as Career Academies and have key features that include, but are not limited to (1) Career or academic content as focal areas or themes, (2) Emphasis on employer engagement, (3) Integration of approved Career and Technical Education programs, (4) Emphasis on content knowledge from themes to real-world application (e.g., work-based learning), and (5) Cross-curricular strategies to embed state standards throughout the curriculum (NC3T, n.d.).

Teachers and school personnel are central to connecting students with CCPs and/or career academies which offer students an opportunity to step out of their normal high school day and prepare students for postsecondary education and employment through "real world" training and experiences. Through CCPs, students are afforded rich opportunities to have authentic experiences in different integrated employment options via work-based learning, apprenticeships, and internships. CCPs hold great promise for students with disabilities because learning is particularly hands-on and applied.

TABLE 7.2 Collaborative Model Examples

Early College High Schools
http://www.jff.org/initiatives/early-college-designs

Early College Designs enable more students, particularly low-income and minority students, to experience rigorous high school and college coursework that leads to improved outcomes.

P21: Partnership for 21st Century Learning
http://www.p21.org

P21 is a national nonprofit organization that advocates for 21st century readiness for every student. P21 recognizes that all learners need educational experiences in school and beyond, from cradle to career, to build knowledge and skills for success in a globally and digitally interconnected world.

StriveTogether Cradle-to-Career Network
www.strivetogether.org/cradle-career-network

StriveTogether Cradle to Career Network is a national, nonprofit network of over 70 partnerships working to improve educational outcomes by bringing together cross-sector partners around a shared community vision and providing strategic assistance, network communications, and high-quality resources.

Four Keys to College and Career Readiness Model (Think, Act, Know, and Go)
www.epiconline.org

EPIC is a nonprofit consulting group that strives to help educators better equip students for success. The Four Keys to College and Career Readiness model incorporates research on what it takes to succeed in college and career.

Concurrent/Dual Enrollment

Concurrent or dual enrollment (CDE) initiatives allow students to be enrolled in high school and college simultaneously (Marken, Gray, & Lewis, 2013). Previously, dual enrollment included only high school students in advanced placement courses, in which students earn high school and college credit simultaneously (Marken et al., 2013). Often, courses are taught by higher education faculty at high school campuses; however, some initiatives have high school students taking college courses on a college campus or via distance education. Today, CDE programs are part of many national and statewide CCR initiatives and are focused on supporting underserved student populations and configured using many different structures and approaches (College and Career Readiness and Success Center [CCRSC] 2016; National Alliance of Concurrent Enrollment Partnerships [NACEP] 2016). Dual enrollment partnerships between high school and community or state colleges may vary regarding requirements to participate. Thus, teachers can facilitate student access, regardless of disability type, by ensuring students and their families are aware of the option, including knowledge of requirements and helping to tailor a CDE plan for students with an interest in participation.

TRANSITION TIP

Prepare a handout for parents explaining CDE and options within their respective school system. Discuss at IEP meetings as well.

This model has emerged as a promising practice for students with disabilities, particularly students with ID/A (Grigal & Deschamps, 2012). College-based dual enrollment programs for students with ID/A are programs that enroll students in secondary education and postsecondary education simultaneously, which usually occurs in order for secondary students ages 18–21, to use local education funds to support participation in higher education. These programs provide opportunities to explore all that college has to offer while still receiving support from high school education staff (Grigal, Paiewonsky, & Hart, 2017). To assist with the collaborative efforts necessary in dual enrollment programs, it is helpful to clearly articulate the role of each partner. While programs differ based upon regional circumstances, most dual enrollment programs for students with ID/A include the four partners noted in Figure 7.3, in some capacity. Figure 7.3 provides detail on the general roles of each partner. For dual enrollment programs for students with ID/A, teachers should make students aware of the opportunity early in high school so that transition goals and the course of study can be focused on college attendance. There may be additional paperwork, application and/or an interview associated with program

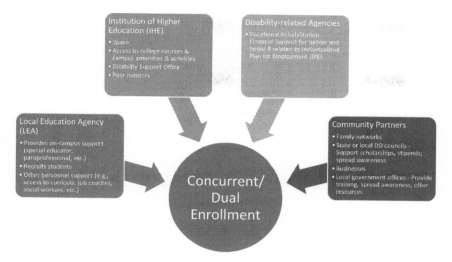

FIGURE 7.3 Dual Enrollment Partners and Related Roles

admission. In addition, engaging students and families in dialogue about college courses of interest as well as differences between high school and college coursework is necessary in order to set the stage for student success.

If your school does not have a dual enrollment program with a local college, teachers can look at other programs in neighboring districts or geographical locations. In addition, school professionals can approach a local college in order to establish a dual enrollment partnership. This can start with a college hosting transition fairs or other informational meetings. Often, colleges are enthusiastic about partnering with local education agencies, which may establish a feeder pattern into their college programs.

The following vignette provides an example of an inclusive concurrent enrollment initiative for students with intellectual disability (ID) in Massachusetts.

Vignette 2: Massachusetts's Inclusive Concurrent Enrollment Initiative (ICEI)

Massachusetts has had a statewide college-based ICEI for students with ID, ages 18–22 who still are eligible to receive education services from their school district. This initiative has been funded by a line item in the state budget since 2007. The funds have been used as seed money to establish partnerships between IHEs and school districts in the surrounding geographic vicinity in addition to the adult service agencies (e.g., workforce development, vocational rehabilitation, developmental disability agencies). Each partnership varies depending on the culture of the host IHE, subject focal areas that in which each IHE may specialize in (e.g., automotive, nursing, teacher preparation, theatre, liberal arts, technology), and how the initiative aligns student services and supports within the existing IHE infrastructure (e.g., registration, orientation, advising, access to inclusive courses, disability services). On average, the ICEI supports between 100 and 125 students annually. This number is expected to increase given the growing number of partnerships. The program is administered by the Massachusetts Executive Office of Education (MEOE), which provides training and technical assistance and general oversight activities for each partnership.

The purpose of the ICEI is to provide students with ID the same opportunities that their peers without disabilities have as they prepare for and enter adult life. The overarching emphasis is to ensure students with ID meet with successful post-school outcomes by having a successful career and become valued members of their home communities. To this end, students with ID are engaged in all campus activities including an inclusive course of study related to their career goals and other personal areas of interest, participating in campus-wide social and academic events, learning to use public transportation to and from campus, obtaining paid and unpaid internships, and ultimately competitive integrated employment rather than staying in a high school or segregated community-based transition program only for students with disability.

In general, the ICEI partnerships are formalized with a Memorandum of Understanding delineating the roles and responsibilities for each participating partner. Staffing often includes the following key personnel: IHE Coordinator; High School Liaison; Educational Coach and/or Peer Mentors; and Career Specialist (MEOE, 2016). If having this full complement of personnel is limited due to budget constraints, these key areas still need to be addressed in order for students to achieve quality post-school outcomes.

Utilizing Technology

Increasingly, faculty members encourage students to use laptops, tablets, or smartphones during class meetings. Additionally, hybrid and fully online courses make up a larger portion of program offerings in higher education. This section will detail how students can prepare for postsecondary education using assistive and instructional technology.

Assistive Technology

Assistive technology (AT) includes assistive, adaptive, and rehabilitative devices used by people with disabilities in their daily lives. The term also encompasses the selection, location, and use of such devices. Each state has an AT program to serve residents who require support when selecting, acquiring, or using AT devices. Accessible educational or instructional materials, referred to as Accessible Educational Material or Accessible Instructional Material (AEM or AIM), are print- and technology-based learning materials designed for use regardless of student variability or type of media. Common examples include Braille, large print, audio, or digital texts, which are developed from print instructional materials.

Accessibility features are built into many devices we use daily, including smartphones, tablets, and computers. Students should learn about their specific AT needs while in middle or high school, which can be facilitated as part of the IEP process. The IEP team can consider the following: (1) Which tasks is the disability impacting? (2) Along with the student, determine whether any AT solutions have already been tried and discuss why they have or have not been helpful. (3) Next, given this information, the IEP team should brainstorm potential AT options for the student while considering alternatives ranging from no tech to high tech (e.g., no tech: specialized pencils; high tech: voice recognition software). Oftentimes, technology may not be available. In this case, there are low, or no tech AT devices available, such as handheld magnifiers, using paper and pen to communicate, devices for reaching or grabbing items, or specialized grips for pens or pencils (Tools for Life Georgia, n.d.). Persons with mobility impairments may use wheelchairs, scooters, walkers, canes, crutches, prosthetic devices, and orthotic devices to enhance their mobility. Another example is the use of closed captioning when showing videos utilized during instruction in order to enable people with hearing impairments to engage with the material as well as others. If training is necessary, assistance may be available through a local AT program or technical assistance provider or through the company that developed the product, if applicable. Parents and family members are also great resources for guidance with regard to the use of AT, whether high or low tech. The team should ensure that the use of any AT is reflected in the IEP and that students have consistent opportunities to receive training and practice with any AT. This will help facilitate effective use of the device(s) while in college, where students may rely more heavily on AT in place of personal services formerly provided in high school but not available in college.

The college program that Tamara attends requires students to have a smartphone for group messaging with program personnel and other students, to receive text alerts from the university, and to use GPS to navigate the campus and community. Tamara received a smartphone as a gift for her birthday last month. The phone salesperson recommended that Tamara install the "Find My phone" application (i.e., "apps"), which can help locate it should it be lost or stolen. Tamara's sister helped her download this and other useful apps. For example, she helped her download audiobooks through Audible, BookShare and LibriVox on French culture and cuisine in preparation for a fall course on Francophone World. Tamara's mother helped her utilize several Google features, such as calendar, task list, and Drive. Tamara has established a routine of daily email communication, setting reminders in her calendar and using the task list to sync with her calendar. These tools will assist Tamara to stay on track since college life will be less structured than high school. Eventually, Tamara will learn how to use Google Maps and Google Transit to navigate the campus and surrounding community near her college, which is two hours away from her hometown. Tamara has documented her college preparation experiences through the SpeechJournal app. She has also taken photos, which she embeds into Speech-Journal. Several incoming freshmen have shared their Speech Journals through social media, like Twitter and Facebook, so Tamara has met people who are preparing for college, too. Tamara and her parents have saved important documents she may need to access electronically, such as emergency contacts and insurance information, in Google Drive, so she can access the documents from anywhere.

TRANSITION TIP

As an assignment, have students contact their respective college Disability Services Office in order to determine AT options available and then reflect on which options would be most helpful. A second suggestion is to invite a guest speaker from a state or local AT center to provide product demonstrations of various AT devices.

There's an "App" for That

Applications (also known as "apps") are designed to assist people in an academic, social, and personal capacity. There are apps that address a wide range of needs, including, but not limited to, time management, document management, and self-monitoring/management.

Ideas for facilitating the use of mobile devices in school settings include allowing students to conduct research related to an assignment while in class using their phone or tablet, encouraging students to set timers with the goal of improving assignment or task focus, and using document sharing to submit assignments. Students with a range of disabilities can utilize apps to assist with daily activities from school to home to work. The following list features a few examples:

- *Time Management and Scheduling*: There are a number of apps specifically intended to assist with time management and scheduling assignments, including MyHomework Student Planner, MyStudyLife, ClassManager, IStudiez, and StudentAgenda, among others.
- *Navigation*: GoogleMaps is one example of technology designed to help all people navigate their community. There are campus and community-specific apps available as well as accessibility apps for certain locations geared towards people with limited mobility or persons using wheelchairs. For example, there is an app that enables users to report obstructions to sidewalks and other mobility-related barriers in Chicago called ChiSafePath. Further, AXSMap allows users to rate buildings based on their accessibility. Certainly, apps of this nature will become more common over time.
- *Text to Speech*: BeMyVoice, is designed specifically for students with learning disabilities, including text disabilities such as dyslexia. The app Lectio can

assist with independent reading as it allows the user to snap a picture of a text-filled page and have the words read aloud.

• *Storyboards Combining Audio and Visuals*: There are a number of apps that allow for easy integration of visuals with audio/voice over narration, which can help with class projects, transition planning, and other related activities. These apps include: SpeechJournal, Proloquo2Go, iConverse, Look2Learn, Tap to Talk, Story Robe, Visules, and Tap Speak Sequence.

TRANSITION TIP

A great first step to help students manage technology is to show students how to use the built-in smart phone accessibility features. Students can utilize technology-based applications while in high school to enhance their skills academically and socially, as well as to increase independence.

Multicultural Implications

Discrepancies sometimes exist between students' and families' culture and may impact interactions with teachers and experiences in the school environment (Povenmire-Kirk, Bethune, Alverson, and Gutmann, 2015). Students with disabilities have poorer post-school outcomes and lag behind peers without disabilities in postsecondary education, employment, and independent living, which are exacerbated for those from culturally and linguistically diverse backgrounds. Educators must partner with students and families to plan for a successful transition; therefore, it is essential that school educators are aware of and understand their own culture, values, and expectations in addition to those of their students'. In

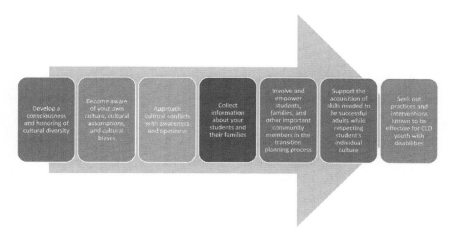

FIGURE 7.4 Approaches to Foster Cultural Competence in Transition

Adapted from Povenmire-Kirk, Bethune, Alverson, & Gutmann Kahn, 2015, p. 325–26 sum, cultural competence should be fostered so that educators better understand how student diversity affects students' future plans (Povenmire-Kirk et al., 2015). Figure 7.4 depicts seven steps to foster cultural competence in transition.

> *While in her junior year, Tamara and her mother were inquiring about continuing her education after graduation. Initially college was not presented as an option. Tamara's older sister, Tatianna, was the first in her family to attend college, and it was not until she mentioned a program at her university for students with ID/A that they were even aware of the opportunity. Although Tamara's case manager did not intentionally leave out options available to Tamara, it may have been that she was not aware of her own cultural assumptions and biases, which hindered her from seeking new opportunities for her students, especially first generation college students and students with diverse abilities. Tamara almost missed out on going to college due to the lack of options presented to her, which may have been a reflection of the case manager's unintentional biases.*

TRANSITION TIP

Recognize that cultural assumptions, values, and conceptions of reality are embedded in the daily work of transition educators, thus it is essential to consider how these might differ between groups (Povenmire-Kirk et al., 2015). The following table provides examples of how to become more self-aware of your own cultural assumptions in order to increase cultural competence.

Recommendations for Developing Cultural Competence for Transition Educators

Skill	Description	Examples of Developmental Activities
Become aware of your own culture, cultural assumptions, and cultural biases	It is a common misconception that understanding cultural diversity is about an awareness of those different from you (or the "other"). Without understanding how one's own thinking patterns and behaviors are culturally bound, one risks assuming that these values are "normal" or "correct" whereas others are "deviant" or "wrong."	• Knowing that our values about postsecondary education, employment, and independent living are not culturally neutral • Developing awareness of what your values are concerning the three domains of transition • Understanding that your values are not more "normal" or "correct" than your students' and their families' values

(Adapted from Povenmire-Kirk et al., 2016)

Conclusion

This chapter has shared strategies and tips for educators to promote school processes, including engaging families and utilizing technology, that support students' success in the transition from high school to college. The difficulties associated with navigating differently structured systems and a lack of both communication and collaboration among various community agencies and organizations have been discussed. Fortunately, the implementation of strategies to promote collaboration between schools, IHEs, and related agencies regarding the transition process has enabled educators to better facilitate student success in college and beyond. Collaborative partnership models between school districts and IHEs have resulted in improved college access for students with disabilities. Resources and practical tips have been included and we encourage readers to learn and apply these strategies.

APPENDIX A: ADDITIONAL RESOURCES

Interagency Linkages

- Transition Fair Toolkit
  http://www.transitionta.org/sites/default/files/Transition_Fair_Toolkit.pdf
  NTACT developed this toolkit to help teams plan, implement, and evaluate
  a transition fair to connect students and their families with resources to help
  with life after high school.

College- and Career-Readiness

- Heath Resource Center
  www.heath.gwu.edu/files/downloads/nhsc_definingccrresourceguide_
  2012_0.pdf. CCR
  Heath has prepared a CCR resource guide that also includes a comprehensive list of CCR organizations.
- The Forum for Youth Investment
  www.Forumfyi.org
  The Forum works with state and local leaders and leadership groups to funda-
  mentally change the way they do business for young people through a variety
  of partnerships at the state and local levels to create opportunities for youth.
- Ready by 21
  www.readyby21.org
  Ready by 21® is a set of innovative strategies developed by the Forum
  for Youth Investment that helps communities improve the odds that all
  children and youth will be ready for college, work, and life. http://www.
  readyby21.org/

Differences Between High School and College

- Think College
  http://www.thinkcollege.net/topics/highschool-college-differences
  This interactive table developed by Think College highlights important differences between high school and college as well as strategies to help people
  with disabilities negotiate and overcome potential issues.

Mentoring

- Check & Connect
  http://checkandconnect.umn.edu/.
  Check & Connect is a comprehensive intervention designed to enhance student engagement at school and learning with students who are disengaged,

through a mentorship model based on relationship building, problem solving and capacity building, and persistence.

- Ohio State University Nisonger Center Electronic Mentoring Program (EMP).
www.ou.edu/content/education/centers-and-partnerships/zarrow/osu-emp.html.
The EMP is a 17-unit online career-focused curriculum for high school students with and without disabilities that teaches key 21st century literacy skills while utilizing an electronic and face-to-face mentoring component to enhance classroom learning. The self-directed career development and skill building in this course results in a customized Transition Portfolio that highlights student accomplishments throughout the course and includes documents and resources that can be used during and after high school.

Summary of Performance (SOP)

- SOP Lesson, Teacher's Guide, Student Script, and Template
www.ou.edu/content/education/centers-and-partnerships/zarrow/trasition-education-materials/student-directed-transition-planning/summary-of-performance.html.
The Zarrow Center for Learning Enrichment at the University of Oklahoma features a teacher's guide and lesson presentation on SOP as well as student script and template available for easy and free download and use.

Technology

- Center for Applied Special Technology (CAST)
http://www.cast.org/
CAST is a nonprofit research organization dedicated to improving education through Universal Design for Learning (UDL).
- National Center on Accessible Instructional Materials
http://aim.cast.org/
The National Center on Accessible Materials is a resource dedicated to implementing National Instructional Materials Accessibility Standard (NIMAS) and Accessible Instructional Materials (AIM) to improve print resources including Braille, audio, large print, and electronic text.
- Digital Citizenship Activities
http://cyberbullying.org/digital-citizenship-activities-for-educators
This website, developed by the Cyberbullying Research Center, features ten ideas to encourage appropriate social media and technology use among students.
- Schools and Online Social Networking
www.nea.org/home/schools-and-online-socil-networking.html.

This page featured on the National Education Association's website provides guidance on how schools can help students stay safe online through providing guidelines for them.

- Technology for High School Students with Intellectual or Developmental Disabilities Dually Enrolled in Postsecondary Education
  www.thinkcollege.net/administrator/components/com_resdb/files/Insight27_day_in_the_life.pdf.
  This article describes a day in the life of Star, a student who is dually enrolled in high school and college, and highlights how she uses technology to support her activities throughout the day. Star attends high school in her hometown and is part of a program for students with intellectual and developmental disabilities (ID/DD) at a college 30 minutes away.

References

Clark, G. (2007). *Assessment for transition planning* (2nd edition). Austin, TX: ProEd, Inc.

College and Career Readiness and Success Center (2016). *College and career readiness and success*. Retrieved from www.ccrscenter.org.

Conley, D.T., and McGaughy, C. (2012). College and career readiness: Same or different? *Educational Leadership, 69*(7), 28–34.

Corbière, M., Villotti, P., Lecomte, T., Bond, G., Lesage, A., and Goldner, E. M. (2014). Work accommodations and natural supports for maintaining employment. *Psychiatric Rehabilitation Journal, 37*(2), 90–98. doi: 10.1037/prj0000033.

Dukes III, L. L. (2010). Gathering data to determine eligibility for services and accommodations. In S. F. Shaw, J. W. Madaus, and L. L. Dukes III (Eds.). *Preparing students with disabilities for college success: A practical guide to transition planning*. Baltimore, MD: Brookes Publishing.

Dukes III, L.L., Shaw, S.F., & Madaus, J.W. (2007). How to complete a summary of performance for students exiting to postsecondary education. Assessment for Effective Intervention, 32(3), 143–159.

Farrington, C., Roderick, M., Allensworth, E., Nagaoka, J., Keyes, T., Johnson, D., and Beechum, N. (2012). *Teaching adolescents to become learners. The role of noncognitive factors in shaping school performance: A critical literature review*. Chicago, IL: University of Chicago Consortium on Chicago School Research.

Federal Partners in Transition (FPT). (2016). *What to know about youth transition services for students and youth with disabilities*. Retrieved from www2.ed.gov/about/offices/list/osers/transition/products/fpt-fact-sheet-transitionservices-swd-ywd-3-9-2016.pdf. http://www.ccrscenter.org/

Grigal, M., and Deschamps, A. (2012). Transition education for adolescents with intellectual disability. In M. L. Wehmeyer and K.W. Webb (Eds.). *Handbook of adolescent transition education for youth with disabilities* (pp. 398–416). New York: Routledge.

Grigal, M., Paiewonsky, M., and Hart, D. (2017). Postsecondary education for students with intellectual disability. In M. L. Wehmeyer and K. A. Shogren (Eds.). *Handbook of research based practices for educating students with intellectual disability* (pp. 471–492). New York: Routledge.

Hamblet, E. C. (2014). Nine strategies to improve college transition planning for students with disabilities. *TEACHING Exceptional Children, 46*(3), 53–59. Retrieved from

www.ctdinstitute.org/sites/default/files/file_attachments/2014NineStrategiestoImpro
veCollegeTransitionforSWD.pdf.

Hobbs, F. (2014). Getting social: Using social media to connect with communities regardless of ability/disability. *Frontline Initiative: A Publication of the National Alliance for Direct
Support Professionals, 12.* Retrieved from www.nadsp.org/communication/frontline-
initiative.html.

Individuals with Disabilities Education Act, 20 U.S.C. § 1400 (2004).

Marken, S., Gray, L., and Lewis, L. (2013). *Dual enrollment programs and courses for high
school students at postsecondary institutions: 2010–11* (NCES 2013–002). U.S. Department of Education. Washington, DC: National Center for Education Statistics.

Martin, J. E., Van Dycke, J., D'Ottavio, M., and Nickerson, K. (2007). The student-
directed summary of performance: Increasing student and family involvement in the
transition planning process. *Career Development for Exceptional Individuals, 30*(1), 13–26.
doi: 10.1177/08857288070300010101.

Massachusetts Executive Office of Education. (2016). *Inclusive concurrent enrollment initiative.*
Retrieved from www.mass.gov/edu/birth-grade-12/higher-education/initiatives-and-
special-programs/inclusive-concurrent-enrollment/.

National Alliance of Concurrent Enrollment Partnerships (NACEP) (2016). *Advancing
quality college courses for high school students.* Retrieved from http://www.nacep.org.

National Center for College and Career Transitions (NC3T) (n.d.). *What is a college-
career pathway and a pathway system?* Retrieved from http://nc3t.com/the-promise-of-
college-career-pathways/.

National Collaborative on Workforce and Disability (NCWD). (2016). *Personal competencies for college & career success: What colleges can do.* Retrieved from www.ncwd-youth.
info/PersonalCompetencies.

National Secondary Transition Technical Assistance Center (NTACT). (2014). *Transition
fair toolkit.* Western Michigan University, Rashell Bowerman, Lydia Schuck, June E.
Gothberg, Jennifer L. Coyle, and Paula D. Kohler. Retrieved from www.transi
tionta.org/sites/default/files/Transition_Fair_Toolkit.pdf.

Povenmire-Kirk, T. C., Bethune, L. K., Alverson, C. Y., and Kahn, L. G. (2015).
A journey, not a destination: Developing cultural competence in secondary transition.
TEACHING Exceptional Children, 47(6), 319–328. doi: 10.1177/0040059915587679.

Rippner, J. A. (2017). State P-20 councils and collaboration between K-12 and higher
education. *Educational Policy, 31*, 2–28. doi: 10.1177/0895904814558008.

Savitz-Romer, M. (2012). The gap between influence and efficacy: College readiness
training, urban school counselors, and the promotion of equity. *Counselor Education &
Supervision, 51*(2), 98–111. doi: 10.1002/j.1556–6978.2012.00007.x.

Shaw, S. F., Dukes, L. L., and Madaus, J. W. (2012). Beyond compliance: Using the summary of performance to enhance transition planning. *TEACHING Exceptional Children, 44*(5), 6–12. doi: 10.1177/004005991204400501.

Sherron Targett, P and Wehman, P. (2011). Planning for the future: One student at a
time. In P. Wehman (Ed.), *The Essentials of Transition Planning. Brookes* (pp. 75–93).
Baltimore, MD: Paul H. Brookes Publishing Co.

Tools for Life Georgia. (n.d.). *What is assistive technology?* Retrieved from www.nichd.nih.
gov/health/topics/rehabtech/conditioninfo/Pages/device.aspx.

8

STRATEGIES TO INCREASE COLLEGE AND CAREER READINESS FOR ALL STUDENTS THROUGH MULTI-TIERED SYSTEMS OF SUPPORT

Allison Lombardi

UNIVERSITY OF CONNECTICUT

Mary Morningstar

UNIVERSITY OF KANSAS

Laura Kern, JD

UNIVERSITY OF SOUTH FLORIDA

> *Mrs. Brooke is frustrated. She has been a high school English teacher for ten years and has seen education "fads" come and go. If you ask her, she thinks that students need to be able to do things on their own to get ready for the "real world." But instead, she feels that she has to get students ready for their SATs so they can get into college. Additionally, one of the students in her class is Monica, a student with autism spectrum disorder. Monica has a special education teacher, Mr. Blake, who has been asking to work with Mrs. Brooke. Mrs. Brooke knows that she has to change her curriculum for Monica and include a bunch of accommodations and modifications. On top of that, Mrs. Brooke's school, Central High School, started to use a multi-tiered system of support (MTSS) a few years ago. Mrs. Brooke was not on the team that started it. She likes the idea of helping more of her students who might have different needs, but she is not sure how this works in high schools. Mrs. Brooke is at a loss—how can she meet the needs of her class and the needs of Monica? How can she help all of her students prepare for life after high school while still making sure she is teaching Monica important skills? How can Mrs. Brooke and Mr. Blake work together?*

Mrs. Brooke's challenges might sound familiar. We know that academic preparation of students, with and without disabilities, is essential for success in college and careers. We also know that setting high expectations and providing equitable opportunities in academic preparation is critical for *all* students. Yet, students with disabilities have not had the same opportunities to participate in a rigorous academic curriculum that prepares them for college and careers (Gregg, 2007). We have to do a better job of increasing the participation of all students with disabilities in the general education curriculum to promote high-quality outcomes for their future.

One way we can address the needs of *all* students is by integrating college and career readiness (CCR) into general education learning and experiences, especially through a multi-tiered system of service delivery (MTSS). By doing this, we challenge the assumption that students with disabilities are on different academic tracks and debunk the notion that they "cannot go to college." All students, with and without disabilities, can be included in school-wide efforts to promote and encourage CCR, while at the same time having most of their academic and behavioral needs addressed in general education through MTSS.

In this chapter, we will discuss school-wide MTSS, and the key components of CCR and how it can work within MTSS, as well as through special education transition policies and procedures. First, we introduce the potential of MTSS in high schools and then propose an organizing framework of CCR that works within an MTSS. We then describe the role of CCR in special and general education. Throughout, we will suggest strategies that can be used in MTSS to make CCR part of your school and classroom.

Multi-Tiered Systems in High Schools

It is important to re-imagine high schools as places where all students, including those with disabilities, are prepared for adult life. MTSS is a school-wide framework within general education that offers all students the potential for equitable access and support. Examples of MTSS include Response to Intervention (RtI), which focuses on academics, and Positive Behavioral Interventions and Supports (PBIS), which focuses on behavior. Under MTSS, academics and behavior are considered essential components that relate to and work with each other in a combined system. Notably, MTSS is situated within general education and is not meant to be exclusive to, or act as a replacement for, special education. Ideally, students with disabilities are included in the general education curriculum, with their needs met through individualized interventions and supports within core curricular and instructional interventions.

Core features of MTSS include: (a) setting consistent school-wide expectations that promote student learning; (b) using evidence-based practices throughout academic and non-academic areas that are accessible to *all* students; and (c) basing decisions on ongoing data collection and assessment. Additionally, one of the most recognizable features of MTSS is that instruction is provided with a tiered system of increasingly more intensive supports. At each tier, students receive instruction based on their individual needs. Assessments of these needs are at each tier, with an increase in frequency and intensity for the students in Tiers 2 and 3. Most students (about 80%) will learn within universal instruction (e.g., general education curriculum and classroom-based instruction). A smaller sub-set of students (about 20%) will benefit from more intense instruction, such as small group interventions. Approximately 5 percent of students will need even more assistance, often requiring individual instruction as a part of their school day (Sugai et al., 2010). Special education students are included across all tiers, and may require additional services tailored to their unique needs that go above and beyond what is typically provided in general education.

> Now that Central High School has initiated MTSS, Mrs. Brooke and some of her fellow teachers have a better understanding of this system. However, they also think it adds more responsibilities for them and may not directly fit within how Central High School operates. They don't see how MTSS helps prepare their students for future success. The school principal has also talked about the importance of college and career readiness for all of the students, but Mr. Blake and Mrs. Brooke do not know what that means or how to consider CCR strategies, let alone through MTSS. They still are not sure what CCR skills can meet the needs of all students, especially the needs of students in special education. It seems to them that CCR and MTSS are two new initiatives that they are required to implement, and don't see how these two efforts can improve student outcomes.
>
> Mrs. Brooke and Mr. Blake head to the internet to find out more about CCR. Some information is focused on academic preparation, while other websites describe non-academic skills. It seems like all of their students need to learn so many skills. How do they prioritize what to focus on?

College and Career Readiness

College and career readiness (CCR) encompasses the skills and experiences that help ensure success of students in their future. In general, CCR incorporates core academic and non-academic skills (e.g., critical thinking, metacognition, self-monitoring, study skills; Farrington et al., 2012; Krauss, Pittman, & Johnson, 2016), student motivation and engagement (Savitz-Romer, 2013), and knowledge of postsecondary requirements (Conley, 2012). CCR can also encompass the needs of certain subgroups, such as students with significant disabilities (Kearns et al., 2011).

The recent shift toward CCR extends policy, research, and practice to ensure all students participate in programs that best prepare them for post-school success. Focusing on CCR initiatives to address the essential, student-centered academic and non-academic factors associated with short-term and intermediate outcomes (in-school learning and engagement) can be an important approach to aligning what takes place in high school with post-school outcomes leading to college and career readiness and success.

TABLE 8.1 CCR Organizing Framework for Secondary Students with Disabilities

Academic Engagement	Mindsets	Learning Processes	Critical Thinking	Interpersonal Engagement	Transition Competencies
Cognitive &Content Knowledge • Language Arts • Math • Science • Social Studies • Career and Technical Education **Knowledge Structures** • Factual • Linking ideas • Organizing concepts • Challenge level **Behaviors** • Attendance • Productivity • Work habits • Class participation • Adaptability/flexibility • Course completion	**Sense of Belonging** • Trusting relationships: academic & nonacademic • Extracurricular engagement **Growth mindset** • Opportunities to practice • Learn from mistakes/progress **Ownership of Learning** • Help seeking • Self-awareness • Self-efficacy • Self-monitoring • Goal-setting **Perseverance** • Persistence • Effort • Motivation • Value • Grit/tenacity	**Accessing Content** • Test-taking skills • Note-taking skills • Time management skills • Organizational skills • Technology skills • Metacognitive skills **Engaging in Learning** • Group/team engagement • Listening and speaking skills	**Problem-Solving** • Recognize/formulate problem • Hypothesize • Strategize actions **Research** • Identify solutions • Collect data **Interpretation** • Analyze • Synthesize **Communication** • Create product • Present product (verbal, written) **Precision/Accuracy** • Monitor progress • Confirm results • Transfer skills	**With Self** • Responsibility • Adaptability **With Others** • Assertion • Accountability • Leadership • Collaboration **Understanding Others** • Social awareness • Empathy • Respect for Diversity	**Early Planning** • Goals tied to interests • Managing application & interview processes • Financial planning • Individual and environmental fit **Career Culture** • Professionalism • Knowledge of career resources • Employer expectations • Workplace fit **College Culture** • Campus resources • Program of study • Faculty expectations • Campus living **Adult Roles/Responsibilities** • Financial literacy • Accessing community resources • Health and wellness • Advocating supports & accommodations • Transportation • Adult living • Community membership • Civic engagement

Morningstar, M., Lombardi, A., Fowler, C., & Test, D. (2017). A college and career readiness framework for secondary students with disabilities. *Career Development and Transition for Exceptional Individuals, 40*(2), 79–91. doi: 10.1177/2165143415589926

In order to address academic and non-academic outcomes systematically, CCR benefits from an organizing framework that will help ensure students with and without disabilities are college and career ready. Morningstar et al. (2017) propose a CCR framework that emphasizes both academic and non-academic factors and includes six CCR categories (or domains). These domains were identified by researchers and those working with students in transition as necessary secondary and transition practices for supporting students with disabilities as they prepare for colleges and careers. The domains include academic engagement, mindsets, learning processes, critical thinking, interpersonal engagement, and transition competencies. Table 8.1 fully describes the organizing framework, identifies the six domains, and provides examples for each domain.

Using CCR within MTSS in High Schools

Many of the important CCR factors identified as essential for success are not systematically taught nor measured in high schools. For example, though both academic and non-academic factors of secondary schools using MTSS have been identified as needed to improve transition outcomes (Fuchs, Fuchs, & Compton, 2010; Morningstar, Gaumer, & Noonan, 2009), the non-academic components are not always addressed. MTSS may help to promote CCR and bridge contextual factors unique to secondary schools and adolescent learners (Morningstar, Knollman, Semon, & Kleinhammer-Tramill, 2012). Such an approach goes beyond academics and behaviors (e.g., RTI, PBIS) by encouraging student engagement, while at the same time directly addressing preparation for life after high school (e.g., college and careers).

Additionally, students with disabilities can benefit from using CCR in MTSS as these students are less likely to receive an academically rigorous curriculum in high school (Gregg, 2007), and their course failure and dropout rates are nearly twice as high as students in the general education population (United States Department of Education, 2012). This is especially troubling given recent evidence that students with disabilities are more likely to pursue two- and four-year postsecondary degrees if they receive instruction in general education classrooms in core subjects (Lombardi, Doren, Gau, & Lindstrom, 2013).

> *Now that Mr. Blake and Mrs. Brooke have learned about what CCR is and how it can be incorporated into MTSS efforts in high school, they would like to use it in their school in order to ensure all students with disabilities have access to the same CCR programs, assessment, curricula, and opportunities that are offered to all students. Mrs. Brooke has been invited to be on the planning team for MTSS for the school and is able to help with the initial development of MTSS. She would like to make sure that CCR is included at every level, but is not quite sure how that would happen.*

Application of the CCR Organizing Framework to MTSS

The CCR framework can be incorporated into each tier of the MTSS. As an initial step, school personnel involved in the MTSS leadership team might consider what they are currently doing in their schools at each of the tiers of support, and then map current resources and activities onto the six CCR domains. This exercise will help them identify areas of strength and gaps to address when considering how to facilitate CCR for all students. If they are not already on the planning team, it is important to solicit feedback from cross-disciplinary members that represent administrators, school counselors, and general and special educators, as well as family members and students themselves. Through this collaborative process, special educators may find that data or programs used elsewhere in the school could be utilized to incorporate CCR. Figure 8.1 shows an example worksheet that can facilitate the process.

Ideally, once planning and consideration of existing programs have occurred, educators can focus on strategies at each level of the MTSS tier. Table 8.2 shows resources by tier and the relevant CCR domain/s. This list is intended to help educators identify strategies at each tier of the CCR framework. The following section will provide a more detailed example of how to use strategies at each tier. First, we will discuss potential strategies for Tier 1, followed by Tiers 2 and 3.

Mapping To What You Currently Do...

	Academic engagement	Mindsets	Learning processes	Critical Thinking	Interpersonal Engagement	Transition Competencies
Tier 1 ALL						
Tier 2 SOME						
Tier 3 FEW						

FIGURE 8.1 Sample worksheet for school teams to consider when evaluating college and career readiness

TABLE 8.2 Examples of Resources by Tier that Map onto the Six Objectives of College and Career Readiness

Tier	Resource	Resource type	Citation(s) and/or website	Description	CCR objective covered
Tier 1	ThinkReady	Performance tasks embedded into content areas	Conley, Lombardi, Seburn, and McGaughy (2009) Website: https://collegereadyinfo.epiconline.org/thinkready/	Intervention that works with existing curriculum by incorporating specific tasks that increase thinking skills such as problem formation	Academic Engagement, Critical Thinking
Tier 1	The Self-Determined Model of Instruction	Instructional framework	Wehmeyer, Palmer, Agran, Mithaug, and Martin (2000) Website: http://www.beachcenter.org	An instructional framework for embedding self-determination skills into the classroom	Mindset, Transition Competencies
Tier 2	EnvisionIT	Curriculum	Izzo, Yurick, Nagaraja, and Novak (2010) Website: http://nisonger.osu.edu/research/envision-it/what-is-envisionit/	Electronic curriculum that increases reading and writing skills, information technology literacy, transition planning, and financial literacy through the development of a Transition Portfolio	Academic Engagement, Learning Processes, Interpersonal Engagement, Transition Competencies
Tier 2	Working At Gaining Employment Skills (WAGES)	Curriculum	Johnson, Bullis, Benz, and Hollenbeck, (2004)	Curriculum for students with disabilities that focuses on social and vocational skills	Critical Thinking, Interpersonal Engagement, Transition Competencies
Tier 2	Post-school Achievement Through Higher Skills (PATHS)	Curriculum	Lindstrom, Doren, Post, and Lombardi (2013)	Curriculum for girls with disabilities for career development including disability awareness and college and career preparation	Mindset, Interpersonal Engagement, Transition Competencies

Tier	Intervention	Type	Citation	Description	Competencies
Tier 3	Rehabilitation for Empowerment, Natural Supports, Education, and Work (RENEW)	Transition planning and wraparound process	Malloy (2013) Website: http://iod.unh.edu/projects/rehabilitation-empowerment-natural-supports-education-and-work-renew/renew-faq	Intervention with a facilitator and individual to develop a plan and goal for their future	Mindset, Interpersonal Engagement, Transition Competencies
Tier 3	Check and Connect	Intervention package	Sinclair, Christenson, and Thurlow (2005) Website: http://checkandconnect.org	Intervention with a mentor matched with a student and family to build student engagement by building relationships and increasing problem solving	Academic Engagement, Mindset, Learning Processes, Interpersonal Engagement

Tier 1

Tier 1, or "universal" supports, addresses the school-wide resources, programs, curricula, assessments, and opportunities that are offered to all students. These practices should be evidence based and offered in academic and non-academic areas in a layered continuum of supports. Below are examples of what Tier 1 might look like in high school settings.

Using Universal Design for Learning: Although UDL is not specific to CCR, it can provide a bridge to include more students with disabilities in the Tier 1 curriculum. UDL is a concept that focuses on increasing accessibility for all, regardless of ability level. Stemming from the field of architecture, specifically building accessibility, UDL has been expanded to include the field of education (Rose, Harbour, Johnston, Daley, & Abarbanell, 2006). UDL complements the principle of differentiation where teachers provide different levels of instruction and ways of presenting material, among other strategies, based on the needs of students in their class. Specifically, Hall Vue, Strangman, & Meyer (2004) suggest several ways to use UDL to guide differentiated instruction: providing multiple examples; highlighting critical features, proving multiple media and formats, supporting background context, providing opportunities to practice with support, offering flexible opportunities for demonstrating skills, adjustable challenge levels, and choice in content, tools, and learning context. For more resources on UDL, the CAST website has included several tools on using UDL to assist with differentiation, and provides many resource for UDL, such as modules and tools (www.udlcenter.org/implementation/examples).

Using UDL can increase access to the general curriculum at the Tier 1 level for all students, including students with disabilities. For example, a school might decide to prioritize financial literacy for all of their students. A teacher could set up a lesson plan related to using comparison shopping skills to buy and finance a car. To differentiate this lesson plan to meet the needs of all students, the teacher will need to consider how information is conveyed, how students engage in learning, and how students share what they have learned. Students may have the choice to read about purchasing a vehicle, or watching a video, or completing an online scavenger hunt. Next, students can engage in learning through small group projects where teams work together to develop the budget and research critical information such as down payments, interest rates and loan terms, and car insurance. For students with diverse support needs, embedding accommodations and modifications will naturally occur within universally designed lessons because of the interactive nature of the activities, and the choices allowed for learning and assessment. For example, small groups might choose to use an auto loan calculator (www.vertex42.com/Calculators/auto-loan-calculator.html), and a role for a student with intellectual disabilities may be as the "recorder" whereby she will input the data to the calculator, thereby meeting her individual needs of number identification. By using UDL to meaningfully increase differentiation as well as embed CCR outcomes within core academic courses, schools can enhance the capacity of Tier 1 curriculum to meaningfully apply to all students.

Embedding CCR into the curriculum: Schools might decide to adopt an approach at the Tier 1 for all of their students that addresses CCR skills as part of the core academic curriculum. For example, a school might decide that they would like to increase opportunities to learn effective problem-solving skills among students. The ThinkReady performance assessment system (Conley, Lombardi, Seburn, & McGaughy, 2009) offers one option to address this goal. ThinkReady is designed to work with the existing academic content by embedding key cognitive strategies known to build problem-solving skills necessary for post-high school success. Students are assessed through performance tasks that require them to problem-solve across multiple disciplines (e.g., English language, arts, mathematics, science). Increasing academic engagement and critical thinking associated with problem solving is a core aspect of CCR. Most importantly, the tasks designed by ThinkReady can meet the needs of all learners, including students with disabilities. Specific information can be found at https://www.inflex ion.org/project/thinkready/.

The MTSS team would also like to work with teachers at the classroom level for Tier 2 and 3 interventions. To do this, they ask their teachers to consider the needs of their students and provide some resources of ideas for teachers to try for small group and individual lessons. In this process, Mrs. Brooke works more collaboratively with other teachers in general and special education, feels more connected with the CCR initiatives happening in the school, and has learned a lot of about embedding career searching and exploration into her content-area instruction from Mr. Blake, given his background in transition planning.

Tier 2

For students who are "non-responders" to Tier 1, more targeted and intensive supports are delivered in Tiers 2 and 3. These students should be identified through systematic assessment, and receive supports in smaller groups and in more frequent duration. Below are examples of what Tiers 2 and 3 might look like in high school settings.

Small group intervention: Tier 2 activities are generally more targeted to smaller groups of students that need intensive instruction, with more opportunities to practice. Small groups can be focused on a specific area of CCR, such as increasing information technology literacy (e.g., the ability to navigate a computer), or increasing the awareness and capacities of students to consider the different types of college experiences and associated skills, such as the Advancement via Individual Difference (AVID) program, which is designed to prepare students traditionally underrepresented in higher education. This program provides small groups of students more intensive instruction through tutorials, mentoring, and peer supports (www.avid.org). In addition, Tier 2 social emotional interventions, such as Check In/Check Out, provide students with daily feedback, adult mentoring relationships, and increased home–school communication to ensure students successfully engage in school (Crone, Hawken, & Horner, 2011).

One of the ways to increase CCR skills related to technological literacy is the evidence-based intervention, EnvisionIT. This curriculum is delivered through a series of online modules for reading and writing skills, improves information technology literacy, transition planning, and financial literacy (Izzo, Yurick, Nagaraja, & Novak, 2010; Lombardi et al., 2017). Students work through the modules and develop a Transition Portfolio. This intervention addresses the needs of a small group of students that might be struggling with technological literacy by incorporating learning experiences on a computer. More information is available online (http://nisonger.osu.edu/research/envision-it/what-is-envisionit/) as well as professional development videos for teachers that demonstrate delivery of particular lessons (http://go.osu.edu/eitpd).

Tier 3

Individualized interventions: For a small number of students requiring more intense and perhaps one-on-one instruction, Tier 3 strategies are specific to the individual student needs of the student. School completion is an area that certain students may struggle with that is directly related to CCR. As a drop-out prevention intensive intervention, Check and Connect matches an at-risk student and their family with a school mentor. The goal is to reduce drop-out and to increase student engagement by building relationships, and academic and personal goal setting, as well as problem solving (Sinclair, Christenson, & Thurlow, 2005). See the following website for more information: http://checkandconnect.org.

> Mrs. Brooke and Mr. Blake realize that if they work together they can include CCR for all the students in their class by incorporating more Tier 2 and 3 interventions. For example, by using small group interventions such as EnvisionIT, Mrs. Brooke will integrate a wider range of CCR skills for all her students by building their technological and career exploration skills. By focusing on a few students who need more individualized intervention at the Tier 3 level, they can make sure that struggling students receive the instruction they need. By using MTSS, they can include more intensive, small group and individualized interventions for students who need more support because the needs of most of her students are met by the Tier 1 interventions.
>
> Now that MTSS is up and running and CCR is included in core content areas, Mr. Blake feels more confident about these changes because he sees that the students with disabilities are participating at every tier of instruction based on their needs. Mr. Blake is still concerned about the progress of some of the students he works with

and would like to make sure that their specialized needs are still being met through special education. He wonders if there is a way to consider CCR specifically in special education.

Special Education

Although students in special education are included in each tier in MTSS, in certain areas, some students require a specific program of instruction that is tied in with their legal rights. The area most relevant to CCR in special education is transition planning, including several key components centered on the development of an Individual Education Program (IEP) and Summary of Performance (SOP).

When Mr. Blake and Mrs. Brooke meet and review Monica's IEP, they notice that Monica has transition goals that describe what she wants to do after high school. One of the goals states: "Monica will attend college." The second goal is: "Monica will live in an apartment with a roommate." Mrs. Brooke and Mr. Blake think that these goals should be more specific and measureable, and better aligned with college and career readiness. However, they are not sure how to fix them or what would be needed to make them specific and measureable. Mr. Blake is not sure if they need to start thinking about a Summary of Performance (SOP) document because Monica is in high school. Mrs. Brooke has never heard of SOP, and is not sure how she can help.

IEP Planning and Goal Development

What sets IEP development apart from special education services during the elementary years is the focus on collaborative planning to facilitate the transition to post-school outcomes, beginning at least by 16 years old, or younger in some states, and lasting until 21 years old for certain students. According to the law, IEP teams need to develop a coordinated set of transition and educational services for students with disabilities that emphasize individual student's post-school goals. This process begins with age-appropriate transition assessments that inform the development of measureable postsecondary goals. As a requirement of the IEP, measurable postsecondary goals must be: (a) measureable, (b) stated to occur after high school, (c) age-appropriate, (d) and based on transition assessments that include the student's interests and preferences (IDEA, 2004, Section 300.320).

Mrs. Brooke and Mr. Blake convened Monica's IEP team. Mr. Blake suggested that they complete several career and learning styles assessments to help identify Monica's post-school interests. He was able to review several on the online Assessment Reviews tool found at www.transitioncoalition.org. Mrs. Brooke thought this sounded like a great idea and was happy to help. Several weeks later, the IEP team had some results from the assessments. They had learned that Monica really enjoys music and would like to work in the music industry, either as a musician or teacher. She would like to start studying music at Maple Community College, a few towns away. She and her family think that starting at a small school will help her complete prerequisites and allow her to test the waters for going to college fulltime. Monica doesn't drive, but she could take public transportation. They realize one of the measurable postsecondary goals might be related to transportation: "Monica will take public transportation to and from school independently 100% of the time." Mrs. Brooke thinks that this is a great goal, as it will help Monica after she graduates in many aspects of her adult life. The team also realize that if Monica is going to go to a postsecondary setting, they need to make sure she has developed both the academic skills she needs, and the non-academic skills that are so essential to success in adulthood such as problem solving, self-advocacy, time management, and social and communication skills.

Mr. Blake has looked over the chart of the CCR constructs and he believes that Monica would benefit from learning organizational and time management strategies. This focus might be an additional CCR related IEP goal. Mr. Blake has also considered how he can include more transition- related skills into his regular expectations for Monica, which would also help her achieve both her post-secondary goals and IEP goals.

CCR initiatives should include students with and without disabilities, and the IEP process required for some students should reflect ongoing high school reform efforts taking place (Fowler, Test, Cease-Cook, Toms, & Bartholomew, 2014). Even though students in special education will receive additional planning and services, it is expected that they also participate in all CCR and MTSS interventions. Thus, it is prudent to align IEP measurable postsecondary goals and the annual goals with state and district CCR efforts. By aligning annual IEP goals with CCR, special educators can leverage existing legal procedures to ensure students with disabilities have access to CCR opportunities. In turn, they will be more likely to satisfy the necessary academic requirements needed for different degree programs in two- and four-year colleges and universities. Table 8.3 shows example IEP annual and measureable postsecondary goal statements that align with the six domains of the CCR framework. These goals were taken from actual student IEPs in an exploratory study that examined alignment between the IEP and CCR framework (for a full study description, see Lombardi, Kern, Flannery, & Doren, 2017).

Mr. Blake decided that Monica's IEP goals would be even stronger if he used the age-appropriate transition assessments to identify areas of strength and challenges and link these with CCR strategies. For example, Monica had many friends with whom she liked spending time. Her interpersonal skills were a source of strength. Mr. Blake realized that if he was able to include some of these friends in group projects, he could increase some of the CCR skills under Learning Processes. He wrote a goal that included group work. He also saw that Monica struggled with organization. He was able to write a goal that included the use of an organizational app for assignments and accommodations, helping Monica and responding to the organizing part of Learning Processes. He was able to share these updated goals with Mrs. Brooke, who realized she could better support Monica in her classroom through these goals and accommodations.

TABLE 8.3 Examples of IEP Annual Goals and Measureable Postsecondary Goals by CCR domain

	CT	AE	M	LP	IE	TC
Annual Goals						
Student will use a self-management system to show his ability to be in class and maintain his grades and attitude.		X	X			
Student will apply decision-making and problem-solving techniques in workplace situations with 4 out of 5 trials measured by staff observation.	X		X			X
Student will research construction trade school opportunities and present findings to classroom staff and students.	X					X
Student will earn a minimum of 70 percent on all pre-algebra/algebra tests and quizzes or will arrange to retake assessment following error analysis and additional practice.	X	X	X			
Student will advocate for his needs related to his hearing impairment by 1) whenever possible sitting in the front of classes and presentations 2) at the start of each new trimester letting his teachers know what his needs and accommodations are.				X		X
Student will obtain 3 letters of recommendation from adults aware of her work experience and ethic to keep in her transition portfolio.					X	X
Measureable Postsecondary Goals						
Student will either gain employment by one year after high school or have contacted vocational rehab services to help him obtain and maintain employment related to the field of computer software or tech program training.		X				X
Student will participate in a transition class to successfully learn to identify job search activities, create a résumé, fill out job application, and prepare for interviews. Student will demonstrate self-awareness by identifying 3 each of work-related strengths, weaknesses, and skills. He will match them to 2 occupational choices.	X		X		X	X
Student will be able to correctly fill out a sample job application starting with: being able to write his address, phone number including area code, and emergency contact. Will improve independence and organization by keeping an updated planner and organizer.				X		X

Note. CT= Critical Thinking, AE=Academic Engagement, M=Mindset, LP=Learning Processes, IE=Interpersonal Engagement, TC=Transition Competencies

Summary of Performance

Under the 2004 reauthorization of IDEA, educators must provide a Summary of Performance (SOP) to exiting students that encourages teams to collect and track data on the successful supports a student uses while in high school. The SOP must be completed during the student's last year of services; however, compiling relevant information throughout high school is encouraged. Bottom line, the SOP must include a summary of a student's academic achievement and functional performance, as well as recommendations on how to assist students in meeting postsecondary goals (Yell, Delport, Plotner, Petcu, & Prince, 2015). To develop the SOP, the student and IEP team should work together to provide information to appropriate postsecondary settings about accommodations that do and do not work well for the student. This process helps the student, particularly when the student is closely involved, learn what to advocate for when arriving on a postsecondary campus or employed in a workplace. Ideally, a student will be able to share the SOP with future employers and postsecondary institutions in order to obtain reasonable accommodations, as well as to share information about what types of supports work best. While there is not a mandatory template for the SOP, sample templates that are considered best practice are widely disseminated by the National Technical Assistance Center on Transition (NTACT). In fact, the NTACT website includes a four-page SOP template with four sections, one of which is meant to track understanding and use of accommodations (see: www.transitionta.org). Additionally, the NTACT website provides sample SOPs, guides, and an annotated bibliography available as resources (http://transitionta.org/transitionplanning). These resources are especially important to consider implementing as students progress towards graduation. Teachers may consider making it a point to complete an SOP on all students with disabilities who have expressed a desire to pursue postsecondary education. Importantly, the SOP could be used for students who have IEPs and/or 504 plans.

Although the team learned they do not need to finish the SOP until Monica is in her senior year, they think it would be best to approach the SOP like a transition portfolio and add to it throughout high school. As Monica was able to try out her new accommodations, she and Mr. Brooke kept track of which accommodations worked well and why on a draft SOP document. Monica intends to take her SOP with her when she graduates and pursues postsecondary education in order to use it as a self-advocacy tool.

Monica has benefited from the Tier 3 interventions focusing on building self-determination. However, Mr. Brooke believes that Monica should be provided even more direct instruction about her special education program. He is worried that she does not understand her accommodations and modifications and how they help her access the regular education curriculum. He is thinking that he should provide some additional instruction for Monica on this topic.

Addressing accommodations and modifications: Students with disabilities often continue to have increasing challenges when transitioning from high school to college and careers. Often their needs can be met by strengthening the general education curriculum and incorporating CCR directly into tiered layers of support within schools that improve their access to essential CCR skills. However, students with disabilities may have specific needs that require additional support in general education. For example, in high school, students often utilize accommodations or modifications. In fact, extra time on tests is the most common accommodation provided to youth across disability types, and youth with one of three disability types (Autism, Intellectual Disability, and Multiple Disabilities) tend to be more likely to take modified tests and receive modified assignments (63–67% and 54–63%, respectively) (Lipscomb et al., 2017). Teachers can assist students in learning about their unique learning needs, and how best to advocate for necessary accommodations to access the general education curriculum. Accommodations should be specified within the IEP document. Moreover, an essential long-term goal for most students would be to have the self-confidence and skills to advocate for support needs, whether they transition to further postsecondary education or employment. Therefore, teachers can play an essential role in supporting students to make a list of their critical accommodations, where and how they are used, and noting how effective they have been. Teachers can also support students to build the self-determination skills necessary to advocate for the use of these accommodations, and for the discontinuation or modification of accommodations that are not effective. The teacher can show the

List out what is contained in the IEP	Check which type		Why do I have this accommodation/modification? How does it help me?	Will I need this Accommodation or Modification in the future?	
	Accommodation	Modification		Yes	No

FIGURE 8.2   A Tool to Facilitate Conversations between Teachers and Students regarding Accommodations and Modifications

student where it will be included in the SOP and how it is the responsibility of the student to bring this information to the attention of an employer or disability services office at a college. The teacher can also explain differences between an accommodation (e.g., change that increases access, such as where someone is being tested) and a modification (e.g., change to the content, such as what is being tested). By having a direct conversation and planning session, students can become more aware of these accommodations and/or modifications, their impact, and the need to advocate for them in the future. It is often necessary to address this specifically as part of special education and within IEP goals. A tool is included to help assist with this conversation (see Figure 8.2).

Concluding Comments

In this chapter, we presented a six-part organizing framework of CCR that promotes academic preparation of students with disabilities by aligning with broader school-wide efforts. Details on the formation of the CCR framework were provided, as well as explicit examples of the application of the framework to both general and special education policies and procedures. School-wide application of the CCR framework will encourage and promote rigorous academic and non-academic standards for students with disabilities. Application of the framework within a MTSS is an important consideration, as school-wide data collection efforts could be both universal (Tier 1), as well as meet the needs of secondary special education transition assessment in order to inform the IEP planning process. Ultimately, aligning general and special education CCR efforts and embedding CCR within existing special education procedures, such as the IEP and SOP, will lead to more coordinated efforts between professionals, and better academic preparation of students with disabilities for post-school pursuits.

> *Now, Mrs. Brooke and Mr. Blake use some of the CCR practices across the school, in the classroom, and for the individual students. They feel more confident that they are meeting the needs of all students. Mrs. Brooke is also able to see how she can help Monica to succeed by working with Mr. Blake and individualizing the CCR skills based on an assessment of her needs and addressing these in her IEP and SOP. Mrs. Brooke is ready for the next year to include even more CCR into her classroom at all levels of instruction. Mr. Blake is also delighted as he feels Monica's needs are being met, high expectations are set for her, and she is getting the instruction she needs to succeed in life after high school.*

References

Conley, D. T. (2012). *A complete definition of college and career readiness.* Educational Policy Improvement Center, Eugene, OR.

Conley, D., Lombardi, A., Seburn, M., and McGaughy, C. (2009). Formative assessment for college readiness on five key cognitive strategies associated with postsecondary success. Paper presented at the 2009 annual conference of the American Educational Research Association, San Diego, CA.

Farrington, C. A., Roderick, M., Allensworth, E., Nagaoka, J., Keyes, T. S., Johnson, D. W., and Beechum, N. O. (2012). *Teaching adolescents to become learners. The role of noncognitive factors in shaping school performance: A critical literature review.* Chicago: University of Chicago Consortium on Chicago School Research.

Fowler, C. H., Test, D. W., Cease-Cook, J., Toms, O., and Bartholomew, A. (2014). Policy implications of high school reform on college and career readiness of youth with disabilities. *Journal of Disability Policy Studies, 25,* 19–29.

Fuchs, L. S., Fuchs, D., and Compton, D. L. (2010). Rethinking response to intervention at middle and high school. *School Psychology Review, 39,* 22–28.

Gregg, N. (2007). Underserved and unprepared: Postsecondary learning disabilities. *Learning Disabilities Research & Practice, 22*(4), 219–228.

Hall, T., Vue, G., Strangman, N., and Meyer, A. (2004). *Differentiated instruction and implications for UDL implementation.* Wakefield, MA: National Center on Accessing the General Curriculum. (Links updated 2014). Retrieved on December 23, 2016 from http://aem.cast.org/about/publications/2003/ncac-differentiated-instruction-udl.html.

Izzo, M. V., Yurick, A., Nagaraja, H. N., and Novak, J. A. (2010). Effects of a 21st century curriculum on students' information technology and transition skills. *Career Development for Exceptional Individuals, 33*(2), 95–105.

Johnson, M. D., Bullis, M., Benz, M. R., and Hollenbeck, K. (2004). *Working at Gaining Employment Skills (WAGES): A job-related social skills curriculum for adolescents.* Longmont, CO: Sopris West.

Kearns, J., Kleinert, H., Harrison, B., Sheppard-Jones, K., Hall, M., and Jones, M. (2011). *What does "college and career ready" mean for students with significant cognitive disabilities?* Lexington: University of Kentucky.

Krauss, S. M., Pittman, K. J., and Johnson, C. (2016, February). *Ready by design: The science and art of youth readiness.* Washington, DC: The Forum on Youth Investment.

Lindstrom, L., Doren, B., Post, C., and Lombardi, A. (2013). Building career PATHS (Postschool Achievement Through Higher Skills) for young women with disablilities. *The Career Development Quarterly, 61*(4), 330–338.

Lipscomb, S., Haimson, J., Liu, A. Y., Burghardt, J., Johnson, D. R., and Thurlow, M. L. (2017). *Preparing for life after high school: The characteristics and experiences of youth in special education. Findings from the National Longitudinal Transition Study 2012.* Volume 2: Comparisons across disability groups (NCEE 2017–4018). Washington, DC: U. S. Department of Education, Institute of Educational Sciences, National Center for Education Evaluation and Regional Assistance.

Lombardi, A., Doren, B., Gau, J., and Lindstrom, L. (2013). The influence of instructional settings in reading and math on postsecondary participation. *Journal of Disability Policy Studies, 24*(3), *169–179.*

Lombardi, A. R., Izzo, M. V., Rifenbark, G. G., Murray, A., Buck, A., Monahan, J., and Gelbar, N. (2017). The impact of an online transition curriculum on secondary student reading: A multilevel examination. *Career Development and Transition for Exceptional Individuals. 40,* 15–24. doi: 10.1177/2165143416681287.

Lombardi, A., Kern, L., Flannery, K. B., & Doren, B. (2017). Is college and career readiness adequately addressed in annual and postsecondary goals? *Journal of Disability Policy Studies, 28*(3), 150–161. doi: 10.1177/1044207317716147.

Malloy, J. (2013). The RENEW model: Supporting transition-age youth with emotional and behavioral challenges. *Report on Emotional and Behavioral Disorders in Youth,* 13(2), 38–46.

Morningstar, M. E., Gaumer, A. E., and Noonan, P. M. (2009). Transition and multi-tiered systems of support: How does it all fit together? Presentation at the KansTran Summit. Wichita, KS.

Morningstar, M. E., Knollman, G., Semon, S., and Kleinhammer-Tramill, J. (2012). Metrics for what matters: Using postschool outcomes to build school and community renewal. In L. C. Burrello, W. Sailor, and J. Kleinhammer-Tramill (Eds.), *Unifying educational systems: Leadership and policy perspectives* (pp. 158–167). Florence, KY: Routledge, Taylor & Frances Group.

Morningstar, M., Lombardi, A., Fowler, C., and Test, D. (2017). A college and career readiness framework for secondary students with disabilities. *Career Development and Transition for Exceptional Individuals, 40*(2), 79–91. doi: 10.1177/2165143415589926.

Rose, D., Harbour, W., Johnston, S., Daley, S., and Abarbanell, L. (2006). Universal Design for Learning in postsecondary education: Reflections on principles and their application. *Journal of Postsecondary Education and Disability, 19*(2), 135–151.

Savitz-Romer, M. (2013). *College readiness and life skills: Moving beyond academics.* Education Week Webinar. Retrieved on January 31, 2013 from www.edweek.org/go/webinars.

Sinclair, M. F., Christenson, S. L., and Thurlow, M. L. (2005). Promoting school completion of urban secondary youth with emotional or behavioral disabilities. *Exceptional Children, 71*, 465–482.

Sugai, G., Horner, R. H., Algozzine, R., Barrett, S., Lewis, T., Anderson, C., . . . Simonsen, B. (2010). *School-wide positive behavior support: Implementation blueprint and self-assessment.* Retrieved from www.pbis.org/common/cms/files/pbisresources/SWPBS_ImplementationBlueprint_vSep_23_2010.pdf.

United States Department of Education, National Center for Education Statistics. (2012). *The condition of education 2012* (NCES 2012–045), Indicator 33. Retrieved from http://nces.ed.gov/fastfacts/display.asp?id=16.

Wehmeyer, M. L., Palmer, S. B., Agran, M., Mithaug, D. E., and Martin, J. (2000). Promoting causal agency: The self-determined learning model of instruction. *Exceptional Children, 66*, 439–453.

Yell, M. L., Delport, J., Plotner, A., Petcu, S., and Prince, A. (2015). Providing transition services: An analysis of law and policy. In B. G. Cook, M. Tankersley, and T. Landrum (Eds.). *Transitions of Youth and Young Adults.* Advances in Learning and Behavioral Disabilities series, volume 28. Bingley, UK: Emerald Publishing Group.

SECTION 4

Resources for Students

9

STUDENT RESOURCE SECTION

Introduction

This section contains resources for high school students with disability that secondary educators, counselors, and transition personnel can use to facilitate self-reflection, as well as college exploration and planning discussions. The resource, "What I Wish I Knew," from Elmore, Veitch, and Harbor and contributors, provides advice from current or recent college students with disabilities to high school students. This resource offers first-hand experiences and suggestions on how students can embrace disability history and culture, advocate for their needs, and build a network of personal supports that can help them achieve their desired goals. Additional downloadable materials include a "Top Ten List" of college advice, a college planning checklist, and a list of recommended organizations and books. Student versions of this section are available for download at www.routledge.com/9781138934733. and can be provided to students. This guide can be used to facilitate discussions with students in high school about their desires for college and the importance of self-knowledge and self-advocacy when preparing for college.

This section includes:

- What I Wish I Knew
- Top Ten List for College Students by College Students
- College Prep Checklist
- National Organizations and Websites
- Recommended Books
- Questions to ask the Disability Services Office During a College Visit
- Disability Specific Resources for College Planning
- Conversation Strategies for Students to Talk to Parents about College

What I Wish I Knew – College Students with Disabilities Advice for High School Students

When students are trying to get through the first years of college, and having problems, or worried about the future, there's nothing quite like getting advice from someone who has been down the same road and really "gets it." Here is some advice to high school students thinking about college, from current or recent college students with disabilities.

What I Wish I Knew was developed by Kim Elmore, Hetsie Veitch, & Wendy S. Harbour with contributions by Nigel Abduh, Crystal Fike, Kings Floyd, Jason Harris, Ann Wai-Yee Kwong, Tara McFadden, Kate Pollack, Katie Roquemore, and K Wheeler.

- **Stop and think about what *you* are looking for in a college, and *then* start looking**. "I would say you need to know what you are looking for in a school," explained Jason:

JASON

> *Look at all your interests and the supports that you might receive. You can always ask for many things in college. Know what programs you might be interested in but also know what kind of environment would work for you. The college that I went to had a large number of commuting students, and there wasn't a lot of people around over the weekends. I didn't like that. You have to look at every aspect of your life when you look for a college. That is important. You have to know what will work for you.*

Ann reminded students that they are the ones who have to live with the choices they make: "At the end of the day, I need to be happy with my choices that determine my life." And both Jason and Crystal suggested students remember that not everyone wants to go to college for a four-year degree, and other options for college exist. As Jason said, "There are many options out there for different people."

- **When choosing a college, think carefully about being the only one with your disability on a campus**. It's easy to ask disability services offices if they have significant experience with your type of disability and how many other students on campus have similar disabilities. It's your right to attend any campus, but it can be tougher if the disability services office doesn't have experience with your disability, and there is no one to talk to when problems arise. Ann and her friend both dealt with this:

ANN

I had one friend in high school who is blind. We both had AP classes and the same vocational rehabilitation services. We were the only blind students using Braille at [our respective] colleges, so ODS [Office of Disability Services] would say, "No one else needs Braille," or "Nobody else is complaining." We would like to have known this might happen when we were in high school.

Kate struggled with a disability resource office that had only one counselor who worked with a handful of deaf and hard-of-hearing undergraduates, and the position had a high turnover rate. Kate had to be very persistent and keep excellent records to support her self-advocacy efforts over the years and eventually graduate with high marks.

KATE

- **Find information for your parents and families if they need it**. Some parents or family members are very nervous about college for students with disabilities. While high schools are supposed to provide college information to students and their families, this is not always the case. Ann told us, "One of our friends was accepted by a [state university] but the parents said, 'No, that's too far, go to the local community college. We're not comfortable with you going to a university far away because we still have to cook for you.'" Ann suggested reaching out for the information and forming connections: "Parents don't get this information [about college] and there are resources out there for parents. Families can also learn from other families, as can students from students." For example, K and her parents found resources when they "joined the International Child Advocacy Network (ICAN) for families and people born without limbs or those who are amputees, and it's an international network, so they can ask questions and connect to others." K told us that "I even connected to [a young adult] in Maryland with almost the exact same thing as me, and they ended up coming to Seattle about three months after we met each other on Facebook, so we were able to meet." K visits this friend every summer and she has influenced K's thinking about college and success. And now K has formed a similar relationship with a younger person with the same disability.

- **Ask for what you need and use the resources to which you are entitled**. Many students are afraid to ask for accommodations or support, but as Kings explained, "asking for help is never a bad thing. I was afraid that if I reached out to parents, my guidance counselor, or anyone about accommodations, that would be seen as a sign of weakness or giving up. But the rewards for asking for help are almost immediate. Overcoming pride and learning to ask for help is very valuable." Nigel adds that you can ask for help without diminishing your pride as a person with a disability: "Come out of your comfort zone. Don't let anybody tell you that you can't and don't be afraid to ask for help. Find out who you are as a person. Don't look at your disability as a bad thing. Don't let anybody keep you from being yourself." And Tara reminded us that real friends will not think differently about us because of an accommodation: "Don't be afraid to use the resources that you are entitled to. I don't mind that it took me longer to fully understand information. It doesn't bother me that I had to take longer just because my brain works differently. Friends who don't get accommodations don't care [that you have] another 30 minutes on a test."

- **Build a support network of friends, professionals, and faculty**. Ann explained how she "needed to step out of my comfort zone to build a support network. I tried different clubs and new activities, and started to be comfortable being uncomfortable." K had difficulty finding friends her first semester because she had only two classes on campus each week and used speech recognition software to do homework, which makes studying with others difficult. "Joining the Harry Potter Club changed that. The club included people from all levels of college, and I discovered I was not necessarily alone in feeling isolated my first semester on campus." Also include students with disabilities in your support network. After having disagreements with her disability resource office, Ann found it helpful "to talk to others with disabilities with similar experiences to get advice because when the ADA officer was disagreeing with disability services and I'd just spent three hours on the phone, sometimes I felt like the only one dealing with this." While many students expressed concerns about making friends at college at first, they found their new friendships fun as well as supportive. Crystal loved "going out, meeting different people, and doing different things" so much that she became president of her program's social gathering committee during her last year.

Ann also encouraged students to go beyond friendships and "build your experiences in academics, and professions, and with disability." For example, Ann and Kate specifically stated that in addition to support from the campus disability resources offices, local support from the state's VR agency is essential for lower income students. When Kate was still in high school, the local VR representative, Kevin Shea, and his service dog approached her and her mom to explain how they would pay for her tuition, books, and rent to help her reach her career goals. Katie adds that building supportive relationships with professors is important: "While the Office of Disability Services certainly was helpful, the most important resource was making connections with professors, especially in my department." She advised new college students to "make an effort to build a relationship with your professors so they see you as a person they want to help be successful. And be confident in expressing what you need to be successful."

- **Learn to advocate for yourself**. Most students stated that learning to advocate for themselves to get the appropriate accommodations is a necessary college success skill, yet it is a skill not often developed in high school. Kate advised students to learn self-advocacy skills and to know their legal rights as a student. Through her experiences at different schools – including a community college, art school, a city university, and a research university – Kate learned the value of self-advocacy in her academic and personal life. She advised students to:

  Try to set up a support network of as many people as you can and learn your legal rights. Learn about the ADA. Learn about what access strategies is going to work for you. Sometimes access is really a trial-and-error thing so don't feel bad if one type of access you thought might work does not actually work. Demand respect. Learn to advocate for yourself. Know that you are going to have to work harder than everyone else. Expect that often your professors are not going to know the first thing about disability and they are likely to not know the law either. That is why you need a disability services office and a [VR] organization like VESID in your corner. Professors may think that access and accommodations is "special treatment" but they have to follow the law.

Ann emphasized that self-advocacy can be an extended process of knowing and stating what you need, proposing a strategy for meeting that need, revising that strategy as needed, and persistently revisiting the negotiation until your need is met. She also recommended cultivating a support community that understands your accommodation needs, empathizes with your experiences as a culturally deaf or disabled student, and can give you advice and support.

- **Learn about yourself.** While you're in college, you'll have a chance to learn more about yourself, both within and outside classwork. For Nigel, this meant not letting disability be the only part of his identity: "Find out who you are as a person, and don't let your disability define you. Don't look at your disability as a bad thing, either. Always know you're going to be a person at the end of the day – don't be anybody but yourself." K agrees that personal growth is part of the college experience: "College is a great thing – it helps you to figure out who you are as a person." Kings reminds us though to "accept that education and self-awareness can come in many different forms. You can learn in the classroom, but also through study abroad or from volunteering."

- **Learn about and share disability history and culture**. Jason described the impact of an undergraduate course in disability culture:

  I took a class about disability, equity and culture at a time when I was very down and negative about my disability. This helped me a lot to better understand that it is not an individual thing and about me the whole time, but that disability is also a cultural thing. I think it is very important for disabled students to know some of the history of disability and so on, to understand it better for themselves. I think it is good to take a course about it. You don't have to major in it and everything, but you will learn more about it. I would recommend that.

Other students valued disability studies so much that they added a disability studies concentration to their major, like K who is double-majoring in Law, Society, Justice, and Disability Studies, Kings who concentrated on Education, Language, and Disability Studies for her bachelor's degree in English, and Jason and Kate who are working on their master's degrees in Education and Disability Studies.

- **Find a mentor**. Mentors during high school and college can be a great help to students with disabilities, guiding students toward opportunities that might have otherwise been missed. Ann noted that mentors are especially important for students who do not have the social capital to personally understand higher education and employment systems or with the help of their families:

To get into a good college you need volunteer and internship opportunities in high school. Many students without disabilities talked about experience and leadership, sports, etc. Disabled students have to know how to highlight their leadership potential, too. When a student lacks social capital or does not have a parent who can do that role, they need a mentor. My mentor helped by just knowing the higher education and disability accommodations terminology. My mentor couldn't provide the actual advocacy piece, but I knew that my mentor could provide emotional support when needed.

CRYSTAL

Crystal realized college mentors could help with much more than academics. Prior to the first semester in her college program, Crystal participated in a Mentoring Matching Party where "we went around and introduced ourselves and got to know each other." Later, each student selected their top three mentors and was then matched with one of the three. Crystal said, "I didn't have mentors before I came to college, but now they help me with everything I need. We go out and meet different people and do different things. My biggest challenge has been working on math skills and reading skills, so I also work with my mentors to build those skills." Finding a mentor isn't always easy, as Ann noted:

I had to be very proactive to seek out mentors. A lot of the mentoring programs for first-generation college students don't go to disability student spaces. A blind friend and I thought we would make a mentoring program since we didn't know of one for disabled students, and most disability services just track students as they progress instead of offering mentoring. We got together with some other students at other colleges, some at independent living centers, and some at community colleges and we started "Survive and Thrive" in California. Since 2012, we've expanded to two workshops per year and social events including families.

Kings told students that she more often discovers mentors informally rather than through mentoring programs:

KINGS

> *You can find a connection with almost anyone anywhere. You just have to be a good enough detective to find it. I didn't think I would necessarily connect with my boss, David, but we started talking about William Faulkner and Mark Twain on my first day of work, and I was super nerdy because I love both of those authors and he really liked both authors. It was a cool connection to find almost right away. So look for ways to connect with people, try to find that connection. Asking questions is the best way to be a detective, even if they're simple open questions like "Oh, how was your day? Or "Oh, where do you live? Or "What do your parents do?" A simple connection can lead to building a bridge that could last a lifetime.*

- **Believe in yourself and your ability to get through difficult experiences or discomfort.**

NIGEL

Nigel advised students to "always stay positive and come out of your comfort zone. Don't let anybody tell you that you can't," and Crystal suggested students "never let anybody tell you no." Tara employed self-advocacy skills when addressing problems, saying, "The biggest thing in having a learning disability is that you need to advocate for yourself, because other people have no idea how your brain works and how you process information." Ann reminded students: "You have to be willing to step out of your comfort zone. Transitions are always difficult and it is going to be uncomfortable, so I would be worried if you felt completely fine. Learn to be okay with that and you will pull through." K worded it differently, telling students to "definitely not underestimate yourself. If you put your mind to it, you can do it. There will be hurdles you'll have to jump through, but you should try because it also helps you figure out who you are as a person."

K

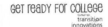

College Readiness Assessment

Description & directions

This assignment will help you determine your present level of knowledge regarding some of the topics related to getting ready for college. **Please complete each section of this assignment as completely as possible without assistance from your family members, teachers, or classmates.**

About me

Learning styles

My two strongest learning styles:

List ways I can use my learning style to enhance my learning:

My strengths, preferences, interests, & needs

My strengths:

My preferences:

My interests:

My needs and weaknesses:

My college interests

Name the major types of colleges or higher education found in the United States?

The ways I will pay for college include:

My top 3 college choices and my reasons for selecting each college:

College	Reasons for Interests
1.	
2.	
3.	

My technology

List pieces of technology than can enhance my learning:

My decision to disclose

Please review the statement and then type in whether the statement is true or false.

Statement	True or False
I can choose to tell or not tell the college I attend that I have a disability.	
I will have a special education teacher who can help me in college.	
Students can always use all of the accommodations they have in high school in college.	
Most colleges require more documentation than just your IEP or 504 plan to qualify for services in college.	
The only thing you need to do get accommodations in college is to sign up with the Disability Support Services Office.	

My plans

My postsecondary employment goal is:

My postsecondary education goal is:

The steps I need to take to reach my postsecondary goals include:

The VCU Center on Transition Innovations is funded by the Virginia Department of Education, #881-62524-H027A15107. For further information about the Center on Transition Innovations, please visit our website www.centerontransition.org

College Action Plan Assignment

Description

This step-by-step plan will assist you in getting closer to reaching your postsecondary and training goal needed for your career. After you complete this activity, follow up on the action plan regularly.

Directions

1. **Review your responses from the previous portfolio activities:**
   - Career Search – Lesson 2
   - Knowing Myself Profile – Lesson 3
2. **Answer questions 1 – 7 starting on page three of this document.**
3. **Review this assignment with your case manager and family. Bring it with you to your next IEP meeting.**

Assignment tips

Education and training section

If you are not aware of the type of training or education required for your career of choice, take the time to research the criteria to enter into this field.

Timeframe section

Based this on the information you have on the type of education or training required for your career choice. For example, if your career requires a Bachelor's degree, than that will take at least four years to complete. If your career will require you to complete on-the-job training, then that may take up to six months.

Postsecondary goals section

For this section, you are to develop postsecondary goals in the areas of employment and education and training. Remember, these goals are your desires for life AFTER high school and are included in your IEP and Academic and Career Plan. Make sure you review the steps for making these S.M.A.R.T. goals, and use the formula to assist in the development of each goal.

Examples of postsecondary **employment** goals:

- By March 2018, I will be employed full-time as a network security technician.
- By June 2019, I will be employed full-time as an officer in the juvenile justice system.
- By June 2021, I will be employed full-time as a mechanical engineer.

Examples of **postsecondary education** and **training goals**:

- By December 2017, I will complete the network security course from J. Sargeant Reynolds Community College Workforce Center and earn my certification in network security basics.
- By May 2019, I will complete my Associate's Degree from John Tyler Community College in the career field of criminal justice.
- By May 2021, I will earn my Bachelor's Degree from VA Tech in the career field of engineering.

Action plan section

For this plan, outline the steps you will need to take to achieve your postsecondary education and training goal listed above. Begin your action plan by thinking about where you are now, and identify the actions that will lead you to accomplishing the education and training required for your career of choice. Make sure to identify at least **five to seven** actions. Use various resources to assist you with this section. Resources can include teachers, family members, the Internet, career services at your high school, and the "Getting Ready for College" checklist listed in the Expanding Your Knowledge section of this unit.

Sample action plan

Action	Deadline	Will you need support?	This person can help me. (Family, friends, school counselor, coach, agency case manager, etc.)
Meet with your school counselor to discuss college entrance requirements	September, 2016	No	
Register for the PSAT in the fall	October 30, 2016	Yes	Mom
Submit request for PSAT accommodations has been submitted	October 30, 2016	Yes	School Counselor

College Action Plan

Career interests

1. What is your top career choice that you are interested in pursuing after you leave high school?

2. Why is this career important to you?

Education and training

3. Which the type of education and training you will need for your career choice? (Check one):

☐ Participate in on the job training to acquire the skills required for the career

☐ Complete course work to earn certification

☐ Complete a vocational/technical training program

☐ Complete an apprenticeship program

☐ Earn a Bachelor's degree

☐ Earn a Master's degree

☐ Enlist in the military and complete a career training program

Time frame

4. What timeframe you are expecting need in order to complete the above education/training?

☐ within 6 months of high school graduation

☐ within 1 year of high school graduation

☐ within 2 years of high school graduation

☐ within 4 years of high school graduation

☐ other, indicate timeframe

Postsecondary goals

Postsecondary goals are your desires for life **AFTER** high school and are included in your IEP and Academic and Career Plan. Develop postsecondary goals in the areas of employment and education and training. Remember to make these goals SMART.

5. **What is your postsecondary employment goal?**

   By _____ (timeframe), I will be employed _____ (full-time or part-time) as a _____ (career title).

6. **What is your postsecondary education or training goal?**

   By _____ (timeframe), I will complete _____ (specific education and training needed) in the career field of _____ (interest).

Action plan

Outline the steps you will need to take to achieve your postsecondary education and training goal. Use various resources to assist you with this section, which can include teachers, family members, the Internet, career services at your high school, and the "Getting Ready for College" checklist listed in the Expanding Your Knowledge section of this unit.

7. **What are the five to seven action steps you need to achieve your postsecondary education and training goal required for your career choice?**

Action to accomplish	Deadline	Will you need support?	This person can help me. (Family, friends, school counselor, coach, agency case manager, etc.)
1.			
2.			
3.			
4.			
5.			
6.			
7.			

The VCU Center on Transition Innovations is funded by the Virginia Department of Education, #881-62524-H027A15107. For further information about the Center on Transition Innovations, please visit our website www.centerontransition.org

Questions to Ask the Disability Services Office During a College Visit

The only way to know how a college responds to these issues important to you is to visit the campus and ask questions. In addition to attending a tour of the college or an open house, students with disabilities and their families should be encouraged to visit the disability services office on campus. Questions to consider include:

- How welcoming and responsive are the staff people?
- Is the office located near the center of campus or far off on the edge of campus, where it might be harder to access?
- What is the minimum number of courses one can take to be considered a full-time student? You should take the minimum number of courses possible, especially the first year.
- Does the college offer a quiet place to take tests? Are you able to take essay tests on a computer?
- Does the college have a writing center? You will need a writing center to assist you in organizing written assignments, especially long-term research papers. Check the hours of operation and inquire whether it is professionally or peer staffed.
- Are organizational coaches available? You may need a coach to assist with staying on task with day-to-day and long-term assignments.
- Are note takers available? How are they selected? You want a note taker that is chosen by the professor or the learning specialist, who hands in notes to the learning specialist, where you can pick them up anonymously.
- Does the college offer priority registration? Being able to register early will help you manage your time better, have later start times, and schedule breaks between classes.
- Is there a contact person who will be able to assess if you are taking a balanced course load each semester? You should avoid having too many heavy reading classes in the same semester.

Reprinted with permission from Bass Educational Service, LLC ©2017

My College Prep ☑ Checklist

BEFORE HIGH SCHOOL

- [ ] Enroll in a well-balanced portfolio of challenging courses, including classes in English, math, science, technology, history, geography, foreign language, and fine arts.
- [ ] Review high school course offerings and pinpoint which classes will prepare you best for college.
- [ ] Make sure your plan of study is added to your IEP transition plan.
- [ ] Work to address any basic skills deficits in reading, math, writing, and oral language.
- [ ] Sharpen your skills with smartphones, computers, and the Internet.
- [ ] Develop a full toolbox of study skills and learning strategies you can use in high school and beyond.

FRESHMAN YEAR

- [ ] Increase your knowledge of your disability and how it may affect academic performance.
- [ ] Practice explaining your own strengths and challenges to others.
- [ ] Work with your transition team and guidance counselor to register for courses and ensure you have the credits needed for your high school diploma.
- [ ] Start a transition portfolio of disability documentation, letters of support, verification of test accommodations used on statewide assessments, copies of past IEPs, and school records.
- [ ] Begin identifying adaptations and modifications you can to use in college to support your learning.
- [ ] Be sure that at least one annual goal on your IEP addresses postsecondary or other vocational transition activities.
- [ ] Prepare for and pass all end-of-course exams.

SOPHOMORE YEAR

- [ ] Conduct research on colleges. Talk to guidance counselors, go to college fairs, and chat with college representatives who visit high schools.
- [ ] Review college disability documentation guidelines.
- [ ] Work with parents to make sure your disability documentation records are current.
- [ ] Find out how to prepare disability documentation for college.
- [ ] Identify and apply for high-stakes test accommodations.
- [ ] Prepare for and take the PSAT to gauge how prepared you are for the SAT.
- [ ] Acquire and expand on specific study skills, such as using the library, reading with auxiliary aids and assistive technologies, and writing a term paper.
- [ ] Develop fluency with assistive technologies you can use in college.

FIGURE 9.1 College Prep Checklist

(Reprinted from Brookes Publishing www.brookes.com)

JUNIOR YEAR

- [ ] Consider possible career goals and college majors that support those goals.
- [ ] Identify a short list of potential colleges that are a good fit for your goals, interests, and abilities (and have the disability support services you need).
- [ ] Use college catalogs and websites to research information about admissions, prerequisites, tech requirements, housing, campus life, and disability services.
- [ ] If the website has a place to submit a question, send queries to admissions and disability services personnel in preparation for your campus visit.
- [ ] Plan campus tours, including a visit to the disability services office. Be prepared to talk to postsecondary disability service personnel about access to support services.
- [ ] Consider retaking high-stakes entrance exams, if necessary.
- [ ] Start working on college application essays (high school English teachers and guidance counselors can usually help you prepare for this).
- [ ] Request letters of recommendation from teachers and other staff.

SENIOR YEAR

- [ ] Meet with your guidance counselor early in the year to review your transition portfolio and identify materials you need for your college application.
- [ ] Talk to the guidance counselor about receiving a Summary of Performance to include in your transition portfolio.
- [ ] Continue to develop self-advocacy skills and study skills for college.
- [ ] If your target colleges require an admissions interview, practice before the interview by role-playing with the transition coordinator or guidance counselor.
- [ ] Go on final campus tours. Bring a list of questions about academics, disability services, and more—admissions procedures, financial aid, housing, social activities, athletics, etc.
- [ ] Review how to complete college application forms online.
- [ ] Fill out college applications (most colleges require applications to be filed by December of senior year).
- [ ] Ask your guidance counselor to review completed applications 2-3 weeks before the deadline.
- [ ] Wait for a letter of acceptance—letters will probably begin to arrive in mid-March.
- [ ] If multiple acceptance letters arrive, congratulations! Consider second campus visits or follow-up phone calls to ease your final decision.
- [ ] Write a short acceptance letter and mail it early along with any deposits and housing requests.
- [ ] CELEBRATE your awesome achievement!

Adapted from *Preparing Students with Disabilities for College Success*, edited by Stan F. Shaw, Joseph W. Madaus, and Lyman L. Dukes III
www.brookespublishing.com
BROOKES
PUBLISHING Co.

FIGURE 9.1 (Continued)

CONVERSATION STRATEGIES FOR STUDENTS TO TALK TO PARENTS ABOUT COLLEGE

PLAN WHAT YOU WANT TO SAY.

Think about what you want your parents to know about your goal to attend college and why you need them to be on board.

BE DIRECT.

Tell them there is something you want to discuss and make sure you have their full attention.

PICK A GOOD TIME TO TALK.

Approach them at a time when they will be able to focus on the conversation. You can even set a time in advance, for example, "There's something I want to talk with you about. Can we make some time when we eat dinner tonight to talk about it?"

WRITE IT DOWN FIRST.

Write down your thoughts in a letter or email before your conversation. If you want to send it, you can. Or, you can just use what you write to get ready and get your thoughts organized.

DISAGREE WITHOUT DISRESPECT.

Remember, you are challenging ideas that your parents have had for a long time. Be sure to use respectful language, listen to them, and stay calm.

National Organizations and Websites

Going-to-College (www.going-to-college.org)

This website provides information about living college life with a disability. It is designed for high school students and provides video clips, activities, and resources that can help get a head start in planning for college.

I'm Determined (www.imdetermined.org)

This website provides direct instruction, models, and opportunities to practice skills associated with self-determined behavior.

I'm First (www.imfirst.org)

Online community for first-generation college students, including stories from college students and resources for finding colleges and getting answers to questions about going to college.

KnowHow2Go (http://knowhow2go.acenet.edu)

Website by the American Council for Education with resources to encourage primarily 8th to 10th grade students to prepare for college.

The National Center for College Students with Disabilities (www.NCCSDonline.org)

The NCCSD provides resources and technical assistance to all college students with disabilities, including undergraduate and graduate students. They have an online Clearinghouse where students can get resources for free (nd DREAM, a national group run by college students for students www.NCCSDClearing house.org) a (www.DREAMCollegeDisability.org).

The National Deaf Center for Postsecondary Outcomes (www.NationalDeafCenter.org/)

If you are a culturally Deaf student, deaf or hard-of-hearing, the NDC can help connect you to resources and information. They can also provide information about deafness, hearing loss, and common accommodations to any parents, high school teachers, college faculty, or disability services staff. For high school students, they also have an online training tool to help students plan goals and a path to college.

Step by Step: *College Awareness and Planning for Families, Counselors and Communities*

https://www.nacacnet.org/advocacy--ethics/initiatives/steps/

Curriculum on college awareness by the National Association for College Admission Counseling with components for middle school, early high school, and late high school. Includes both learning activities for students and guides for leading parent workshops. A workshop on financial aid is also included.

Think College (*www.ThinkCollege.net*)

Think College focuses on information and resources on college options for students with intellectual disability. The website has student stories, a college search directory, a resource library, and many videos about college students with intellectual disability. It also offers information about financial aid and college planning.

Recommended Books

- *Preparing Students with Disabilities for College Success: A Practical Guide to Transition Planning* by Stan F. Shaw, Joseph W. Madaus, and Lyman L. Dukes. While this was written for professionals, parents and students can find everything they need to know about getting ready for college, and what high schools should be doing during the transition process. It includes comprehensive information about the ADA and Section 504, and how college disability services offices work.
- *Learning Outside the Lines: Two Ivy League Students with Learning Disabilities and ADHD Give You the Tools for Academic Success and Educational Revolution* by Jonathan Mooney and David Cole. This book can help students with any type of disability consider how they learn best, and practical strategies for dealing with college-level academics.
- *Empowering Leadership: A Systems Change Guide for Autistic Students and Those with Other Disabilities* by the Autistic Self-Advocacy Network. This handbook by and for disabled students helps develop leadership and organizing skills to foster change on campus. Students may also find the information helpful for dealing with administrators when problems occur.
- *Navigating College: A Handbook on Self-Advocacy* by the Autistic Self-Advocacy Network. While written for students who are on the Autism Spectrum, the information could easily apply to students with many other disabilities, including mental and emotional illnesses. With tips for academics, housing, social situations, and talking about disability with others, it covers practical information that most students could use during their first years of college.

- *The K&W Guide to College Programs and Services for Students with Learning Disabilities or Attention Deficit/Hyperactivity Disorder, 13th (2016) Edition by Princeton Review.* This book provides a good starting point in researching the learning support services and programs at more than 350 colleges and universities in the U.S.

BLINDNESS	
www.accreditedschoolsonline.org/resources/helping-students-with-visual-impaiments/	A webpage from Accredited Schools Online that provides information on accommodations for students with visual impairment, tips for finding the right school, and links to resources and scholarships
http://ods.rutgers.edu/faculty/visual	A webpage for faculty at Rutgers University with information on accommodating students with visual impairment that may be useful for understanding the many strategies that can be used
DEAFNESS	
http://www.jsu.edu/dept/dss/nuts&bolts/introduction.pdf	A guide for students from Pepnet on college success for students who are deaf or hard of hearing
MENTAL HEALTH	
http://www.nami.org/collegeguide/	A downloadable guide for college students from the National Alliance on Mental Illness to begin the conversation about mental health issues during college
www.mentalhealthamerica.net/whats-your-plan-college-mental-health-disorder	A webpage from Mental Health America with information on planning for college for students with a mental health disorder
INTELLECTUAL DISABILITY	
www.thinkcollege.net	A website that provides information and resources on college for students with intellectual disability, including interviews and advice from college students
LEARNING DISABILITIES	
https://www.washington.edu/doit/sites/default/files/atoms/files/Academic-Accommodations-Learning-Disabilities.pdf	A guide from DO-IT on academic accommodations for students with learning disabilities
https://www.understood.org/en/school-learning/choosing-starting-school/leaving-high-school	A webpage from Understood.org that gives tips for families to ease the transition to college for students with learning disabilities
www.greatschools.org/gk/articles/college-planning/	A webpage from Great Schools that provides information for families to understand college for students with learning disabilities
ADHD	
https://add.org/college-students/	A list of resources for college students with ADHD from the Attention Deficit Disorder Association
https://www.additudemag.com/category/parenting-adhd-kids/school-learning/college/	A college survival guide from ADDitude magazine, with articles and tips for students and parents
MOBILITY	
www.usnews.com/education/best-colleges/articles/2011/12/05/4-tips-for-college-applicants-students-with-physical-disabilities	A list of tips for college applicants and students with physical disabilities from U.S. News and World Report
AUTISM	
www.navigatingcollege.org	A downloadable guide for autistic college students written by adults on the autism spectrum, with a focus on self-advocacy
CHRONIC HEALTH CONDITIONS	
www.onlinecolleges.net/for-students/chronic-health-issues/	A website by the Center for Online Education that provides information and resources on attending college for students with a chronic health condition

FIGURE 2.2 Disability-specific resources for college planning

Students involved in DREAM: Disability Rights, Education, Activism, and Mentoring, a national online group for college students with disabilities, produced the following list of top tips for college students:

TEN TIPS
FOR STUDENTS WITH DISABILITIES...
FROM STUDENTS WITH DISABILITIES

1. **Disability accommodations are rights, not special help.**
   Ask for what you need. Advocate for yourself.

2. **You are an important and valuable part of campus diversity.**
   Diversity includes disability.

3. **College disability services offices can be gatekeepers.**
   Most are good allies for students, but some are not. Demand professional, individualized, respectful services and file a complaint if you don't get them.

4. **Feed your soul and body.**
   Balance your valuable time, energy, and health.

5. **Stay focused on your career.**
   If it won't help you get a job or maintain your passion for college, don't bother.

6. **Find a community.**
   Never go it alone. Consider connecting with others who have disabilities.

7. **Universally design your own learning.**
   Learn how you learn best, and then use your strengths and unique learning style.

8. **Never apologize for your disability or your accommodations.**
   If you apologize, people may think you are ashamed.

9. **Fight oppression and bullying in any form.**
   Ableism is just one "ism." If one of us is oppressed, all of us are oppressed.

10. **Learn disability history.**
    Learn about the people and movements that made it possible for you to be in college.

DREAM Disability Rights, Education, Activism, and Mentoring
NCCSD National Center for College Students with Disabilities

This is available in other formats upon request. Funding for NCCSD and DREAM is from the Fund for the Improvement of Postsecondary Education (FIPSE) at the US Dept. of Education (P116D150005)

FIGURE 9.3 Top Ten List for College Students by College Students

INDEX